THE PRESIDENT'S LEGISLATIVE POLICY AGENDA, 1789–2002

Jeffrey E. Cohen asks why U.S. presidents send to Congress the legislative proposals that they do and what Congress does with those proposals. His study covers nearly the entire history of the presidency, from 1789 to 2002. The long historical scope allows Cohen to engage competing perspectives on how the presidency has developed over time. He asks what accounts for the short- and long-term trends in presidential requests to Congress, what substantive policies and issues the recommendations are concerned with, and which factors affect the presidential decision to submit a recommendation on a particular issue. *The President's Legislative Policy Agenda, 1789–2002*, argues that presidents often anticipate the congressional reaction to their legislative proposals and modify their agendas accordingly.

Jeffrey E. Cohen is Professor of Political Science at Fordham University. He is the author of twelve books, including *Presidential Responsiveness and Public Policy-Making: The Public and the Policies that Presidents Choose* (1997), which won the Richard E. Neustadt Award from the Presidency Research Group of the American Political Science Association for the best book on the presidency, and *Going Local: Presidential Leadership in the Post-Broadcast Age* (Cambridge 2010), which also won both the Neustadt Award and the Goldsmith Award from the Joan Shorenstein Center at the Kennedy School, Harvard University, for the book that best fulfills the objective of improving democratic governance through an examination of the intersection between the media, politics, and public policy.

The President's Legislative Policy Agenda, 1789–2002

Jeffrey E. Cohen

Fordham University

CAMBRIDGE
UNIVERSITY PRESS

CAMBRIDGE UNIVERSITY PRESS
Cambridge, New York, Melbourne, Madrid, Cape Town,
Singapore, São Paulo, Delhi, Mexico City

Cambridge University Press
32 Avenue of the Americas, New York, NY 10013-2473, USA

www.cambridge.org
Information on this title: www.cambridge.org/9781107634978

First published 2012

Printed in the United States of America

A catalog record for this publication is available from the British Library.

Library of Congress Cataloging in Publication Data

Cohen, Jeffrey E.
The president's legislative policy agenda, 1789–2002 / Jeffrey E. Cohen.
  pages cm
Includes bibliographical references.
ISBN 978-1-107-01270-7 (hardback) – ISBN 978-1-107-63497-8 (paperback)
1. Presidents – United States – History. 2. Political planning – United States – History.
3. Legislation – United States – History. 4. United States – Politics and
government. I. Title.
JK511.C62 2013
320.60973–dc23   2012006451

ISBN 978-1-107-01270-7 Hardback
ISBN 978-1-107-63497-8 Paperback

Contents

List of Figures

List of Tables

Introduction

Two Puzzles

Since the presidency of George Washington, presidents have submitted legislative proposals to Congress. These proposals compose the president's *Legislative Policy Agenda*. This book asks why does the legislative policy agenda takes the shape that it does. What affects presidential decisions to include some proposals on their legislative agendas but not others? Do these presidential agenda-building decisions have consequences for congressional treatment of the presidential agenda? When building their legislative agendas, do presidents take into consideration the congressional context? Based on past research, the answers to these questions are not clear. Consider, for instance, the two following puzzles, the *divided government puzzle* and the *modern president puzzle*.

PUZZLE 1: THE DIVIDED GOVERNMENT PUZZLE

Research consistently finds presidents are more successful when their party controls Congress than with opposition control. For example, from 1953 to 2007, presidents received 30.5% more support in the House and 17% more in Senate with their party in control rather than the opposition (Ragsdale, 2009, pp. 500–502). A general consensus now exists that party control is one of the most, if not *the* most important factor conditioning presidential success in Congress.

Fleisher et al. (2008, pp. 198–199) detail the theoretical rationale for the large impact of party control on presidential success in

Congress. First, members of the president's party are more likely to share policy preferences with the president than opposition party members. Second, party loyalty might motivate presidential co-partisans to support the president more than opposition party legislators. Third, the electoral fate of co-partisans is tied to the president; they run on their record as well as the president's, providing them with an incentive to help and support the president. Finally, the majority party determines Congress's organization and agenda, including committee memberships, workload, which bills reach the floor, and the rules governing floor action on those bills. Congressional leaders can use their control over these organizational and agenda levers to advantage the president's legislative aims and proposals.

The strong effect of party control on presidential success raises a puzzle. Being defeated can be costly to a president. Defeat can harm a president's leadership image and undermine his public support (Brace and Hinckley, 1992; Rivers and Rose, 1985). Defeat on one proposal can spill over to affect the prospects of enactment of other proposals. During the health care debate of 2009 and 2010, journalists and pundits commented on the broad implications of victory versus defeat for President Obama. One journalistic review said this about Congress's finally giving President Obama much of his health care proposal: "Historians and political experts said that Sunday's passage of the Democrats' health care overhaul by the House of Representatives, together with the Senate's expected passage of its final terms in coming days, rescues Obama from being branded a political loser in only the second year of his presidency ... " (Talev and Thomma, March 21, 2010). Another journalistic analysis pointed to the possible foreign policy implications of the health care victory: "President Barack Obama's domestic success on healthcare reform may pay dividends abroad as the strengthened U.S. leader taps his momentum to take on international issues with allies and adversaries" (Mason, May 26, 2010). Given the costs of defeat, the consequences of winning or losing, why do presidents allow themselves to be defeated *so often* in the face of opposition congresses when they can lessen the likelihood of defeat by modifying or refraining from submitting their legislative proposals?

PUZZLE 2: THE MODERN PRESIDENT PUZZLE

Since the mid-twentieth century, presidents have submitted several times the number of proposals to Congress than their predecessors. Using data collected for this book, from the 79th (1945–1946) Congress to the 107th (2001–2002), presidents submitted on average 313 proposals per congress compared with 60 for presidents serving during the first 78 congresses, a fivefold increase. Viewed from the perspective of the literature on presidential-congressional relations, most of which covers the modern period, this high rate of modern presidential legislative activism is puzzling. That literature emphasizes the difficulties presidents have with Congress. In the terminology of Krutz et al., there is a "presumption of failure" when presidents take positions on legislation (1998, p. 871). Empirical evidence documents the high legislative "failure" rate of the legislative proposals of modern presidents (Cameron and Park, 2008; Edwards and Barrett, 2000; Edwards, Barrett, and Peake, 1997; Peterson, 1990; Rudalevige, 2002).

Why do modern presidents allow themselves to be defeated so often, which imposes previously noted costs, when they have alternative means of making policy? Modern presidents can use unilateral tools like executive orders, thereby sidestepping Congress in making many policies (Mayer, 1999, 2001, 2009; Moe and Howell, 1999). Only rarely does Congress challenge an executive order. Why are modern presidents so *stubbornly legislatively active* in the face of these high expected failure rates and the availability policy-making alternatives?

CONVENTIONAL EXPLANATIONS OF PRESIDENTIAL BEHAVIOR

Conventional explanations of the legislative proposing of presidents take the number and nature of presidential proposals behavior as a given, not something worthy of explanation. With regard to the divided government puzzle, the conventional view argues that presidents do not care whether their proposals will be defeated, what I will call the presidential sincerity perspective (e.g., Peterson, 1990). Thus, presidents send proposals to Congress that they like, without considering whether Congress accepts or defeats their proposals. For the reasons laid out in Fleisher et al. (2008), as noted earlier, presidents will be defeated more often when confronting an opposition-controlled Congress than one controlled by the president's party.

The conventional view about the high level of modern presidential activism argues that presidents are primarily reacting to public and political expectations to supply legislative leadership (e.g., Greenstein, 1988; Shaw, 1987). Like the sincerity perspective, this reactive perspective implies that presidents care little whether Congress defeats their legislative proposals. Instead, modern presidents submit numerous proposals to Congress only because of public and political expectations that they should.

Both the divided government and modern presidency perspectives suggest that presidents do not care much about success with Congress, a somewhat odd position given that the bulk of the research on presidential-congressional relations studies the conditions that help or hinder presidential success with Congress. Second, both puzzles suggest that presidential agenda-building decisions are divorced from the rest of the legislative process. In effect, there is a presidential agenda-building process and another distinct legislative policy-making process.

CONGRESSIONAL ANTICIPATIONS AND PRESIDENTIAL AGENDA BUILDING

In *The President's Legislative Policy Agenda, 1789–2002*, I offer a theory, *congressional anticipations*, that resolves both of these puzzles. The core tenet of the theory is that presidents take into account the congressional environment when deciding which proposals to submit to Congress: That is, they calculate the likelihood that Congress will enact a proposal. For reasons noted earlier, presidents want to avoid being defeated by Congress. If presidents expect a proposal to be defeated, they have several ways to minimize being defeated. First, a president can decide not to submit a proposal to Congress. Second, presidents can modify their proposals to increase the likelihood that Congress will enact them. Third, presidents can collect resources to improve their bargaining situation with Congress, using those resources to increase the likelihood that Congress will approve and not defeat their proposals. Presidents engage in these strategic behaviors to minimize being defeated because presidents view congressional defeat of their legislative proposals as costly.

This congressional anticipations theory thus begins with a simple assumption: that presidents do not want Congress to defeat their legislative proposals because of the cost of such defeats. As I show in the pages to follow, this simple assumption helps us to resolve the seemingly disparate divided government and modern president puzzles. This assumption also allows us to integrate the presidential agenda-building process to the later congressional policy-making process: Presidential agenda choices affect the congressional policy-making process. Finally, especially with regard to the modern president puzzle, we can understand the institutional development of one important aspect of the presidency.

I am not the first to argue that the presidential agenda-building and congressional policy-making processes are linked, or that presidential agenda-building decisions have consequences for the latter congressional policy-making process, nor am I the first to argue that presidents take into account the congressional context in constructing their legislative policy agendas (cf. Cameron and Park, 2008; Larocca, 2006; Light, 1991). But compared with the vast literature on presidential-congressional relations, this is a decidedly minority position. Moreover, as I detail in this text, there are important limitations to the existing studies arguing that presidential agenda building is linked to congressional policy making.

To test these ideas, I use a data set that consists of every presidential proposal submitted to Congress from 1789 to 2002, over 14,000 proposals. The proposals from 1789 to 1992 come from the Presidential Request Table, under the direction of Michael Malbin, a part of the larger *Database of Historical Congressional Statistics* project, supported by the National Science Foundation (Swift et al., 2000). Andrew Rudalevige updated the presidential request data through 2002, which he graciously made available to me. As I discuss further in this book, I also matched each proposal from 1789 to 1992 to specific congressional roll calls by using the Rollreq Table of the *Database of Historical*

Congressional Statistics. These data represent the most comprehensive and temporally extensive data sets in existence on presidential legislative proposals to Congress.

The vast historical scope of these data allows us to test the modern presidency puzzle, which requires that we have data on presidential proposals and congressional roll calls spanning the traditional and modern presidency epochs. Not only do these data allow such a comparison but also, by covering almost the entire history of the presidency, we can be quite confident about the generality of the findings unearthed. Unlike so much of the research on the presidency and presidential-congressional relations, this study is not time bound.

In addition to the temporally sweeping data for this study, I classify each presidential proposal by policy area. The policy classification of proposals allows us to test whether the logic of strategic presidential anticipations applies across policy areas or is restricted to only some types of policies. As a side benefit, the policy data allow us to describe the historical trend in the policy emphasis and direction of the president's legislative agenda. We are sorely lacking in basic description of this type of presidential behavior, among other important presidential behaviors. In this sense, this study makes two contributions, one theoretical and the other descriptive and empirical.

To foreshadow some of the key findings presented in *The President's Legislative Policy Agenda, 1789–2002*, I show in these pages:

- The president's legislative agenda is smaller during divided than united government, as presidents strip proposals destined for congressional defeat from their agenda.
- Once the size of the president's agenda is taken into account, divided government no longer has the pronounced direct effects on success in Congress as found in the extant literature. Most of the effect of divided government on success is mediated through the size of the president's agenda.
- Presidents moderate their policy positions during divided as opposed to united government. Such policy moderation improves the odds for presidential success during divided, but not united, government.

- Beginning with the full implementation of the legislative clearance process in 1949, the size of the president's agenda grew remarkably. The legislative clearance process gave modern presidents a newfound institutional resource that increased their prospects for success in Congress. Consequently, the legislative agendas for modern presidents are larger than those of traditional, pre-1949 presidents.

- Modern presidents are more successful with Congress than traditional presidents, and there is a positive relationship between the size of the agenda and success for modern presidents, but there is no relationship between agenda size and success for traditional presidents. Modern presidents have larger agendas than traditional ones partly because they foresee greater success with Congress than their traditional counterparts.

PLAN OF THE BOOK

Chapter 1 lays the foundation for the study. It provides a historical discussion of presidential legislative proposals, showing that the practice of submitting legislative proposals to Congress began early in George Washington's term. Submitting legislative proposals to Congress has been a mainstay activity for presidents ever since. In 1946, under Harry Truman, proposing legislation to Congress became more formalized, creating what we now call the *president's program*. In Chapter 1 I define and distinguish important terms, such as the president's legislative policy agenda, other presidential policy agendas, the presidential program, and presidential position taking on congressional roll calls. Doing so helps to clarify what we are talking about and delimits the scope of this study. Finally, in Chapter 1 I briefly introduce the data used in this study, which consists of all presidential proposals submitted to Congress for legislative consideration, more than 14,000 proposals.

Chapter 2 reviews the literature on building the president's agenda, pointing out three major limitations: The research on presidential agenda building looks at only the modern presidency, that literature also looks at only domestic policy, and rarely does that literature test hypotheses about agenda building or the consequences of agenda building. *The President's Legislative Policy Agenda, 1789–2002* looks at presidential agenda building across virtually the entire history of the presidency, considers foreign as well as domestic policy proposals, develops hypotheses about factors that affect the construction of the president's agenda and the implication of the composition of the president's agenda on presidential success with Congress, and tests those hypotheses. Chapter 2 also discusses the major approaches to the study of agenda building, process and agenda comparison. Process approaches trace the life history of issues, whereas agenda comparison looks at the similarities and differences across agendas. In this book, I employ the agenda comparison approach.

Chapter 3 offers a theory of presidential agenda building, congressional anticipations. The theory is offered to resolve the two puzzles that motivate this study, the divided government and modern president puzzles. Underlying the theory of congressional anticipations is a simple assumption, namely, that presidents want to avoid congressional defeat of their legislative proposals. They want to avoid defeat because of the costs of defeat. Chapter 3 reviews the two puzzles and why the extant literature does a poor job of accounting for those puzzles. The theory of congressional anticipations is presented, and hypotheses from the theory are derived. Importantly, the theory of congressional anticipations views presidential agenda building and congressional action on presidential proposals as two phases of the same process, not two separate processes, as implied in some research. Finally, the chapter reviews other factors that can affect presidential agenda-building decisions. Incorporating these factors into the analysis provides a more well-rounded understanding of presidential agenda building and also acts as a statistical control in the analysis that follows. If we detect support for the hypotheses from the theory in the face of these controls, our confidence in the theory will be bolstered.

The next four chapters present the empirical tests of the hypotheses of the theory of congressional anticipations. Chapter 4 looks at the trend in the overall number of presidential proposals. The first part of that chapter describes this trend, finding a large surge in the number of presidential proposals in the year immediately after the end of the Second World War, coinciding with the creation of the legislative clearance process. The second half of the chapter statistically accounts for this trend, in particular testing for the effects of divided government on the size of the agenda. Consistent with the theory proposed here, presidents submit smaller agendas during divided government, except during reelection congresses, when they appear to engage in a "blame game" with Congress. A final section in Chapter 4 looks at the trends in the size of the agenda for the modern period, when public opinion data are available. That analysis indicates that the agenda seems to grow when the public is in a liberal mood.

Chapter 5 disaggregates presidential proposals into policy type, focusing on four major policy domains: government operations, national sovereignty, international affairs, and domestic policy. Disaggregating by policy type allows us to trace presidential attention to different policies over time, to test whether the congressional anticipations theory applies to all types of policies, and to raise the question of the interrelations among policies that appear on the president's agenda. The first part of the chapter describes the trends for the four policy domains. The major point revealed by this description is that most of the surge in presidential proposals in the post-World War Two era is a function of increased presidential attention to domestic policy, and social welfare policy in particular. Analysis in this chapter also found that congressional anticipations affect agenda choice for all policy domains except for national sovereignty. Finally, the analysis revealed that the presidential decision to place proposals from one policy domain had implications for placement of proposals from other policy domains. The president's legislative policy agenda needs to be viewed as a package, not a set of discrete, separate proposals.

Chapter 6 tests the moderation hypothesis, the idea that minority presidents modify their policy proposals to bring them closer to the position of key decision makers in Congress. Instead of the presidential proposal data, I use roll call–based measures to test this hypothesis, because we cannot locate a presidential proposal in a policy space. Results of the analysis in Chapter 6 find support for the divided government-moderation hypothesis and also show that party polarization conditions the degree to which minority presidents will moderate. When polarization between the parties is wide, presidents moderate less than when the parties are not so highly polarized.

Chapters 4 to 6 tested various aspects of the theory of congressional anticipations as related to presidential agenda building. Support was found for all of the major hypotheses developed from that theory, but the theory has implications for presidential success with Congress, the topic of Chapter 7. Chapter 7 presents tests of several hypotheses derived from the theory of congressional anticipations. The first is that with controls for the size of the agenda, the large effect of divided government so often found in the literature will fall. Second, there is a positive direct impact of size of the president's agenda on success in Congress. The next relates to the modern presidency puzzle, hypothesizing that the resources of the modern presidency should be associated with increases in success. Finally, Chapter 7 tests the strategic moderation hypothesis, that policy moderate presidents are more successful with Congress than extreme presidents, but only during divided government. Using data at various levels of aggregation, the chapter presents support for all of these hypotheses, making the larger point that congressional factors that influence presidential agenda building in turn affect presidential success with Congress. The presidential agenda building and congressional policy-making processes are not two distinct, divorced processes but form one process. Finally, Chapter 8 concludes the book, putting the findings into perspective, raising several unresolved questions, and posing directions for future research.

ACKNOWLEDGMENTS

In writing this book, I have incurred numerous debts. I want to thank Timothy Lynch, currently working on his Ph.D. in Political Science at the University of Wisconsin-Milwaukee. While a graduate student at Fordham University working on his M.A., Tim led the coding of each presidential proposal by policy area, overseeing undergraduate coders, coding proposals, and working with me on this important aspect of data collection. These data on the policy area of each proposal greatly enriched this study. Fortunately, in Tim I had someone on whom I could rely to produce high-quality data.

I receive considerable financial and other support to carry out this study. Fordham University supplied me with a summer research grant in 2005 that allowed me to hire a team of coders to complete data collection and prepare the data for analysis. For academic year 2008/2009 I was fortunate enough to receive a faculty fellowship from Fordham as well as a Visiting Senior Research Scholar fellowship from the Center for the Study of Democratic Politics (CSDP), Woodrow Wilson School of Public and International Affairs, Princeton University. Most of this manuscript was written during my fellowship at CSDP. I thank Larry Bartels, then the Director of CSDP, Michele Epstein, the Assistant Director of the Center, and Helene Wood, also of the Center. They, CSDP, and Princeton provided me with good working conditions and a congenial environment. At CDSP I was able to renew old friendships, make new friends, and take part in a vibrant intellectual community.

I presented some of the research in these pages at several seminars, including two presentations at CSDP, another at the Embedding Laws in the American State Conference, University of Virginia, May 2–3, 2008, hosted by Jeffrey Jenkins and Eric M. Patashnik, and a fourth paper at the "Going to Extremes Conference: The Fate of the Political Center in American Politics," Nelson A. Rockefeller Center for Public Policy and the Social Sciences, Dartmouth College, June 18–20, 2008. I want to thank all of the seminar participants for their comments. The paper presented at the Virginia conference is to be published as "Durability and Change in the President's Legislative Policy Agenda, 1799–2002," co-authored with Matthew Eshbaugh-Soha in *Living Legislation: Political Development and Contemporary American Politics*, Jeffrey A. Jenkins and Eric M. Patashnik, eds. (Chicago: University of Chicago Press, 2012). Some of the material from that chapter is included in Chapter 5 of this book. The paper at the Dartmouth conference was published as "Presidents, Polarization, and Divided Government," *Presidential Studies Quarterly*, September 2011, and provides the foundation for Chapter 6 in this book.

Many people gave of their time, through conversation and by reading papers that became this manuscript. Several deserve special mention. Warmest thanks go to my department colleague, Richard Fleisher. Over the years we have had many conversations about our research. Rich's comments, wisdom, and good judgment have not only made me a better political scientist but also a better person. Another department colleague, Bob Hume, read papers that became chapters in this study, helping me to clarify my presentation and thinking.

Costas Panagopoulos, also a member of my department, let me bend his ear often about ideas for this book. His boundless energy and enthusiasm provided inspiration and encouragement. I am quite lucky to have so many members of my department at Fordham able and willing to help me in doing the research and writing this book.

My sometimes co-author, Matthew Eshbaugh-Soha, also deserves a heartfelt thank-you, especially for his patience with my questions about statistical modeling. I also want to thank Chuck Cameron, whom I have pestered over the years with many silly ideas. Chuck's enthusiasm is infectious, and his encouragement and hard questions improved this study. Importantly, Chuck prodded me to combine my interest in agenda setting with presidential success in Congress and to think about the underlying story, rather than just present a string of findings. I also want to extend a thank-you to Dave Mayhew. At the Virginia conference mentioned previously, Dave raised several questions and comments on a figure that I presented on trends in the size of the president's agenda. Dave was right; the figure had a more interesting story to it than I had originally thought. Fred Greenstein also deserves another special thank-you. While we were together at CSDP, Fred and I had many occasions to discuss the presidency, his and my research, and research in general. Although the style of research contained in this study differs from Fred's approach, I hope that he will agree that we share similar concerns about the presidency and political science.

The intellectual seeds of this study began thirty-five years ago, while I was a graduate student at the University of Michigan. There I met two people who would have profound effects on my thinking and my research both at Michigan and for the rest of my career, Paul Light and John Kingdon. With Paul, another graduate student, I had someone who shared some of my interests in the presidency and agenda setting. Citations and references to Paul's work appear repeatedly in these pages. John Kingdon was my dissertation adviser, working on his important agenda-setting book while I was a graduate student. John's work, like Paul's, gave us much of our vocabulary for studying agenda setting. Throughout my career, John always reminded me to address the "why" question, why does something occur, and why should we be interested in this question or that study? Hopefully I have addressed the why question in these pages.

Finally, I am the luckiest man alive to be married to my wife, Phyllis.

CHAPTER 1

The President's Legislative Policy Agenda

He shall from time to time give to the Congress information of the state of the union, and recommend to their consideration such measures as he shall judge necessary and expedient. (United States Constitution, Article II, Section 3)

Article II, Section 3 of the Constitution, quoted here, had among the most profound implications for the presidency of any words written in the Constitution. That passage planted the seeds for two presidential institutions, the State of the Union Address (SUA) and the president's legislative policy agenda, the latter becoming the legislative program in 1946. These institutions breached the strict wall of separation between the president and Congress and transformed the president into an important policy leader and participant in the legislative policy-making process.

Perhaps only the presidential inauguration can rival the SUA as a high-state ceremonial occasion. George Washington complied with the constitutional requirement for a "state of the union" message to Congress less than a year after taking office, on January 8, 1790.[1] The 1091-word document congratulated Congress on its legislative actions of the previous year and informed Congress on the general health of the economy. The document, however, also raised the specter of foreign policy problems and the need for the nation to prepare for hostilities with several Indian tribes.

Washington not only used his first annual message to inform Congress on the state of the nation but also to recommend issues on

---

[1] Washington took office on April 30, 1789.

which Congress might legislate. He asked for congressional legislative action on eight issues: 1) establishing a uniform system for the militia, 2) establishing independent manufactures for military supplies, 3) providing compensation for troops, 4) providing for the protection of southern and western frontiers, 5) establishing a uniform rule for naturalization, 6) establishing uniform currency, 7) establishing uniform weights and measures, and 8) ratifying a treaty with the Creek Nation of Indians.[2]

From this beginning, the SUA developed into a regular, recurring, expected feature of the presidency; in other words, it became an institutionalized aspect of the presidency.[3] Washington interpreted the phrase "from time to time" as once a year, presenting his second "Annual Message," as the SUA was then called, on December 8, 1790. He proceeded to deliver the SUA to Congress every year thereafter, a practice that each subsequent president continued.

THE FOUNDATION OF THE PRESIDENT'S LEGISLATIVE POLICY AGENDA

George Washington breached the strict wall of separation in policy making between Congress and the president by asking Congress to legislate on matters that he identified as important, but this earliest generation of political leaders, like Washington, took separation of powers seriously. They viewed it almost literally, seeing it, with federalism, as a way to disperse power and thereby reduce the potential for concentration of power and tyranny that would result (e.g., Carey, 1978; Casper, 1995; McDonald, 1994). Viewed strictly, separation of powers locates responsibility for legislating with Congress; any

---

[2] The initial SUA was not the first occasion on which Washington asked Congress for legislative action. In 1789, prior to his first SUA, he made eight requests, most concerning Indian and defense matters, including ratifying three treaties.

[3] My usage of the term *institutionalization* follows from Huntington (1968) and Polsby (1968), the latter of whom identifies three characteristics of institutionalization: organizational boundedness, organizational complexity, and organizational use of universalistic and automatic criteria for conducting business and recruitment of personnel, among other tasks. Institutionalization has been an important concept for understanding the development and evolution of the presidency, too. See for instance Wyszomirski, 1982; Burke, 1992; Ragsdale and Theiss, 1997; Krause and Cohen, 2000; Krause, 2002.

presidential involvement in that process would violate strict separation of powers.

Thus, for Washington and other early presidents to cross the wall of separation between the branches required an unassailable justification. Washington found that justification in Article II, Section 3, as quoted previously. In his first Inaugural Address, before a joint session of Congress, he quoted the passage, informing the legislature that at a later date he would act on that constitutional duty:

> By the article establishing the executive department it is made the duty of the President 'to recommend to your consideration such measures as he shall judge necessary and expedient.' The circumstances under which I now meet you will acquit me from entering into that subject further than to refer to the great constitutional charter under which you are assembled, and which, in defining your powers, designates the objects to which your attention is to be given.

Possibly fearing a congressional counterreaction to this foray into the legislative process in this way, Washington preempted criticisms and attacks by providing a rationale literally grounded and rooted in the Constitution. In so doing, Washington built a case that the SUA, and his submission of legislative requests, did not constitute an expansion of presidential power, nor was it an exercise in interpreting the Constitution. Instead, Washington was merely carrying out the constitutionally prescribed duties of the presidency. In effect, he was arguing that there should be no debate over his annual message to Congress or his submitting requests for legislation, because the Constitution required him to do so.[4]

Armed with this constitutional justification and duty, Washington submitted legislative recommendations to Congress. During the first Congress (1789–1790), he made twenty-five such recommendations, with sixteen mentioned in that first annual address. In each and every State of the Union Address to follow, presidents followed Washington's lead and submitted legislative recommendations to Congress.

---

[4] Even at the Constitutional Convention, the idea of a state of the union address and presidential recommendations for legislation was not highly controversial. Gouverneur Morris, among the most ardent proponent of a strong presidency at the Constitutional Convention, wanted presidential recommendations to Congress to be a "duty," not merely an option (Milkis and Nelson, 2008, p. 49).

Washington and subsequent presidents also submitted legislative recommendations to Congress through other documents, outside of the SUA. Never has anyone seriously questioned presidents about submitting requests for legislation to Congress.[5]

A primary justification for replacing the Articles of Confederation with the Constitution was to ensure greater "energy and dispatch" through the presidency, especially in foreign policy and other national emergencies that required swift action. Based on the experience of government under the Articles, the attendees at the Constitutional Convention had come to think that foreign relations could not be run effectively through a deliberative body like Congress. Consistent with this policy responsibility, in his first year in office Washington asked that Congress ratify four treaties. Many of the remaining twenty-one legislative recommendations that he made that year concerned foreign policy and national defense matters. His legislative recommendations also touched on other, non–foreign policy matters, however: immigration and naturalization, admission of states into the Union (Kentucky), organization of the Post Office, monetary issues, establishing uniform juridical sentencing, and creating a uniform system of weights and measures.

Admittedly, Washington's legislative recommendations did not cover as many policy issues as do those of modern presidents, which

[5] Many thought, however, that presidential involvement would have to stop with the recommendation and that presidents should not further lobby Congress in behalf of those recommendations. Washington, for instance, stayed on the sidelines, whereas his Treasury Secretary, Alexander Hamilton, coordinated and oversaw legislative strategy with key members of Congress. As early a president as John Quincy Adams attempted "to lead Congress openly toward an active program of legislative achievement" (Milkis and Nelson, 2008, pp. 112–113). Thomas Jefferson mobilized his party in Congress behind his legislative goals, but he worked with the congressional party leaders, letting them do the actual work of building support for policies that Jefferson identified (Malone, 1974, vol. 4 & 5; Milkis and Neslon, 2008, 108–109). Greenstein's (2006, p. 381) analysis suggests that Jefferson actively engaged in Congress's business for the furtherance of his policy goals: Jefferson "typically worked through intermediaries, sometimes taking it upon himself to draft legislative measures for introduction by sympathetic lawmakers" and that "Jefferson minced no words in private about the importance he placed on influencing Congress." George Hoar, a Republican Senator in the Grant era, summarizes the general congressional attitude in the nineteenth century to presidential involvement in the legislative process: "... Senators ... would have received as a personal affront a private message from the White House expressing a desire that they should adopt any course in the discharge of their legislative duties that they did not approve. If they visited the White House, it was to give, not receive advice" (Milkis and Nelson, 2008, p. 182).

we will see in greater detail in later chapters. Using the SUA to submit most of his legislative recommendations would protect and legitimize the practice. At times Washington still submitted requests for legislation outside of the SUA, as needs required, laying the foundation for broader and more concerted presidential activity in the legislative policy-making process. George Washington, in interpreting the Constitution as he did, sowed the seeds of modern legislative policy activism. Presidents after Washington continued the practice of submitting legislative recommendations to Congress.

If Washington based his legislative policy agenda on constitutional, and perhaps policy grounds, other early presidents saw the political implications of their legislative proposals. Some thought that their administration would be judged partly on what they had asked for, and whether Congress enacted their proposals into law and policy, a perspective usually associated only with modern, legislatively active presidents.[6] James K. Polk, commenting to his nominee for secretary of the navy, George Bancroft, could not be more explicit in this regard:

> There are four great measures which are to be the measures of my administration: one, a reduction of the tariff; another, the independent treasury; a third, the settlement of the Oregon boundary question; and lastly the acquisition of California.[7]

[6] Just because presidents refrained from asserting policy leadership as frequently and across as many issues as modern presidents does not mean that premodern and less policy-active presidents did not have preferences over public policy. Both Edwards (2003, p. 114) and Phelps (1989, p. 65) contend that Washington held strong views across several important policy controversies, such as immigration and internal improvements, two of several topics for which Washington made legislative recommendations in the data used here. Others square the lack of visible or overt acts of Washington's policy leadership, noting that he worked through intermediaries or surrogates like Hamilton, calling Washington the first "hidden-hand" president (Leibiger, 1999, p. 10), a model of "behind-the-scenes" presidential leadership first applied to Eisenhower by Greenstein (1982). Without reviewing each and every premodern president, based on these accounts of these early presidents, it is an overstatement to suggest that because premodern presidents were not as policy active as modern executives that *all of them* did not care about policy.

[7] I want to thank Fred Greenstein for pointing this out to me; also see Merry (2009, p. 133). Merry also reports that "Polk never went beyond Bancroft in discussing the daring goals he set for himself and his country." (p. 133). Merry suggests that something about Polk's personality kept him publicly silent about his policy ambitions, although his public reticence might also have to do with the political culture of the time, which did not yet accept such bold and public presidential policy leadership.

Without amendment to the Constitution, presidential involvement in the legislative policy-making process continued to grow. By the Truman administration in the late 1940s, the president packaged his proposals into what came to be known as the *president's program* (Berman, 1979; Dickinson, 1997; Larocca, 2006; Neustadt, 1955; Rudalevige, 2002; Seligman, 1956). Presidents also lobbied Congress actively about bills before the legislature, including bills that the president had submitted to Congress and those that the president did not submit. The aims of presidential lobbying were to produce legislation that the president supported and to stop legislation that the president opposed. Presidents increasingly engaged in the details of building and shaping individual pieces of legislation at all stages of the legislative policy-making process.

By the mid-twentieth century, Congress and the public alike had come to expect presidential involvement in the legislative process from beginning to end, that is, from agenda setting, to shaping, to passing of legislation (Greenstein, 1988; Huntington, 1973). Presidential activism in legislating would be more than a congressional expectation, more like a demand for presidential leadership (Light, 1991, pp. 155–157). Neustadt (1955) recounts the now-famous story of Eisenhower's resistance to provide legislative leadership in the first year of his presidency. Eisenhower's reluctance to supply strong legislative policy leadership met with criticism from all political quarters, including his own party. Feeling the public and political pressures to be more legislatively active and assertive, Eisenhower submitted a full-fledged and sweeping legislative program to Congress in his second year in office. For the past three-quarters of a century, if not more, these legislative chores and activities rivaled, if not surpassed, other tasks in occupying presidential time and attention, and a president's legacy and reputation rested heavily on his legislative accomplishments (Light, 1991, pp. 66–68).

MULTIPLE PRESIDENTIAL POLICY AGENDAS: DEFINING THE PRESIDENTIAL LEGISLATIVE POLICY AGENDA

This book is about the president's legislative policy agenda. What is it? How does it differ from other presidential policy agendas? What are the differences between the president's *legislative policy agenda,* presidential *legislative position taking,* and the *president's program?*

This book begins by reviewing how others define the policy agenda. Doing so provides a foundation for defining the president's legislative policy agenda, to distinguish it from other presidential policy agendas, presidential position taking on congressional roll calls, and the president's program. Existing research tends to use terms like the *president's agenda* rather loosely and rarely distinguishes between presidential position taking on roll calls from the president's legislative policy agenda. Although presidential policy agendas, presidential position taking, and the president's program are related and overlap, they are conceptually distinct. Clarifying this terminology is important for theory development, comparing empirical results, generalizing from those empirical results, and raising new research questions and directions.

DEFINING AGENDAS

John Kingdon (1995, p. 3) defines the *agenda* as "the list of subjects or problems to which government officials, and people outside of government closely associated with those officials, are paying some serious attention at any given time." This is a somewhat narrower definition than that used by Cobb and Elder (1972, p. 14), who define the agenda as "a general set of political controversies that will be viewed at any point in time as falling within the range of legitimate concerns meriting the attention of the polity."

There are several differences in Kingdon's and Cobb and Elder's definitions of the agenda. Cobb and Elder allow the agenda to include all legitimate concerns of the polity, whether they are receiving attention at a specific point in time or not – what we might think of as the *potential agenda.* Kingdon further distinguishes between the governmental agenda, or those issues receiving attention, and the decision agenda, or those items up for active decision (1995, p. 4). Thus, it might be useful to distinguish among the potential governmental agenda, the actual governmental agenda, and government's decision agenda, with the potential governmental agenda consisting of all issues of legitimate government concern, the actual governmental agenda as those issues receiving active consideration, and the governmental decision agenda as those issues for which some government officials are ready to make a policy decision, even if that decision is to do nothing (Bachrach and Baratz, 1963).

In addition, Cobb and Elder distinguish the institutional from the systemic agenda, the former being "a set of concrete, specific items scheduled for active and serious consideration by a particular institutional decision-making body" (p. 14), in other words, the agenda as Kingdon uses the term. The systemic agenda is broader, more abstract, and more general than the institutional agenda (Cobb and Elder, 1972, p. 14). Recent usage generally equates the systemic agenda with public opinion, or what the public views as pressing problems, issues, and policies (Cohen, 1995).[8]

MULTIPLE PRESIDENTIAL POLICY AGENDAS

Within the broad governmental agenda, Kingdon identifies several *specialized* agendas (1995, pp. 4–5). These specialized agendas can relate to different governmental decision-making bodies or venues. Thus, each of the three branches of government has its own agenda, and within the legislature we can distinguish between the agendas of the House and Senate, and within those chambers, each committee has its own agenda, and so forth.

Similarly, presidents have several policy agendas. The legislative policy agenda is only one. For present purposes, I define the *president's policy agenda* as the list of problems, issues, and policies to which the

---

[8] Although Cobb and Elder (1972) suggest that the systemic agenda may be broader and more encompassing of problems and issues than "any institutional agenda" (p. 14), if we restrict the systemic agenda to issues of concern to the public, then it is more likely that the governmental agenda is broader than the public agenda. Perhaps more important, however, than the scope of the governmental versus the systemic agenda is their overlap or discrepancy. Cobb and Elder also suggest a time lag from an issue arising on the systemic agenda and its appearance on an institutional or governmental agenda. In a later formulation, however, Cobb, Ross, and Ross (1976) allow for the possibility that an issue on an institutional agenda might travel on the systemic or public agenda. Agenda setting becomes a *representational process* when an issue arrives on the systemic or public agendas prior to a governmental agenda (Jones and Baumgartner, 2005), while we can think of it from a leadership perspective when an issue moves from a governmental agenda to the public agenda (Cohen, 1995; Hill, 1998).

president has committed some attention and resources. Three specialized presidential policy agendas merit attention: the rhetorical, administrative, and legislative.

First, the president's *rhetorical policy agenda* consists of those issues that the president speaks about in public, usually targeting the mass public, the news media, and/or members of interest and other groups for his communications efforts. In Cobb and Elder's terminology, the systemic (public) agenda is one target of the president's rhetorical policy agenda. Speeches, public announcements, press secretary briefings of the news media, and modern methods of "going public" (Cohen, 2008, 2010; Kernell, 2007) are the primary methods of publicizing the president's rhetorical policy agenda. The president's rhetorical policy agenda may have several aims or goals, such as to alter the public agenda to align more closely with presidential policy priorities, to build public support for specific pieces of legislation or other policy actions, to demonstrate presidential responsiveness to the public (Cohen, 1997), to inform the nation of presidential actions, or to burnish the president's leadership image.[9]

Presidents do not so much make policy through their rhetorical policy agendas as announce their policy intentions and preferences. Rendering authoritative governmental decisions is an objective of the presidents' other two policy agendas, the executive (or administrative) and the legislative. The executive and the legislative policy agendas differ in the way that policy is made and in their content. For their executive or administrative policy agenda, presidents primarily employ unilateral and/or executive tools, such as executive orders, for translating policy agenda into actual policy.[10] At times, especially in foreign policy, decisions might be masked in secrecy, without a paper trail or formal documentation. In contrast, the legislative policy

---

[9] A considerable body of research has investigated the linkages and causality between the president's rhetorical agenda and public agenda, as well as the agenda of the news media, Congress. See for instance Barabas, 2008; Canes-Wrone, 2006; Cohen, 1995, 1997; Hill, 1998; Edwards and Wood, 1999; Eshbaugh-Soha and Peake, 2004, 2005; Horvit et al., 2008; Peake, 2001; Peake and Eshbaugh-Soha, 2008; Wood, 2007; Wood and Peake, 1999; Yates and Whitford, 2005; Young and Perkins, 2005.

[10] Recent years have seen a flurry of research on this type of presidential policy making. See Cooper, 2002; Dickinson, 2004; Howell, 2003; Mayer, 2001.

agenda consists of those items that require congressional action, such as the passage of legislation.

Formally, the *president's legislative policy agenda* consists of all the president's recommendations that Congress legislate on a particular problem, issue, or policy. The legislative policy agenda, as defined, is overt and public. Presidents might have ideas and preferences on other issues, but for terminological clarity, if the president did not recommend them to Congress, they are not on the legislative policy agenda, but only on the president's *potential legislative policy agenda*. To be part of the president's legislative policy agenda, the president must formally and publicly submit a proposal to Congress. (The potential legislative agenda, discussed in more detail later in this chapter, poses important complications for the study of presidential agenda building and the implications of presidential agenda decisions on success with Congress.)

By recommending congressional action on particular items, the president is providing legislative policy leadership in the minimal sense of aiming to set the congressional agenda. Presidents can also aim to affect the shape of policy outcomes by providing Congress with ideas concerning the content of the resulting legislation. They can offer broad outlines or directions for legislation to take or provide highly detailed ideas, such as through drafts of bills for Congress to use, and from the president's perspective, hopefully adopt. Presidents also can lobby Congress extensively in support of their legislative agendas, but presidents may not do anything else in support of a recommendation once it is submitted to Congress. This study does not directly address the question of presidential lobbying effort, despite the importance of that question.[11]

There might be some substantive overlap in these three presidential policy agendas. As noted previously, the rhetorical policy agenda can be important in building support for items on the legislative policy agenda, the famous "going public" strategy. Once Congress has

---

[11] The question of the conditions under which presidents lobby Congress for or against proposals and bills, and the effectiveness of such lobbying, is central in research on presidential-congressional relations, found in the work of Neustadt (1960, 1990) of persuasion, Bond and Fleisher's (1990) analysis of skill, and Cameron's (2000) veto bargaining model, to name several prominent examples. See Beckmann (2010) for a recent and detailed treatment of presidential lobbying.

enacted an item from the president's legislative policy agenda, the president may take executive actions, issuing executive orders and the like, because he possesses the authority to do so or because the enacted legislation requires him to do so. Presidents may also try to make policy through executive means when Congress fails or refuses to enact an item on the president's legislative policy agenda, however (Howell, 2003). Presidents might see either legislative or executive action as a means for implementing policy, depending on circumstances.

A complete theory of presidential policy making needs to take into account these several presidential policy agendas, their similarities and differences, and their implications for presidential policy making. The more narrow aim of this book is to understand the factors that affect the composition of the president's legislative policy agenda, the decisions of presidents to include some items on their legislative agenda but not others, how these presidential legislative policy agenda-building decisions affect success with Congress, and the impact of presidential agenda-building decisions on the importance of resulting legislation. Answering these questions provides one necessary step in building the fuller theory of presidential policy agendas and policy making.

DISTINGUISHING THE LEGISLATIVE POLICY AGENDA FROM POSITION TAKING

The president's legislative policy agenda differs from presidential positions on roll call before Congress, the aspect of presidential-congressional relations that has received the most empirical attention. Presidential roll call positions are both broader and narrower than the president's legislative policy agenda. Figure 1.1 presents a schematic to distinguish the differences between roll call positions and presidential requests.

The two large ovals represent the president's legislative agenda on the left, and on the right the universe of bills introduced by members of Congress. These "active agendas," to use Kingdon's (1995) phrase, represent only a subset of the potential presidential and congressional agendas. Not included in the illustration are issues that the president and members could have submitted but did not, as well as the set of

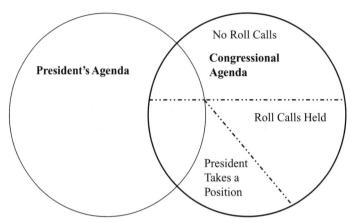

Figure 1.1. Presidential Agendas, Congressional Agendas, and Congressional Actions on Those Agendas.

possible issues of concern to someone else in the polity but that did not make the list of potential presidential or congressional legislative proposals.

In the congressional oval, the dashed line separates congressional bill introductions into two sets, those receiving roll call votes (below the line) and those not receiving roll calls (above the line).[12] As the figure also illustrates, some presidential proposals receive roll calls, but others will not, the latter designated by the area of the presidential proposal oval that does not overlap with the congressional agenda. The figure also shows that presidents may take positions on some congressional roll calls not from the president's legislative agenda.

Presidential roll call position taking, as used commonly in the literature, thus consists of items from the president's legislative policy agenda as well as from bills that members of Congress introduced, what we might call "on-agenda" versus "off-agenda" roll calls (Covington et al., 1995). For the latter group, presidents might not have taken a formal position until long into the legislative policy-making process, perhaps near the time of the roll call, and might do nothing more than

[12] We could have made the figure more realistic and complex by detailing other aspects of congressional attention to bills, such as committee hearings and differences in treatment between the House and Senate. Doing so would unnecessarily clutter the figure and obscure the more basic point aimed at here, namely, the difference between presidential proposals and presidential positions on roll calls.

announce support or opposition to the bill in question. Unlike bills from the president's agenda, for off-agenda items, "the president is merely responding to their [members of Congress] initiative by recommending adoption or defeat of the bill" (Covington et al., 1995, p. 1004).

Very few studies differentiate "on-agenda" and "off-agenda" bills. Covington et al. (1995) argue that such a distinction is warranted and necessary. The factors that affect passage differ between "on-agenda" and "off-agenda" bills. According to Covington et al. (1995), presidents also should enjoy higher congressional success for on-agenda than off-agenda bills: "If a proposal is on a president's agenda, then the president is able to shape the bill's content in ways that are not true of proposals initiated by others. By shaping the language of a bill, the president is defining the terms of debate. The opposition may deal with the president's issues on the president's terms" (p. 1004). Their analysis indicates higher presidential success for on-agenda than off-agenda roll calls.

Both presidential proposals and position taking are worthy topics for investigation. Inasmuch as their prospects for and factors leading to success differ, we need to keep these two phenomena conceptually and empirically distinct. As I review later in more detail, there are some studies that look solely at congressional treatment of presidential proposals, like this study, but most studies focus on presidential roll call positions without distinguishing between on- and off-agenda items.[13]

THE PRESIDENT'S PROGRAM VERSUS THE LEGISLATIVE POLICY AGENDA

The president's legislative policy agenda also differs from the president's program, but for the modern period, they are synonymous. As argued in the opening pages of this book, a presidential legislative policy agenda has existed since the earliest days of the presidency. One difference between the legislative policy agenda and the presidential

---

[13] A useful but as yet unaddressed question asks why and under which conditions presidents take positions on roll calls not from their agenda, the off-agenda. Presidents may do so to claim credit for issues headed for passage, to stop some from being enacted, among other possible reasons.

program therefore is length of existence, but second, the presidential program is more formalized and routinized than the legislative policy agenda. Importantly, the presidential program grew out of the legislative policy agenda.[14]

The idea of a presidential program emerged in the late 1940s with the presidency of Harry Truman. Several forces moved Truman to the idea of identifying a presidential program. First, a president program provided Truman with a handy reference for his 1948 reelection campaign, especially his charge that the Republican-controlled Congress had failed to enact necessary legislation, dubbing it a "do nothing" Congress (Donaldson, 1999; Hartmann, 1971; Neustadt, 1954, 1955; Williams, 1979). In addition, after nearly two decades since the first election of FDR, the public, media and Congress had come to expect presidential legislative leadership, or at least the identification of important issues to address. Moreover, a decade of depression, followed by five years of war, had stalled progress on many domestic concerns and issues. Finally, both the administration and Congress desired some way of distinguishing departmental legislative proposals from those of the president, the assumption that the president did not view every bureaucratic proposal as a high priority (Rudalevige, 2002, pp. 41–47; Wayne, 1978).

To some degree, the idea of a presidential program identifies more a process than a list of presidential proposals. This is because, as Rudalevige (2002, pp. 63–64) points out, different presidents have employed different methods of tallying their legislative success and accomplishments, that no agreed-on standard exists for defining the president's program, and that no document or standard compilation of documents exists that formally identifies the president's program.

---

[14] Landy and Milkis use the term *presidential program* in describing John Quincy Adams's legislative policy ambitions. "Adams was far bolder. He produced his own legislative program and used the occasion of his first annual message to Congress to enumerate it and press for its passage. Among other things, he proposed the establishment of a national university and a vigorous and expensive program of internal improvements" (2000, p. 84). Landy and Milkis are correct that Adams was more legislatively ambitious than many of his predecessors and that his separate proposals formed a cohesive set or package, but he did not have a legislative program in the modern sense, which uses staff agencies to clear proposals from the bureaucracies, incorporate them with other proposals, and establish priorities among the various proposals.

Under Truman, the process of identifying the president's legislative proposals and positions was formalized. The Legislative Reference Division of the Bureau of the Budget cleared all legislative drafts written in the agencies, stamping some of them presidential (Neustadt, 1954; Rudalevige, 2002). That clearance process would allow those nonpresidential drafts to be submitted to Congress as long as they were not contrary to the president's program and policies, thus distinguishing between presidential proposals and departmental ones that the president did not oppose. Further, the Legislative Reference Division reviewed all enrolled legislation, bills under active congressional consideration, to determine if the president should support, oppose (and threaten to veto), or take no stand on them (Wayne, Cole, and Hyde, 1979). Finally, the process reviewed all bureaucratic testimony or communications to Congress for consistency with the president's program and policies. Without an agreed-on guide or definition of the presidential program, scholars have used different techniques to determine the content of the program. Light's (1991) pioneering work on the president's agenda relies on the State of the Union Address for identifying the composition of the president's program.[15]

There are several issues with using the SUA as a comprehensive accounting of the president's program and legislative policy agenda. First, it is incomplete. Presidents may identify legislative proposals in other documents, such as the budget, as well as special messages to Congress. Second, the president's legislative policy agenda is dynamic. Between one SUA and the next, it can change especially when unexpected events occur, events that shift presidential attention to new

---

[15] Light also used OMB legislative clearance records, in combination with the SUA, to identify the president's agenda. Specifically, to be included in his database, each item or proposal had to meet two criteria, had to be cleared by OMB, and had to be mentioned in at least one SUA during the president's term, producing a total of 266 items from 1961 to 1980 (1991, p. 9). Furthermore, Light does not include foreign policy items, and of domestic policy, he does not consider economic policy either (p. 7). He updated his study to include Reagan's two terms, using the same criteria. According to Light, Reagan added another sixty items during his eight years in office (p. 241). In a 2000 publication, Light adds George H. W. Bush and Bill Clinton's first term, for an additional forty-one and forty-two items, respectively (p. 118). All told, Light includes 409 items in his domestic policy tallies. It is not clear what the implication is for generalizing about the president's legislative policy agenda by restricting items to domestic social policy.

problems and issues. For example, George W. Bush came to office in 2001 emphasizing economic and domestic policies as his top agenda priorities. The terrorist attacks of September 11, 2001 redirected his agenda to combating terrorism and international affairs, leaving much less time and attention for the president to pursue his economic and domestic policy aims. Bush delayed pushing for Social Security reform until after the 2004 reelection, possibly because of his preoccupation with foreign affairs.

The legislative policy agenda, as defined here, helps to overcome some of these limitations of using the SUA as the sole document for identifying the president's program. At the same time, because the legislative policy agenda existed long before the establishment of the more formalized presidential program, we can investigate an aspect of presidential engagement with congressional policy making across the entire sweep of U.S. history. This lets us address empirically the question of the impact of the presidential program on presidential agenda building and on presidential relations with Congress, rather than merely assuming that matters changed radically with the creation of the presidential program (Skowronek, 2002; Woolley, 2005).

THE PRESIDENT'S LEGISLATIVE POLICY AGENDA DATABASE, 1789–2002

Rudalevige's (2002) study of centralization in the preparation of the president's program employs the most extensive and inclusive operational definition of the president's program/legislative agenda. To Rudalevige, any item that a president specifically mentions in a request for legislation belongs in president's program. To identify specific presidential requests, Rudalevige turns to the *Public Papers of the Presidents*, in particular any written message sent to Congress asking for legislation. The *Public Papers* have been published from the Hoover presidency onward: Rudalevige begins his study of centralization in preparation of the presidential program with 1949, the first year that we can say an identifiable presidential program existed.

I employ the same operational definition as Rudalevige for identifying the president's legislative policy agenda, the only distinction between the presidential program and legislative policy agenda being temporal. Presidents have always had a legislative policy agenda, but in the late 1940s this agenda transformed itself, becoming the presidential program.[16] Did the development of a formal presidential program have any implications on presidential-congressional relations and the policy-making process? The chapters that follow address this question. In fact, as we will see, the creation of the presidential program and the attendant legislative clearance process helps us to unravel the modern president puzzle, one of the puzzles that motivates this research.

I use several data sets to identify presidential legislative requests from 1789 through 2002. The primary data source is the Presidential Request file of the *Database of Historical Congressional Statistics*, which was funded by the National Science Foundation. The Presidential Request file was collected under the direction of Michael Malbin. That file contains 12,505 presidential requests made from 1789 through 1992. In a second data set, Andrew Rudalevige has essentially replicated the Malbin Presidential Request file for the years 1993 to 2002. He has generously made those data available to me, adding another 1,687 requests and bringing the total to 14,192. I have combined the two data sets into one.

Identifying congressional policy proposals, or requests, is relatively easy. Before Congress can formally consider an issue or proposal, a member of Congress must submit a bill.[17] It is not as easy to identify presidential requests to Congress. Presidents cannot introduce bills themselves, nor must the president fill out any special forms that

[16] Presidential effort on behalf of their proposals, that is, presidential lobbying of Congress, also seems to have intensified in the mid-twentieth century, but systematic overt presidential lobbying seems to predate the establishment of the presidential program, arriving by early in Franklin Roosevelt's tenure, if not before (Greenstein, 1988). Presidential lobbying efforts in behalf of legislation prior to FDR do not appear systematic, varying from president to president, across policies, and the presidency did not have institutional resources, like the Office of Legislative Relations, to help (Wayne, 1978). Still, the historical record indicates that several pre-FDR presidents were actively involved in trying to move legislation forward, even if they did not do so publicly, like Jefferson (Malone, 1974), although John Quincy Adams (Hargreaves, 1985), James K. Polk (Bergeron, 1987), and Woodrow Wilson (Macmahon, 1956) among pre-FDR presidents seemed more public in the legislative lobbying of Congress.

[17] Congress can informally consider issues without a bill introduction, and a member may spend time and effort working with other members prior to introducing a bill, but for Congress to take formal action, like holding a committee hearing, a bill must be introduced.

identify his proposals. Tracking down each presidential request for legislation thus becomes a laborious task.[18] The Malbin/Rudalevige efforts undertook the laborious task of reading every public presidential message to Congress to locate the president's legislative requests. Coders were provided with detailed instructions for determining whether a presidential statement constitutes a request for legislative action.

First, to be considered a presidential request, a request must appear in a message from the president to Congress. According to the codebook, "Requests or recommendations delivered privately, verbally, or through an intermediary (including official, approved Administration requests from a Cabinet Secretary) are not included."[19] Furthermore, the data collections exclude requests that Congress not act, as well as vetoes, items subject to legislative veto, nominations, and executive branch reorganizations plans. Treaties are included if they meet the publication tests. The data collections also exclude appropriations requests unless that request asks for new policy initiatives. Discrete requests are listed separately, even if they form part of a policy package, following how the president presents the request to Congress. Beginning with Truman, presidential requests made after the last day of the final congressional session in that president's term are not included, with the exception of treaties. Finally, for the years during which the *Congressional Quarterly* (CQ) published its "box score," coding began with CQ's list of requests and eliminated ones that did not meet the above criteria. The president's *Public Papers* for these years are used as a second pass to catch what CQ might have missed and to double check CQ coding decisions.

This data collection process also excludes other public comments that presidents make about preferred policies, as well as presidential efforts on legislation that are not announced publicly. Sometimes

---

[18] For instance, in my earlier studies (Cohen, 1982a, 1982b), I used only the SUA as a source for identifying presidential proposals. As noted earlier, this provides an incomplete listing of presidential requests to Congress.

[19] Sources for presidential messages are James P. Richardson, ed. *A Compilation of Messages and Papers of the Presidents*, for years 1789 to 1917, the *Congressional Record* from 1917 to 1929, the *Public Papers of the President* for presidents Hoover plus Truman through George H. W. Bush, 1929 to 1932 and 1944 to 1992, and for Franklin Roosevelt, *The Public Papers and Addresses of Franklin D. Roosevelt*.

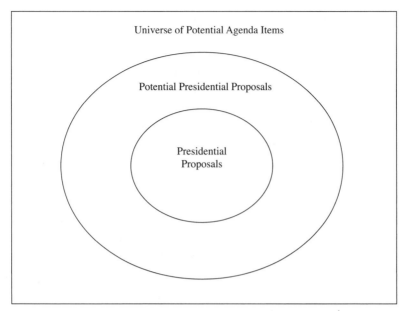

Figure 1.2. Potential and Actual Presidential Agendas.

presidents make a public comment, but not in a direct message to Congress and often vague, about support for a policy direction or initiative – what we normally think of as a "trial balloon." Trial balloons are used to test the political waters, to estimate political support and opposition before the president commits himself to the policy. Sometimes a surrogate for the president, like an administration official or member of Congress, floats the trial balloon, which allows the president to distance himself from the proposal if it receives stiff resistance or the president decides not to pursue the topic further. We should not consider such trial balloons as part of the president's legislative policy agenda unless the president subsequently submits a formal proposal to Congress. Trail balloons are items that reside in the president's *potential policy agenda* (see Figure 1.2). If the president decides to submit a proposal to Congress based on the results of floating the trial balloon, the proposal moves into the president's agenda. It is better to think of using trial balloons as one process that presidents may employ in building their legislative policy agendas. Until a president submits a proposal to Congress, however, we should not consider such public comments as part of the president's legislative policy agenda.[20]

Presidents may also take a stand on a policy or issue but not reveal that position in public. They may work behind the scenes, with members of Congress, on behalf of or against legislation. Why would a president fail to "go public" on issues of concern to him? Canes-Wrone's (2001, 2006) theory of strategically going public suggests that presidents stay private if their position is not popular with the public. By going public, presidents, according to Canes-Wrone's theory, activate opinion, raising the salience of the issue. This intensifies public opinion pressures on Congress and increases the likelihood that Congress will enact legislation that the president dislikes. Examples of presidential "staying private" exist (Covington, 1987). Identifying occasions when presidents remain private is the primary obstacle to their systematic study. Records of meetings on the issue between the president and legislative leaders might not exist and presidents may even rely on surrogates to liaise with members of Congress, making recovery of the president's involvement even more problematic. Although presidents pursue legislative goals in instances when they stay private, these cases differ from legislative proposals that presidents submit to Congress by the mere fact of the president's not submitting a public proposal. Staying private with regard to his legislative wishes is an important topic, as both Canes-Wrone (2001) and Covington (1987) show, but because of the reasons mentioned previously, it remains outside of this research.

SUMMARY

The main goal of this chapter is to define the president's legislative policy agenda, distinguishing that agenda from two other presidential policy agendas, the rhetorical and administrative policy agendas. This

---

[20] Other than case studies of particular trial balloons, or passing references in textbooks on the presidency or policy making, I have been unable to locate a single systematic study of presidential trial balloons, when presidents decide to use them, under which conditions, for which types of policies, or their outcome, whether they result in legislative proposals, executive actions, and so forth. Presidential trial balloons should be a topic for future research.

chapter also differentiates the president's legislative policy agenda from presidential position taking on roll calls and from the president's program. Despite overlap between the legislative policy agenda, position taking, and the president's program, these topics differ conceptually and represent different populations of events. Finally, this chapter introduces the legislative proposal database, a compilation of all presidential proposals for legislation made public from 1789 to 2002, the most comprehensive such data set in existence. The next chapter reviews the literature on agenda building, discussing how this study differs from past efforts to study agendas.

CHAPTER 2

Studying Agenda Building

This chapter reviews the literature on agenda building, with special emphasis on the president's legislative policy agenda. The existing research on presidential agenda building, as well as agenda building in general, provides the building blocks for this study. As this review details, however, the existing literature is not without its limitations.

Research on agenda building has blossomed in recent decades. Among the important and highly influential studies on the general question of the agenda building process include Bachrach and Baratz (1963), Cobb and Elder (1972), Kingdon (1995), Light (1982, 1991), Baumgartner and Jones (1993, 2009), and Jones and Baumgartner (2005). That research has provided some of the terminology that has come to define how we study the agenda and the agenda-building process, such as Bachrach and Baratz's nondecisions; Cobb and Elder's distinction between the systemic and institutional agenda; Kingdon's concepts of the active agenda, and the policy, political, and problem streams; and Baumgartner and Jones's policy venues, to list just a few of the central ideas.

The rational choice literature has also grappled with agenda setting but generally in a more formalized sense of an agenda setter who acts as a gatekeeper who controls access to decision-making venues and the sequence of voting on alternatives. The theory of committees and the median voter theorem provide the underpinnings of this brand of agenda-setting research, with Romer and Rosenthal (1978) the seminal work in this vein. Krehbiel's (1998) pivotal politics theory, as well as Cameron's (2000) veto bargaining model, and Canes-Wrone's

(2006) strategic "going public" model, among others, grew out of this research tradition.

This book is concerned primarily with the presidency. Considerable research now exists on the president's agenda, and both of the research traditions noted earlier, agenda processes and rational choice, have contributed to our understanding of the president's agenda (see Wood, 2009b, for a review of the literature). Larroca's (2006) information model and Cameron and Park's (2008) burden-sharing model are two examples of studies that combine the two agenda-setting research traditions with regard to the presidency.[1]

As reviewed in more detail later in this chapter, research on the president's agenda is limited in several regards, however; those limitations and gaps restrict what we can say about presidential agenda building and the implications of the president's agenda on policy making. These limitations include 1) an almost exclusive focus on the post–World War Two era, 2) an emphasis on domestic as opposed to foreign policy, and 3) hypotheses about the factors that affect the presidential legislative policy agenda choice that are only rarely tested.[2]

TEMPORAL LIMITATIONS

Almost all research on presidential agenda building, in fact the bulk of all research on the presidency, considers only the era from the New Deal, the era of the modern presidency. Light's (1982, 1991) seminal study of the president's agenda provides an instructive example. He focuses on the process of agenda building since the Kennedy administration, relying on interviews with White House staffers and others who participated in the process of building presidential agendas. Similarly, the burgeoning empirical literature on the president's

---

[1] Larocca (2006, pp. 5–7) makes the important point, namely that the rational choice literature on agenda setting, with its emphasis on monopoly agenda setters who determine the sequence of voting on alternatives, has limited applicability to presidential agenda setting. Presidents do not possess such formal authority over the congressional agenda. In fact, one puzzle for agenda-setting research to address is why the president seems to have such an easy time getting onto the congressional agenda (e.g., Edwards and Barrett, 2000) without any formal authority over the congressional agenda.

[2] Wood (2009b) also argues that there has been more research attention to the president's rhetorical than to the legislative or executive policy agendas.

rhetorical agenda (cf. Cohen, 1995, 1997; Edwards and Wood, 1999; Eshbaugh-Soha and Peake, 2004, 2005; Hill, 1998; Peake, 2001; Peake and Eshbaugh-Soha, 2008; Wood and Peake, 1998) also looks only at the modern era. The same can be said for other notable studies of the president's agenda (Cameron and Park, 2008; Cummins, 2008; Eshbaugh-Soha, 2005; Light, 2000; Peterson, 1990).[3]

Understandable reasons exist for the emphasis on modern presidents. Data availability and the costs of collecting data affect the ability to study premodern presidents as fully as modern ones. For instance, participants in past presidential administrations may have passed away, obviously making it impossible to interview them. Diaries, biographies, and histories might not cover or document the questions of interest. Only recently have newspapers digitized their collections, which has enabled more efficient collection of news stories about presidents, but newspapers do not present a complete public record of information relevant to agenda building and the presidency. Some types of relevant data, such as polls and surveys, came into existence only in the modern era.

We possess long-term historical data on some important aspects of presidential behavior, however, like proposals submitted to Congress, executive orders, vetoes, nominations and appointments, and speeches. Although the existing historical and official documentary record might not be as rich as one might hope, we have not mined these records deeply in studying the presidency. As Woolley (2005, p. 9) comments: "Still today, relatively little systematic work, by standards of contemporary social science, has been done on the pre-modern period. Very few examples exist of research that actually spans the pre-modern and modern periods. . . . " McCarty's (2009) recent examination of veto use during the early years of the office illustrates the value of studying traditional presidents for understanding presidential behavior and the development of the office.

There are important theoretical implications of the dearth of research on traditional presidents and the lack of comparison between traditional and modern chief executives. Again, Woolley: "One of the

---

[3] In citing these studies, I do not distinguish between those that look at the effects of the president's agenda versus those that look at factors that affect the composition of the agenda.

unfortunate modernist legacies has been to legitimate a dismissal of the past as too dissimilar to be of serious interest and thus not capable of informing us about the present" (Woolley, 2005, p. 10). Moreover, debate exists over the development of the presidency, and whether Greenstein's (1988) modern presidency notion, Tulis's (1987) rhetorical presidency thesis, or Skowronek's (1993) political time theory better characterize the development of the office and presidential behavior. By focusing so much research attention on the modern era and neglecting research on the premodern era, we implicitly assume that modern presidents differ from premodern (traditional) presidents, but rarely do we test this assumption.[4] Even if modern and premodern presidents differ in important and fundamental ways, empirical documentation on the ways and the extent to which they differ would be useful. Obtaining that information can be done only if we test the modern–premodern differences hypothesis.[5]

This study employs data on presidential proposals submitted to Congress for virtually the entire history of the office, 1789 to 2002. I will test the implications of the modern presidency on building the president's legislative agenda and the prospects for success with Congress, the modern presidency puzzle noted in the introduction:

[4] In two early studies, Cohen (1982a, 1982b), using long-term historical data tests of whether modern presidents have higher success with Congress than earlier presidents, if the processes leading to success for modern and traditional presidents varies, and whether the advantage in foreign policy for modern presidents holds for traditional presidents. From a completely different research tradition, American political development and political thought, David Nichols (1994) argues that one can see elements of the modern presidency in both the design of the institution at its founding, as well as the behavior of early presidents.

[5] Woolley (2005) also argues that the literature on the development of the office emphasizes major breaks or jumps, what Skowronek (2002) labels "big bang" accounts of presidential transformation, but aspects of the office and presidential behavior might have developed incrementally. There is the possibility of different development patterns for different aspects of the office and presidential behavior. For instance, incrementalism might account for some aspects of presidential behavior, whereas sudden breaks account for others. Moreover, the "sudden break" literature is not always clear about the casual mechanism that led to this marked change in the office and/or presidential behavior. The rhetorical presidency literature, for example, tends to ask if rhetorical style changed with Theodore Roosevelt or Woodrow Wilson, as Tulis (1988) argues. Generally, such studies present univariate time series of aspects of presidential rhetoric, visually inspecting them for breaks and changes in level, but do not test hypotheses relating to the impact of competing independent variables on these series (cf. Teten, 2003, 2007, 2008; Lim, 2002; Murphy, 2008).

How can we square the fact of such a pronounced increase in the size of the president's legislative agenda between the traditional and modern epochs with the difficult time that modern presidents have with Congress and the availability of alternative means for policy making, such as the executive order?

DOMESTIC POLICY EMPHASIS

Studies of the president's agenda tend to focus on domestic policy choice. Very little attention has been paid to presidential agenda setting for foreign policy. This imbalance in research attention between the two policy areas parallels the state of political science research more generally, in which research on domestic and foreign policy generally has developed separately from each other. Most agenda-setting research has been conducted by domestic policy scholars. Moreover, scholars of domestic policy development often know little about foreign policy and vice versa. Recent years have witnessed some scholars merging the study of the two types of policies, for example Howell and Pevehouse (2007). Some studies also have begun to look at foreign policy and presidential agendas, often comparing foreign and domestic policy (Cohen, 1995, 1997; Edwards and Wood, 1999; Hill, 1998; Peake, 2001; Wood and Peake, 1998; Young and Perkins, 2005); these studies focus almost exclusively on the rhetorical agenda.[6] The general point, however, that studies of domestic and foreign policy making do not speak to each other or use each other's research and insights and contributions, still holds.

To my knowledge, only Durant and Diehl (1989) explicitly address the question of whether theories about domestic agenda building, in particular Kingdon's (1984) multiple streams model, are applicable to the foreign policy case. They find Kingdon's model wanting as an explanation of presidential foreign policy agenda setting.[7] Durant

---

[6] To be fair, Canes-Wrone's (2006) study of presidential policy responsiveness to and leadership of public opinion compares domestic and foreign policy, as does Cohen (1997).

[7] A few studies have picked up on Durant and Diehl's lead. Travis and Zahariadis (2002) use the policy streams approach in their study on foreign aid, but foreign aid as a policy area clearly differs from national security and defense.

and Diehl argue that many domestic issues are discretionary and compete with each other for presidential (and congressional and public)
attention, but the most important foreign policy issues are not discretionary. Presidents have to attend to foreign policy when important issues and/or crises happen. Many foreign policy issues/crises
arise from the often-unanticipated action of other nations. Foreign
policy crises might have national security implications and require
immediate responses; time is a luxury that might not be possible with
these crises, unlike most domestic policy issues. Policy makers generally think that they must attend to foreign policy crises quickly and
with dispatch. If they do not respond quickly, the situation may grow
out of control, lead to more severe consequences like armed conflict
and war, and possibly undermine the nation's security. The founding
fathers recognized these aspects of foreign policy and fashioned the
presidency to handle foreign policy with "energy and dispatch."

Moreover, despite the advantages of the president in foreign compared with domestic policy (e.g., the two presidencies thesis, see Shull,
1991; Canes-Wrone, Howell, and Lewis, 2008), much presidential
policy making on foreign policy remains hidden from public view.
As Baum (2004) argues, the high public opinion cost of "bad" foreign policy crisis outcomes creates incentives for presidents to refrain
from publicizing certain foreign policy issues and actions. Presidents,
according to Baum, will go public in foreign policy when the probability of success is high and when the public will reward them for that
success. This tends to limit foreign policy issues that the president will
speak about publicly to those with important national security implications, for which the president might need broad-based political and
public support. Thus, presidential rhetorical attention to foreign policy is a highly selective subset of presidential activity and interest in
foreign policy. For this reason, the research on presidential rhetorical
attention to foreign policy may present a distorted or biased portrait
of presidential foreign policy making. An understanding of presidential agenda attention to foreign policy requires looking beyond the
president's rhetorical policy agenda.[8]

---

[8] There is an irony here, too. Whichever advantages that presidents possess in domestic
policy making derive in part from being able to mobilize public support, a resource

Neglecting foreign policy in studies of presidential agenda building, as well as policy-making studies more generally, restricts and perhaps biases our understanding of how presidents build their policy agendas. It is useful to think of agendas as a scarce resource. Policy makers can attend to only a certain number of issues at any one time, and almost always the number of issues seeking agenda status outnumbers available placements. If foreign policy issues have an easier time getting onto presidential agenda, then the failure of domestic issues to gain agenda status might have a lot to do with the ability of foreign policy issues to get on the president's agenda. Studies that look at the rise and fall of issues on the president's agenda but address only competition among domestic issues and fail to incorporate agenda competition between domestic and foreign policy issues could be wrong about the dynamics and processes that lead to the rise and fall of issues on the president's agenda. Only by incorporating foreign policy into studies of agenda building can we begin to compare the differences and similarities between foreign and domestic policy in the agenda-building process, and the implications of each type of policy for the ability of the other to secure agenda status.

Moreover, accepting that foreign policy constitutes one of the president's most important policy responsibilities, we overlook this important aspect of presidential policy making when we limit research to domestic policy matters. Neglecting foreign policy in the study of presidential agenda building, and presidential policy making more generally, can provide at best a partial and incomplete portrait of what presidents do and how they do it.

Furthermore, foreign versus domestic policy could have implications for our two puzzles. For instance, if presidents win more on foreign than on domestic policy, as the two presidencies thesis argues, will divided versus united government have as much impact on foreign policy as on domestic policy proposals? Might presidents, when facing opposition congresses, displace domestic policy proposals in favor of

that other policy makers cannot as easily obtain. From Durant and Diehl (1989), however, the presidential advantage in foreign policy making may come from secrecy and control over information, not public support. The irony is that presidents might have an easier time mobilizing public support for foreign as opposed to domestic policy.

foreign policy ones, given the higher prospects of success for foreign than domestic policy? Owing to the reasons stated earlier, this study makes use of both foreign and domestic policy proposals from the president to Congress.

LACK OF HYPOTHESIS TESTING

Only a small number of studies develop and test hypotheses regarding presidential legislative policy agenda building (Cameron and Park, 2008; Eshbaugh-Soha, 2005; Rudalevige, 2002),[9] whereas several others suggest hypotheses concerning presidential agenda choice. Inasmuch as developing hypotheses and testing them are necessary steps for theory building, limited theoretical progress has been made on presidential agenda building. First let us consider some key studies that offer hypotheses but do not put them to systematic testing, and then let us review the studies that develop and test hypotheses regarding presidential agenda building.

In terms of research from which we can extract testable hypotheses, Paul Light's work stands out. Light (1982, 1991) lists numerous factors that affect different stages of presidential agenda building, gleaned from his interviews with staffers who served in the White House since Kennedy. Light discusses how timing, presidential resources, the congressional environment, and a host of other factors affect the construction of the president's legislative agenda. Nowhere, however, does he use his interview data to test specific hypotheses formally, which would enable him to provide us with a sense of the relative importance of these various factors on presidential agenda decision making.

Similarly, consider Light's (2000) review of trends in the presidential agenda, the secular decline in the number of large and new policy proposals. He suggests several reasons for such a decline in the "importance" of presidential legislative policy ambitions. These reasons include 1) the rise of party polarization, which makes it

---

9   This contrasts to the empirical theory building and testing of the president's rhetorical agenda. See for example Barabas, 2008; Cohen, 1995; Hill, 1998; Edwards and Wood, 1999; Eshbaugh-Soha and Peake, 2004, 2005; Horvit et al., 2008; Peake, 2001; Peake and Eshbaugh-Soha, 2008; Wood, 2007; Wood and Peake, 1999; Yates and Whitford, 2005; Young and Perkins, 2005.

harder to pass big policies; 2) the legacy of the Reagan revolution, which undermined support for governmental solutions to problems; 3) large budget deficits, which limit financial resources to tackle problems with government programs; 4) the American state has played itself out, in part by implementing policies and programs across all aspects of life and society; and 5) that demographic change, the aging of society, and the burgeoning size of related programs (e.g., Social Security, Medicare) have created a massive problem for government that will push most other problems off of the nation's agenda (pp. 126–129). These are thoughtful hypotheses, although some now might be dated. Light never systematically tests these competing explanations of an important trend in the presidential agenda, however.

Several studies, however, do present and test hypotheses about presidential legislative agenda building. Rudalevige (2002) looks at the factors that affect the degree of centralization in preparation of legislative proposals from 1949 to 1996; that is, whether the White House/Executive Office of the President or departmental agencies authored the proposal. For instance, he finds greater centralization when a proposal involves several departments or agencies, when the proposal is new, when the proposal has a reorganizational impact, and when the White House/EOP possesses larger staff. Authorship is decentralized the more technically complex the proposal. Somewhat surprisingly, neither the presence of divided versus united government nor presidential party affect centralization, but wider ideological distances between the president and Congress are associated with greater White House control (centralization) in the preparation of legislative proposals.

Eshbaugh-Soha (2005) offers another systematic test of presidential agenda building. He constructs a two-dimensional typology, in which policy proposals vary in degree of importance (important versus less important) and by temporal impact (long-term versus short-term). These two dimensions produce a fourfold typology: *major* (important, long-term), *incremental* (unimportant, long-term), *meteoric* (short-term, important), and *minor* (short-term, unimportant). Using data from 1949 to 2000, Eshbaugh-Soha finds that "The numbers of *major* and *incremental* policy types as well as the president's total domestic policy agenda decrease in the face of budget deficits and unfavorable Congressional makeup," (p. 266), but that contextual factors like these do not seem to affect minor agenda items.

Cameron and Park (2008) develop a formal model that integrates presidential legislative agenda choice with legislative success, their burden-sharing model. The burden-sharing model argues that presidents assume some of the cost of the legislative process by providing Congress with drafts of legislation, but presidents will engage in such behavior only if they sense that Congress is in a mood to legislate on the matter at hand. Presidents benefit when they submit draft legislation by bending Congress toward the president's preferred policy solution on the matter under consideration. Using data on the total number of presidential submissions to Congress for the years 1949 to 1996, they find that the volume of presidential submissions increases as Congress appears ready to produce legislation.

The Rudalevige, Eshbaugh-Soha, and Cameron-Park studies represent important advances in the study of presidential legislative agenda building. They identify key attributes of presidential agendas, and most critically develop hypotheses to account for variation in those attributes, which they test systematically, in Rudalevige's words, "replacing anecdote with evidence" (p. 85). The three studies look at only the modern period, however. Moreover, centralization/decentralization, importance, temporal impact, and legislative activism (size) do not exhaust the characteristics of the presidential agenda of theoretical interest.[10] Perhaps more to the point, there are only three such studies in the literature on presidential agenda building.[11] Clearly more such work is needed. This book offers a theory in which presidential anticipations of Congress play a large part in

[10] There are issues with Eshbaugh-Soha's definition of the president's legislative agenda and his data collection techniques. He includes presidential positions on congressional issues as part of the president's agenda. As argued previously, we must distinguish between such presidential positions and presidential proposals. Research might determine that they are fundamentally alike, but it is premature to make that case, and Covington et al. (1995), as noted earlier, suggest and find systematic differences between on- and off-agenda items when it comes to success with Congress. Plus, to be considered part of the president's agenda, Eshbaugh-Soha first turns to the State of the Union Address (SUA) and then requires that an item from the SUA also be mentioned in a second presidential message. This may be an unduly restrictive and rhetoric-focused method for identifying the president's legislative agenda. This study stands out for its systematic testing of hypotheses, however.

[11] There is a somewhat larger literature that looks at the success of the presidential agenda in Congress, which I review in more detail later. Generally, that literature

presidential agenda building. That theory leads to several hypotheses concerning presidential agenda-building decisions and the implications of those decisions on the actions that Congress takes on the president's proposals.

AN APPROACH TO STUDYING PRESIDENTIAL
AGENDA BUILDING

The primary question that agenda-setting research asks is why some issues make it onto government agendas but other issues do not. Such a question conceptualizes agenda setting as a decision, a choice between placing an issue on an agenda or not. A type of sample-selection bias, what an older literature has termed *nondecisions* (Bachrach and Baratz, 1962, 1963), afflicts all empirical studies of agenda setting.

Figure 1.2, from the previous chapter, illustrates this point and its consequences. We can with some precision identify the issues or items on the president's legislative agenda because the president forwards them to Congress in the form of a proposal. We do not possess a similarly well-defined list of "potential presidential proposals" or the "universe of potential agenda items," however, unless the administration made an overt decision to reject an item for the president's legislative agenda.

Peterson (1990, p. 46) aptly summarizes the difficulty in collecting empirical evidence on presidential legislative agenda-building decisions prior to submission of a proposal:

> [T]he processes are so complex, the participants are so varied and numerous, and executive decisions about legislative issues are often not discrete events. Ideally, one would like first to have an accurate assessment of the president's operational goals and sincere policy preferences, and then be able to examine the record of each proposal, before its submission by the president, for traces of congressionally inspired changes. So many events and maneuvers never enter the paper trail, however, and those that do are so voluminous that the task of identifying them all is probably beyond the capabilities of even the most encompassing research enterprises.

takes the presidential agenda as fixed, that a president does not modify his agenda based on expectations for success in Congress.

In other words, we know little about the parameters of our population, that is, all potential presidential proposals. We possess information only about proposals that the president submitted to Congress, the president's legislative policy agenda, but the proposals that the president forwards to Congress do not constitute a random sample from the set of potential proposals. Thus, although we know that submitted proposals differ from those not submitted, we do not know how or in which way(s) they differ, because we cannot compare the characteristics of submitted proposals from those not submitted, the characteristics of the latter set not being observed. Our inability to determine the parameters for the president's potential legislative agenda, to measure characteristics of potential proposals that the president does not submit to Congress, has serious consequences for the empirical study of presidential agenda building and the implications of agenda-building decisions on later policy making, like presidential success with Congress. Some research designs, however, as explained more fully later in this chapter, allow us to develop and test hypotheses about some differences between submitted and nonsubmitted proposals, thus expanding our empirical store of knowledge about presidential legislative agenda building.

PROCESS VERSUS COMPARISON APPROACHES TO STUDYING AGENDAS

Empirical research on agenda setting generally employs two major approaches, what I call *process modeling* and *agenda comparison*. Neither approach fully comes to grips with the sample selection bias issue detailed earlier, however. Rather than thinking of the two approaches as competing, we should view them as complementary.

Process modeling is the dominant approach to studying the presidential agenda, and perhaps to studying agendas in general. The work of John Kingdon (1984) and Paul Light (1984) exemplifies the process approach to understanding agenda building, as does the work that employs the policy stages approach (e.g., Anderson, 2003; Jones, 1977). My study employs the *agenda comparison* approach, which in many regards is similar in spirit of the Baumgartner and Jones Policy Agenda Project, which we can also view as a type of agenda comparison approach.

The process approach generally takes the policy, issue, or proposal as the unit of analysis and asks whether and when the issue arrives onto a policy-making agenda. This approach looks at the "life history" of a policy, compares the life history of one issue to others, and often emphasizes the complexity of the agenda-building process. Hence, in Kingdon, a confluence of streams (i.e., policy, problem, political) must converge for government to attend to an issue.[12] This approach does not lend itself easily to hypothesis testing, a necessary element of scientific advance.[13] As will be apparent later, however, Kingdon and Light are the source of many of the hypotheses that I generate and test in the empirical chapters of this study.

Because the process approach begins with an issue on the agenda and traces the progress of that issue across the policy-making process, this approach has a difficult time with the question of why some issues get onto the agenda and others do not. The process approach, however, can say something about the timing and conditions under which the issue(s) under consideration get onto the agenda. For instance, Kingdon's model suggests that the policy, problem, and political streams must be coupled before an issue gets onto a governmental agenda.

The agenda comparison approach begins with the assumption that we can identify agendas and measure their attributes.[14] For example, the president's legislative policy agenda consists of all proposals for legislation that the president submits to Congress. Second, this approach assumes that agendas are dynamic, that they change over time. Thus, across two points in time, we can compare the attributes and composition of the president's legislative policy agenda, and from this we can assess the degree of change or stability in the agenda. For instance, we can look at the proposals that the president submits to the 39th Congress and compare them to proposals submitted to the 40th Congress. We can assess the similarities and differences of the

[12] The process-modeling approach gets a partial handle on the selection bias problem by comparing times when an issue across its life cycle fails to obtain agenda status from times when its gets onto the agenda.

[13] For a critique of Kingdon's "garbage can" model, especially that it is too abstract or general of a level to enable hypothesis generation and testing, see Mucciaroni, 1992.

[14] We cannot measure potential agendas for reasons already noted, however.

proposals for the 39th and the 40th Congresses. (Admittedly, there is a degree of arbitrariness or artificiality when deciding which time units to employ for comparison. For much of this study I use the "natural" congress as the time unit, because once a congress has ended so also does the proposal if the legislature did not take positive action on it. The president must recommend the proposal again in the next congress for the legislature to consider it. Here the rules and structures of the political system define for us an appropriate time unit.[15])

The analytic leverage of the agenda comparison approach comes from being able to measures differences (and similarities) across agendas. How many proposals did the president submit during the two congresses? What is their policy composition? How many concerned foreign as opposed to domestic policy? How innovative and ambitious were the proposals on the two (or more) agendas? These attributes or characteristics of the president's legislative policy agenda become variables that we can measure.

Our empirical aim then becomes accounting for the variance in these characteristics of interest across agendas. We can do this by developing testable hypotheses, asking which factors are systematically associated with change in this characteristic across presidential agendas. For instance, are presidential agendas larger and more innovative when their party controls Congress than if they face opposition party control? Do certain characteristics of presidential agendas vary by the party of the president, when an election is near, or if the president is serving in his first or second term? I test hypotheses like these and others in this study. Before going on to hypothesis testing, however, we need a theory to guide us to relevant hypotheses for testing; this is the task for the next chapter.

---

[15] Alternatively, I could have used years as the time unit for comparison, but doing so raises the complication of what to do with proposals submitted in the first year of a "natural congress" that Congress works on during the second year. Such complications arise with any other time unit besides the natural congress.

CHAPTER 3

A Theory of Presidential Agenda Building and the Congressional Response

This research seeks to resolve two puzzles introduced in the opening pages of this book, the divided government and modern president puzzles. Although these puzzles initially appear different, they raise the same basic question: Why do "divided government" and "modern" presidents seem to allow themselves to be defeated so often in Congress? Adding to this puzzling behavior is that presidents can do several things to reduce the rate of legislative defeat. For instance, presidents can refrain from submitting proposals destined for defeat, they can modify their proposals to make them more acceptable to Congress, and/or they can gather resources that will strengthen their bargaining position with Congress. Current explanations of presidential behavior with regard to Congress do not offer satisfactory resolutions to these two puzzles. In this chapter, I present the theory of congressional anticipations as a resolution to both of these puzzles.

That theory argues that in building their legislative agendas, presidents factor in the congressional context to estimate the likelihood that Congress will accept or defeat a legislative proposal. When the expected likelihood of defeat is high, presidents might decide to refrain from submitting such a proposal to Congress, they can alter the proposal to decrease congressional opposition, and/or they can acquire resources that enhance their bargaining situation with Congress. All of these actions will reduce the frequency with which Congress rejects or fails to enact a presidential proposal for legislation. Unlike much past research, the congressional anticipations theory connects presidential agenda building to later congressional action on the president's legislative policy agenda. From the theory of congressional anticipations, we can derive hypotheses about presidential agenda-building decisions and presidential success with Congress. Some of these hypotheses differ from conventional perspectives on presidential agenda-building decisions and the factors that directly affect presidential success. This theory too is parsimonious because it focuses on one driving motivation for presidents, avoiding the cost of legislative defeat.

This chapter proceeds as follows. First, I review the two puzzles and the conventional explanations to account for presidential behavior when faced with divided government or modern expectations for presidential leadership. I then present the congressional anticipations theory and detail how hypotheses derived from that theory differ from hypotheses culled from conventional perspectives. Because more than anticipations of congressional action affects presidential agenda-building decisions, the third section reviews other factors that might have an impact on presidential agenda building. These other perspectives serve as controls and as alternative explanations of presidential behavior. Inasmuch as the hypotheses of the theory hold with controls for these other factors, our confidence in the theory of congressional anticipations will be bolstered.

THE TWO PUZZLES REVISITED

The Divided Government Puzzle

Presidents "do better," often by a wide margin, when their party controls Congress than when Congress is under opposition party control. As noted in the introduction, from 1953 to 2007, presidential support is 30.5% higher in the House and 17% higher in the Senate under united than divided government (Ragsdale, 2009, pp. 500–502). Nor does it does appear to matter how we measure "doing better," with support scores or wins on roll calls. *Congressional Quarterly*'s House and Senate combined victory rates from 1953 through 2008 show 23.1% higher victory rates with united (81.9%) than with divided government (58.8%; Stanley and Niemi, 2009, Table 6.7). Instances of split party control, when the president's party controls one chamber and the opposition the other, are also quite instructive. During the eight years of split party control from 1953 to 2008, the president won 82.7% of the time in the chamber that his party controlled compared with 60.8% in the opposition-controlled chamber, a 21.9% difference (Stanley and Niemi, 2009, Table 6.7).[1] As a result of these types of facts, repeated in study after study, the impact of divided government on presidential success has become a nearly lawlike proposition: "Party control in Congress is by far the most important factor affecting presidential success in the legislative arena" (Barrett and Eshbaugh-Soha, 2007, p. 102).[2] Most studies now treat divided government as a control variable, rarely discussing the effects of divided government on presidential success in much detail.

Fleisher, Bond, and Wood (2008, pp. 198–199) provide the most detailed theoretical rationale to account for the impact of divided government on presidential success in Congress. First, they argue that members of the president's party are more likely to share policy preferences with the president than with opposition party members. Second, presidents can call on the party loyalty of co-partisans in Congress to build support for their policy proposals.

---

[1]   The years of split party control are 1981 to 1986 under Reagan, when the Republicans held the Senate but the Democrats the House, and 2001 to 2002 under George W. Bush, with Democratic control of the Senate and Republican control of the House. Democrats narrowly gained control of the Senate when Jim Jeffords (VT) switched party from Republican to Independent, allowing the Democrats a one-seat margin over the Republicans. The difference in presidential support in 2001/2002 are slight, with 89.9% for the Senate and 83.1% for the House, the opposite of what we would expect, but presidential support balloons in the Senate, especially in the first years in office, because of the large number of confirmation votes on nominees to the president's administration, most of which receive handy support from members on both sides of the aisle. Restricting our attention to the six years of split party control during the Reagan years, Reagan won 82.6% in the Senate, which the Republicans controlled, compared with 51.1% for the Democratic-controlled House, a 30.5% difference.

[2]   Relevant research on this point is truly massive. Among the most important studies include Barrett and Eshbaugh-Soha, 2007; Bond and Fleisher, 1990; Bond, Fleisher, and Wood, 2003; Covington et al., 1995; Edwards, 1989; Lockerbie et al., 1998; 2008; Marshall and Prins, 2007. Bond, Fleisher, and Wood (2003, p. 105) further demonstrate that the percentage of members in Congress of the president's party does not affect success beyond that found for the simple party control dichotomy. In contrast to the bulk of the literature, which makes the simple distinction between divided and united control, Richard Conley (2003) argues that there are a variety of divided government contexts that presidents face. For a review of the relevant literature on divided government, see Coleman and Parker (2009).

Shared electoral fate between members of Congress and the president is the third factor connecting partisanship and presidential support. Members of the president's party run for reelection partly on their own record as well as the president's. There is a two-step linkage here, which begins with the assumption that public attitudes toward the president affect voting for Congress: Positive evaluations of the president lead voters to cast ballots for congressional candidates of the president's party, whereas negative presidential evaluations lead them to support opposition party candidates (Gronke, Koch, and Wilson, 2003). Inasmuch as legislative defeat might harm the president's image among voters (Brace and Hinckley, 1992; Rivers and Rose, 1985), members of the president's party have incentives to support the president on legislative issues whenever possible. By shoring up the president's image with the public, members of Congress aid their own reelection efforts.

The fourth element for explaining the impact of divided government considers the implications of majority party status on congressional organization and the congressional agenda. For instance, the congressional majority determines the organization and agenda of the legislature, including committee memberships, workload, which bills will reach the floor, and the rules governing floor action on those bills. Congressional leaders can use their control over these organizational and agenda levers to advantage the president's legislative aims and proposals. For these reasons, the literature argues, presidents find more support from Congress when their party controls the legislature than the opposition party.

The strong effect of party control on presidential success is puzzling, however. Being defeated can be costly to a president. Defeat can harm a president's leadership image and undermine his public support (Brace and Hinckley, 1992; Rivers and Rose, 1985). Another cost is that defeat on one proposal could spill over to affect the prospects of enactment of other proposals. It is common for commentators and pundits to remark on the implications of legislative defeat for presidents and their presidencies. We see this in the recent debates over the health care reforms of 2009/2010, which Barack Obama not only supported but also made one of his highest legislative priorities. For example, David Kendall, of the Third Way think tank, termed passage of the health care legislation a "defining moment for the presidency," arguing further that it would affect Obama's ability to lead if he lost. "If you can't lead, you look weak, and Americans don't like weakness" (Zengerle, 2010).

Presidents not only seem aware of the implications of legislative victory versus defeat but also that they will meet greater resistance from an opposition-controlled Congress than one controlled by their party. Light's interviews with presidential staffers from the Kennedy through Reagan administrations indicate that administrations take into account the congressional context, especially divided government, in deciding to submit or modify proposals that they submit to Congress for legislative consideration (Light, 1991, pp. 27–28, 53–58, 137–139, 161–166).

If a president expects that Congress will defeat a proposal, the president can refrain from submitting it or modify it to make the proposal more acceptable to Congress. If the president withholds a proposal, he cannot be defeated. Modification of a proposal to meet objections in Congress can increase the likelihood that something will be passed, that a president might get "half a loaf" instead of none. In some instances, receiving "half a loaf" from Congress might be enough for a president to claim a legislative victory. Presidents even seem to be willing to modify high-priority legislative proposals. For instance, Barack Obama jettisoned the public option to dampen opposition to his health care package in 2010 (Stolberg and Herszenhorn, 2010). Later that year, in the face of strong Republican resistance, he ceded his opposition to extending the 2001 Bush tax cuts to the wealthiest Americans (Herszenhorn and Calmes, 2010). Eventually Congress produced legislation, and the president claimed a legislative victory on tax policy. These are but several obvious examples of presidents modifying their position to lessen opposition to their legislative priorities.[3]

Given the costs of defeat noted earlier, why do presidents allow themselves to be defeated so often when facing opposition congresses, when they can refrain from submitting or modify their proposals? Although it not surprising that presidents succeed more when their party controls Congress, given their ability to anticipate resistance

[3] On such presidential bargaining with Congress see Beckmann (2010).

from opposition congresses and these simple strategic responses, the large effect of divided government on presidential success in Congress is puzzling.

The Modern President Puzzle

Since the mid-twentieth century, presidents have been more legislatively active than their predecessors, commonly termed *traditional* or *premodern* presidents. Figure 4.1, to be discussed in more detail in the next chapter, traces one indicator of legislative activism, the number of proposals that presidents submit to Congress for legislative consideration from 1789 to 2002 (Cameron and Park, 2008; Rudalevige, 2002). Although most research that uses the modern presidency paradigm considers Franklin Roosevelt to be the first fully modern president (e.g., Greenstein, 1989),[4] the figure reveals a large surge in proposals beginning with the 79th (1945/1946) Congress and continues through the present. This aspect of *modern* presidential behavior, the high level of legislative proposing, begins with Truman, not FDR.

Truman submitted 135 legislative proposals during the 79th Congress, 89 more than for the previous Congress. Since the 79th Congress, presidents have submitted on average 313 proposals per congress compared to 60 for presidents serving during the first 78 congresses, a fivefold increase.

At least with regard to this type of legislative activism,[5] there appear to be two presidential eras, 1) the traditional pre-modern era (1st–78th Congresses, 1789–1944), in which presidents submitted a modest number of proposals to Congress, and 2) the modern era from 1945 to the present (79th Congress–present), in which presidents submit a significantly larger number of proposals, packaging those proposals into what has come to be termed *the president's program.*

---

[4] The modern presidency idea is not without controversy. Some, like Skowronek (1996), question the utility of the concept. Others question the date of arrival. For example, if we view Jeffrey Tulis's (1987) concept of the rhetorical presidency as an expression of presidential modernization, then the modern presidency appeared with Wilson. Scott James (2009) reviews many of the relevant debates over the development of the presidency.

[5] Lobbying Congress behind legislation from the president's agenda, bills submitted by members, and vetoes, can be thought of as other types of presidential legislative activism.

Although the utility of drawing sharp lines to distinguish presidential eras has been questioned (Woolley, 2005), the legislative proposing data in Figure 4.1 suggest a major, rapid, and sustained transformation of one important aspect of presidential behavior. Modern, post-World War Two presidents have legislative agendas that are multiples larger than their predecessors.[6] What are the implications of this heightened legislative activism of modern presidents on their success with Congress?

From the perspective of the literature on presidential-congressional relations, most of which covers the modern period, the high rate of modern presidential legislative activism is puzzling. That literature emphasizes the difficulties that presidents have with Congress. In Krutz, Fleisher, and Bond's terminology, there is a "presumption of failure" when presidents take positions on legislation (1998, p. 871).[7] Empirical evidence documents the high legislative "failure" rate of modern presidents' legislative proposals. Although estimates vary owing to differences in time frames and definitions of success and of importance, presidents can expect about 40% of their important proposals to be defeated, rising to 50% to 60% or higher under divided government (Cameron and Park, 2008; Edwards and Barrett, 2000; Edwards, Barrett, and Peake, 1997; Peterson, 1990, Rudalvige, 2002).

Why do modern presidents allow themselves to be defeated by Congress so often? This is the same question asked about presidents serving during divided government. As noted previously, being defeated on a proposal can harm a president's leadership image and spill over, undermining the enactment chances of other proposals. In addition, modern expectations for presidential leadership can render legislative defeat more consequential for modern compared with premodern presidents. In the modern age, legislative accomplishment, getting Congress to enact the president's policy initiatives, might be the most important definition of what constitutes a successful

---

[6] Chapter 5 also details that modern presidential agendas cover a broader array of policies than those of traditional presidents. See Cohen and Eshbaugh-Soha, 2012, for more on this point.

[7] In contrast, they argue that a "presumption of success" exists for presidential nominations.

presidency. This expectation tells us much about why modern presidents work so hard on legislating, but not why they spend so much time on legislative proposals that will not result in enactment.

Beside the costs of legislative defeat already noted, there are opportunity and coordination costs to building a large legislative agenda. Opportunity costs come in two varieties. The first relates to allocating time across the president's legislative proposals. For instance, assume that presidential lobbying of Congress (lobbying effort) can influence the roll call behavior of legislators. Up to a point, more lobbying effort will result in a larger number of members of Congress supporting the president's proposal (Beckmann, 2010), but lobbying effort entails consuming presidential time (among other possible presidential resources). Assume further that presidential time is finite, at least in the short term. Now assume that a president has only one lobbying effort time unit to allocate but has submitted two proposals to Congress, of equal priority to the president. Proposal A is very short of congressional acceptance, and the lobbying effort time unit will not result in congressional enactment, although the lobbying effort will narrow the final vote margin. In contrast, Proposal B is close enough that allocating his lobbying effort will result in Congress's enacting Proposal B. A rational president will allocate his lobbying effort to Proposal B but not Proposal A. In fact, allocating lobbying effort to Proposal A will result in neither proposal being enacted. Why would a modern president elevate proposals like A onto his legislative agenda? The literature on the modern presidency and legislative activism is silent on this quandary.

The second opportunity cost relates to nonlegislative activities. Again assuming finite presidential resources, such as time, the more time allocated to building and lobbying for a large legislative agenda, the less time is available for nonlegislative activities, such as meeting with foreign leaders, burnishing the president's image through public speaking engagements, and the like.

A large legislative agenda also increases presidential coordination costs. To build a large legislative agenda requires staff support and processes to manage that staff. The White House and Executive Office staff has grown since the mid-twentieth century (Dickinson and Lebo, 2007). Some of these additional staffers are assigned to legislative agenda-building tasks, like the legislative clearance processes. Although a larger staff can allow the president to fashion a larger number of legislative proposals across a wider range of policy areas, having a larger staff also increases the amount of time and attention that presidents must pay to staff management issues, such as recruitment and mediating disputes among staffers (Dickinson, 1997). At some point it becomes more costly to a president to add an additional staffer than the benefit received. In this sense there are limits to staff size, which should place limits on the size of the president's legislative agenda. Why is the legislative agenda of modern presidents so large given these various costs to large legislative agendas?

The large modern presidential agenda becomes all the more puzzling when one considers that presidents possess nonlegislative means for much policy making. Presidents can use unilateral devices like executive orders, allowing them to sidestep Congress in the policy-making process (Mayer, 1999, 2001, 2009; Moe and Howell, 1999). Howell (2005) demonstrates that as prospects for congressional passage of important legislation wane, presidential use of executive orders rises. Moreover, only rarely does Congress challenge an executive order.[8]

Further adding to this puzzling aspect of modern presidential behavior is Cohen's (1982a, 1982b) research, perhaps the only studies that quantitatively compare the legislative success of traditional and modern presidents. He finds little difference in the legislative success rates of modern and traditional presidents.[9]

Why are modern presidents so stubbornly legislatively active in the face of these high expected failure rates, institutional costs, and the availability of policy-making alternatives? The theory of congressional

---

[8] Presidents must possess legislative or constitutional authority before they can employ an executive order, however. Presidents have been quite creative at times in "locating" such authority. Ruth Morgan's (1970) early study of Truman and civil rights is quite instructive here.

[9] Cohen argues that the factors that promote success differ across the two eras: Party conditions in Congress are more important for traditional than for modern presidents. There are important limitations to Cohen's work. He uses the SUAs for identifying the president's legislative proposals, missing all proposals submitted to Congress outside of that message. Second, his statistical analysis techniques are now dated.

anticipations argues that the modern office acquired institutional resources, such as staff, and developed processes, such as legislative clearance, not merely to increase the presidency's capability to respond to heightened expectations for presidential policy leadership but also because these resources strengthened the president's bargaining position with Congress. A strengthened bargaining position leads to higher success rates with Congress. According to this theory, modern presidents will be more successful with Congress than their traditional predecessors.

Summary

Despite different substantive problems, the divided government and modern president puzzles raise the same question: Why do divided government and modern presidents allow themselves to be defeated so often, especially when there are things they can do to minimize or lessen the rate of defeat? Asked this way, both questions assume that presidents care whether they are defeated or are victorious in the legislative arena. The theory of congressional anticipations, developed later in this chapter, begins with that assumption. Before turning to that theory, let us review the common explanations for presidential relations with Congress as related to these two queries.

CONVENTIONAL EXPLANATIONS FOR PRESIDENTIAL BEHAVIOR: SINCERITY AND RESPONSIVENESS TO EXPECTATIONS

This section reviews the conventional understanding of presidential relations with Congress as it relates to the high defeat rate during divided government and the high proposal rate of modern presidents. The existing literature generally argues that divided government presidents lose so much because presidents are sincere in proposing and position taking. The modern presidency thesis implies that the high rate of legislative activism is a function of presidential responsiveness to the climate of expectations for presidential leadership. Both of these conventional views assume that presidents care little about whether they win or lose with Congress.

PRESIDENTIAL SINCERITY AND CONGRESS

The sincerity perspective argues that presidents submit legislative pro-posals to Congress without much regard for the congressional context. Instead, presidents submit all of their most preferred policy proposals, no matter what the odds of enactment are. Hence, presidents rarely modify their legislative proposals to increase acceptance in Congress and rarely refrain from submitting proposals certain to be defeated. Steger (2005) argues that the sincerity perspective is "prevalent in studies of presidential-congressional relations" (p. 312).[10]

Peterson (1990; also Fett, 1992) identifies several reasons why pres-idents are sincere in taking positions on policy and in submitting proposals to Congress. First, according to Peterson, the congressional policy-making environment is too complex for presidents to predict easily or reliably what Congress will do with their legislative proposals. Second, unforeseen events can occur that can alter legislative policy preferences and priorities. Some unexpected events will enhance the enactment prospects of a presidential proposal, whereas other events will undermine those prospects. Presidents cannot predict if and when such events will occur or the implications of such events for their leg-islative agendas. The uncertainties associated with the congressional policy-making process and unexpected events lead presidents to sub-mit to Congress their most preferred policy alternatives. Third, pres-idents are (overly) confident in their ability to persuade Congress to support their proposals.

Presidents also might be sincere because they propose legislation for nonlegislative reasons. For instance, presidents might submit a proposal to Congress to repay a group of voters for their support in the last election or to attract their support in the next election. Pres-idents also might submit a proposal because they promised to do so in their electoral campaign. Research suggests that rather than being idle promises, campaign pledges are important to presidents and they do try to act on them (Fett, 1992; Fishel, 1985; Krukones, 1984;

---

[10] Steger goes on to say that "No published presidential agenda-setting study argues for the strategic agenda-setting perspective" (p. 312), but here I review several studies that argue for strategic presidential behavior.

Pomper and Lederman, 1980). Proposing can be used for symbolic, as opposed to policy, reasons, for instance, to suggest presidential attention to important and salient issues and problems (Cohen, 1997).

Evidence of Presidential Sincerity. Surprisingly, little evidence exists that presidents are sincere in submitting proposals to Congress or taking positions on legislation before Congress. Peterson (1990, pp. 32–76) gleans from his interviews that eventual success with Congress plays only a minor role in presidential proposal development. His respondents also report that the White House might take Congress into account when forging legislative proposals, for instance, by consulting with Congress before sending up legislation (pp. 49–60). Furthermore, "the overwhelming majorities of the informants . . . agreed that predictions of likely congressional action could or did influence the content of executive proposals" (p. 61).

Why then does Peterson argue that presidents are sincere and that the congressional context does not influence presidential agenda building very much? Prior consultation, according to Peterson, rarely has major impacts on the substance of legislation. The administration instead consults with Congress as part of intelligence gathering about the congressional mood, which informs the politics rather than the substance of legislation (pp. 55, 58). Consultation is also used to inform congressional leadership of presidential policy intentions (p. 55) and for making "technical" adjustments to legislation (i.e., fine-tuning legislation to make it more appealing to Congress [p. 58]) but does not alter the direction or thrust of the proposal. Anticipation of congressional reactions could also lead to the administration's "dropping a proposal" (p. 62) or modifying it, but his informants also cited instances in which the president sent a proposal even when the administration expected a negative congressional reaction (p. 65). To Peterson, because the congressional environment is one of uncertainty and unpredictability, presidential commitment, the belief that a proposal is the best policy course, better explains presidential agenda building.

Where Peterson uses interview data, Fett (1992) uses behavioral data to test the sincerity assumption. He compares the amount of public support by presidents for their legislative initiatives with the closeness of roll calls on those proposals. Fett argues that the volume of presidential public rhetoric on behalf of a proposal indicates presidential priorities. High-priority proposals receive a larger volume of presidential public rhetoric; lower-priority proposals do not receive as much presidential attention. Fett hypothesizes that "success-oriented" presidents, those who want a high "batting average" with Congress, will talk more about proposals with a high prospect for enactment than proposals with lower enactment prospects, measuring enactment odds by the congressional vote margin for a proposal. Presidents interested in "legislative output," those interested in the policy consequences of their proposals, will expend their effort on proposals with lesser enactment prospects, evidenced by narrow roll call results. To Fett, "sincere" presidents will spend more effort on their highest priorities, regardless of their enactment prospects. Using data from the first year of the Carter and Reagan administrations, Fett detects no relationship between the volume of public rhetoric and the roll call divide, leading him to argue that presidents are sincere rather than strategic with regard to their legislative programs. As Fett notes (p. 900), however, his procedure "does not completely eliminate the possibility of 'anticipated reactions'. . . . We can never know for sure what the president would have proposed were he totally unconstrained by the consideration of whether or not the proposal would have a chance for success in Congress."

Presidential Sincerity Hypotheses. The presidential sincerity perspective leads to several hypotheses. One, the size of the president's agenda should not covary with divided versus united government. Presidents will submit essentially the same agenda no matter which party controls Congress. Two, presidents will not alter or moderate their legislative proposals depending on whether Congress is united or divided. These first two hypotheses argue that presidents will not accommodate their legislative policy agendas to conditions in Congress. The final hypothesis refers to success in Congress, rather than the composition of the president's legislative agenda: Presidents will be more successful with a united than a divided Congress. The logic underlying this hypothesis is that because presidents submit legislative agendas irrespective of the congressional context, and because they receive more support from their party than the opposition, success will be substantially lower during divided than united government.

Modern Presidents and the President's Legislative Agenda

Like the sincerity perspective, the modern presidency thesis sees legislative activism arising from nonlegislative sources, primarily expectations for presidential leadership. Also similar to the sincerity perspective, modern presidents do not take into account the congressional context when building their legislative agendas.

The modern presidency thesis, most fully articulated by Greenstein (1988), is far from noncontroversial. Skowronek (2009) reviews many criticisms of the modern presidency concept, importantly, that pre-modern presidents often exhibit modern behaviors. For this research it is important to note the sudden and large increase in presidential proposing once the Second World War ended. Rarely do we find such clear sustained changes in presidential behavior (e.g., Woolley, 2005). At least for presidential proposing rates, we can speak of two periods, from 1789 to 1945 and 1946 to the present.

The modern presidency thesis offers one account for the sudden, sustained rise in presidential proposing. Greenstein (1988) dates the emergence of the modern presidency with Franklin Roosevelt's presidency. Roosevelt's personality, the exigencies of the Great Depression, and the slow accretion of resources in the presidency coalesced to forge the modern presidency. The establishment of the Executive Office of the Presidency in 1939 institutionalized the modern presidency such that FDR's successors would continue the modern office (Leuchtenburg, 1983).

Greenstein (1978, 1988) lists four characteristics of modern presidents that differentiate them from their traditional predecessors: 1) they have greater formal and informal power to make decisions on their own initiative, such as executive orders and other unilateral policy-making tools; 2) they have come to be the chief agenda setters in federal level policy making, with the consequence of creating expectations that they can rarely fulfill; 3) they have accumulated major staff and advisory capability; and 4) they have become the most visible actors in the political system (Shaw, 1987).

Public and political expectations for presidential leadership are critical. Presidents are often portrayed as reacting to such expectations. For instance, there is the famous story, reported in Neustadt (1954), that Eisenhower failed to present a full-fledged presidential program to Congress in his first year in office. Severe criticism, especially from Republicans in Congress, forced the president's hand. In 1954, his second year in office, and each year thereafter, Eisenhower, like Truman before him, presented Congress with a presidential program. Rather than trying to shape or scale back expectations for presidential leadership, Eisenhower caved in to those pressures.[11] From this perspective, many of the developments associated with the modern presidency, such as staffing, heightened levels of going public, and legislative activism, are designed to help presidents to live up to these expectations for presidential leadership.

This modern presidency-expectations dynamic not only offers an explanation for the comparatively high level of proposing by post-World War Two presidents but also has implications for presidential success with Congress in the postwar years. First, like sincere presidents, by this account modern presidents are not sensitive to the congressional context in submitting proposals to Congress for legislative consideration. Instead, responsiveness to public expectations affects presidential proposing decisions – presidents will submit proposals to Congress when the public expects presidential leadership on the issue. Over time this has come to include the entire range of policy issues. The president's agenda thus consists of proposals of varying prospects for success. Some will have strong prospects for congressional enactment, and others, lesser prospects.

It is quite difficult to derive testable hypotheses from this modern presidency-expectations perspective. One hypothesis, obviously, is that modern presidents will have larger legislative agendas than traditional presidents. This hypothesis, however, does not take us very far. A more discriminating hypothesis would predict the factors that affect the size

---

[11] Waterman et al. (1999) and Jenkins-Smith et al. (2005) document the importance of public expectations for evaluating presidential performance and the sources of the expectations gap. Simon (2009) reviews the literature on public expectations. Other notable studies of public expectations of the president include Kinder et al. (1980) and Wayne (1982).

of modern presidential agendas. As Figure 4.1 shows, modern presidential agendas vary in size. One possible hypothesis from the modern presidency-expectations perspective is that agenda size covaries with public demand for presidential leadership. Measuring public demand for presidential leadership is difficult and problematic, especially given the dearth of relevant public opinion surveys on the topic.

Furthermore, the modern presidency-expectations perspective fails to offer a precise hypothesis regarding success with Congress. It is not clear, for instance, whether modern presidents will be more successful than traditional ones, because the modern presidency thesis does not inform us about the agenda-building calculus of traditional presidents. Returning to Figure 4.1, we see a gradual growth in the legislative agendas of traditional presidents. What accounts for this growth? The modern presidency perspective cannot help us to address this question.

The modern presidency thesis also does not tell us why the success rates of modern presidents vary. Because public expectations and not prospects for success determine whether an issue gets onto the president's agenda, there should not be a relationship between agenda size and success. This leaves us with the null hypothesis of no relationship between agenda size and congressional success for modern presidents. Thus, other than the observation that modern presidents will have larger legislative agendas than traditional presidents, the modern presidency-expectations perspectives does not offer any clearly testable hypothesis about either the relative legislative success of modern versus traditional presidents or the variation in the success levels of modern presidents.

Summary

Although they are concerned with substantively different problems, the sincerity and modern presidency perspectives have some similarities. Of importance for this research, the congressional context does not enter into the presidential decision to submit a proposal to Congress for legislative considerations. The motivation for legislative proposing resides elsewhere, in the president's belief that the proposal offers good public policy for the sincerity perspective or the president's reaction to public expectations for presidential leadership for the modern presidency perspective. Consequently, neither perspective views congressional defeat of presidential proposals as problematic.

The next section develops the congressional anticipations theory of presidential proposing. That theory argues that presidents take into account the congressional context when submitting proposals for legislative consideration. As a result, the theory leads to several hypotheses about presidential proposing and the sources of presidential success with Congress that differ from the sincerity and modern presidency perspectives. Moreover, the congressional anticipations theory accounts for both the divided government and modern presidency puzzles.

THE THEORY OF CONGRESSIONAL ANTICIPATIONS

This research asks two questions: Why do presidents allow themselves to be defeated so often during divided government? Why do modern presidents submit such large legislative agendas to Congress when they too can expect to be defeated frequently? The presidential sincerity and modern presidency perspectives, as detailed earlier, imply that presidents do not care very much whether Congress defeats their proposals for legislation.

I take a different tack here, arguing that congressional defeat can be costly to presidents and that presidents want to avoid or minimize that cost. The theory of congressional anticipations further contends that presidents can reduce the incidence of legislative defeat. For instance, they can refrain from submitting proposals to Congress that they expected to be defeated. Second, they can modify their legislative proposals to make them more acceptable to Congress and to overcome congressional resistance. Third, presidents can acquire resources to strengthen their bargaining situation with Congress, which will improve the prospects that Congress will enact their legislative proposals. From all of this, the theory of congressional anticipations leads to several predictions about presidential proposing behavior and the sources of presidential success with Congress that differ from hypotheses derived from the sincerity and modern presidency perspectives. Subsequent chapters present empirical tests of these competing hypotheses.

Existing Research

A small amount of literature has begun to explore, both theoretically and empirically, the implications of presidents engaging in strategic behavior with regard to congressional relations, in opposition to the sincerity perspective that has dominated most thinking.

First, Light's interviews with White House staffers who served from the 1960s through the 1980s indicate White House sensitivity to political costs in developing policy proposals. Political costs include assessment of prospects for congressional defeat and how much effort it will take the administration to rally support in Congress. One Kennedy staffer is quoted as saying, "The first question was always, 'Will it fly on the Hill?'" A Nixon staffer recalled, "We didn't want to send legislation that had no chance of success, but we also didn't want to hold back on legislation that had an opportunity" (p. 138). Seat ratios were the primary indicator of potential presidential support, according to these White House staffers (p. 138). The Johnson administration consulted with Congress in the early stages of proposal development to decrease later political costs and increase the chance for later victory (Light, 1991, pp. 138–139). As a result, prospects for enactment affect how presidents prioritize which proposals get onto their legislative agendas: "[I]n the definition of top priorities the President and staff emphasize programs that have a greater chance of legislative success" (Light, 1991, p. 60).

Larocca (2006) develops and tests an informational model of presidential success with Congress. His model argues that the strategic provision of information about an issue can influence congressional enactment. Larocca contrasts two types of information that the president provides to Congress, information from presidential "going public" activities and information from draft legislation that the executive submits to Congress. Although both types of information might increase presidential success with Congress, information from draft legislation seems to have greater impact on congressional behavior than going public information in Larocca's analysis.

Cameron and Park (2008) develop and test a related model of strategic presidential behavior, burden sharing. They (2008) ask, "Why does the president expend executive branch resources by providing Congress with detailed draft legislation?" Their answer is that presidents pay this cost because it provides policy benefits that outweigh the cost of writing and submitting bill drafts. The burden-sharing model assumes a congressional cost to legislating.[12] Executive branch bill drafts might reduce that cost of legislating, allowing Congress to work on more legislation and reducing congressional uncertainty about policy outcomes. By getting Congress to adopt the president's draft bill, the executive "bends" the policy outcome closer to his ideal point, providing the president with a policy benefit. Presidents, of course, will supply Congress with draft legislation only if the policy benefit is greater than the cost of drafting the legislation, and the policy benefit depends on expectations of passage. Presidents have no incentive to supply draft legislation if it will not be enacted. Cameron and Park hypothesize that when Congress is in a mood to legislate, presidents should submit more proposals to Congress, capitalizing on this mood. Using annual data from 1963 to 1996, they find that the president's legislative program expands with the interaction of a small gridlock interval and external demand for legislation.

Rudalevige (2002) focuses on whether presidential proposals are written within the White House (centralized) or in a department (decentralized). He hypothesizes that when presidential and congressional preferences converge, presidents worry less that bureaucrats will write bills that drift away from the president's policy preferences (pp. 93–94). Rudalevige provides support for this hypothesis (pp. 105–108). Presidents may centralize bill drafting when enactment prospects fade, in hopes of improving the odds of enactment (Rudalevige, 2002, pp. 116–118). By centralizing, presidents maintain more control over legislative strategy, the content of legislation as it progresses through the legislative process. They also are more likely to mobilize White House resources in support of legislation, which signals to Congress how important the president deems the proposal. Although controlling legislative strategy and mobilizing White House

---

[12] Such costs include the time it takes for Congress to learn about an issue so that it can produce a good piece of legislation. Such opportunity costs can limit how many bills Congress can work on – working on one bill might preclude working on another (or attending to other legislative matters, like casework).

resources could marginally improve the odds of enactment, Rudalevige detects little support for the notion that centralization helps
enactment (pp. 143–150). As Rudalevige summarizes, "centralizing
program formulation has its managerial uses, but is not an effective
strategy for success in Congress" (p. 149). There appears to be a
trade-off between policy control and success with Congress. Rudalevige's results suggest that presidents are willing to pay the price of
lower success for greater control of policy development.

Eshbaugh-Soha (2005) hypothesizes, "Acting rationally and strategically, presidents consider those factors that will influence a policy's success and support or propose policies that are most likely to
pass Congress. Indeed, the rule of anticipative reactions holds that
presidents who face an opportune environment will advocate more
expansive policies; presidents who face a set of constraints will advocate less expansive legislation" (2005, pp. 258–259). Using data for
the period from 1949 to 2000, Eshbaugh-Soha finds that the overall size of the presidential agenda shrinks under divided government
(p. 265).

Finally, Marshall and Prins (2007) detect support that presidents are
strategic in taking positions on roll calls before Congress. Presidents
are more likely to take roll call positions when they expect to be
on the winning side. They present evidence comparing the sources
of roll call success for a "nonstrategic" versus a "strategic" model.
Unified government always influences success but is half as strong
for the strategic as opposed to nonstrategic estimations. This decline
in strength results from the large impact of united government on
position taking – presidents take more roll call positions when they
expect success (pp. 272–278).

As Wood (2009b) maintains, "[T]here is little past work that cap-
tures the strategic nature of the agenda setting game between presidents and other political institutions and its potential importance
for the *substantive make-up* of institutional agendas . . . with respect to
Congress presidents may decline to initiate legislation . . . under periods of divided government because there is little probability of achieving success" (p. 126, italics in original). This small body of research
reviewed here suggests that presidents take into account Congress
when submitting proposals to the legislature or in roll call position

taking.[13] The theory of congressional anticipations offered here builds on those past efforts. Unlike that past research, which looks at either the implications of strategic behavior on proposing or success with Congress, my study offers and tests hypotheses about both proposing and congressional success. Furthermore, where the existing research looks at only presidents in the modern, post–World War Two era, I look at the implications of congressional anticipations across nearly the entire history of the presidency, from 1789 to 2002. That enables me to test for the impact of the modern presidency on presidential proposing and success, arguing that the modern presidency effects are but a special case of presidential anticipations of what Congress will do with their legislative proposals.

Basic Assumptions

The theory of congressional anticipations is built on the following assumptions. First, presidents care whether Congress defeats or accepts their legislative proposals, because being defeated can be costly to presidents. Not only does being defeated mean that one of the president's policy proposals will not be enacted, but defeat can undermine the president's leadership image and public support (Brace and Hinckley, 1992; Ostrom and Simon, 1985; Rivers and Rose, 1985). Furthermore, defeat of one proposal can also spill over to affect other proposals. Once having defeated a president's proposal, congressional opponents to the president might be emboldened to attack other proposals, sensing the executive's weakened position. Moreover, Lebo and O'Geen (2011) find that success affects the number of seats that

---

[13] Other studies look at whether Congress affects presidential *rhetorical policy* attention. These studies also present a mixed picture. Edwards and Wood (1998) find that presidential attention does not covary with Congressional activity on five issues. Peake (2001) finds that congressional attention affects presidential attention on three less visible foreign policy issues. Yates and Whitford (2005) detect no congressional influence on presidential attention to criminal justice. Flemming, Wood, and Bothe (1999) find that congressional attention to civil liberties and the environment affects presidential attention to those policy areas, but congressional attention does not affect presidential attention to civil rights. Andrade and Young (1996) find that as congressional support for the president declines, presidents give more foreign policy speeches, arguing that declining prospects with Congress lead presidents to emphasize policy areas where they hold natural advantages, such as foreign policy. Thus Congress can affect presidential attention on some issues, but it is not clear whether characteristics of the issue will affect the degree of presidential responsiveness in their rhetorical agendas.

the president's party holds in the next Congress. Success leads to gaining seats while defeat reduces the number of seats held in the next Congress.[14] Because defeat imposes costs on presidents, they would like to avoid being defeated and paying the cost of defeat, if possible.[15]

The second assumption pertains to the complexity of the congressional environment. The sincerity perspective reviewed previously contends that the congressional environment is too complex and uncertain for presidents to predict the odds of enactment versus defeat (e.g., Peterson, 1990). In contrast, I argue that the congressional context provides presidents with relatively easy-to-collect information about their likely success with the legislature. Cameron and Park (2008) make a similar argument in their burden-sharing model, arguing that presidents generally can determine whether Congress is in a mood to legislate on a given issue. In their model, Cameron and Park identify two indicators of the legislative mood on Capitol Hill: policy differences between the parties, indicated by the span of the gridlock interval, and interest group demands for policy. Similarly, unified versus divided government presents presidents with reliable information about the receptivity of Congress to their policy proposals. Presidents can generally expect greater support from Congress controlled by their party than the opposition.

To minimize or avoid the cost of expected defeat, presidents can engage in three behaviors. First, they can refrain from submitting a proposal to Congress if they expect that proposal to be defeated. Second, the president can modify or alter his proposal, moving it closer to congressional preferences, thereby increasing the prospects that the proposal will be enacted rather than defeated. Third, the president can acquire resources to improve his bargaining position with Congress, which also will improve the likelihood of congressional enactment.[16]

---

[14] They estimate that each 1% increase in the success rate leads to a gain of two-thirds of a seat.

[15] In other words, think of the president as a rational "proposer," who will submit a proposal to Congress if the benefit of proposing is greater than its cost. In this conceptualization, expecting to be defeated raises the costs of proposing in some instances to the point that the cost of proposing exceeds the benefits of proposing.

[16] Whether the president would engage in any of these behaviors to avoid defeat can also be thought of in benefit-cost terms. In particular, it could be quite costly for

The next section applies the logic of the congressional anticipations approach to the divided government and modern presidency puzzles. I derive several hypotheses regarding presidential proposing and success with Congress. Importantly, these hypotheses differ in their predictions from those of the presidential sincerity and modern presidency perspectives.

CONGRESSIONAL ANTICIPATIONS AND DIVIDED GOVERNMENT

The Agenda Size Hypothesis

Presidents can expect higher defeat rates for their proposals with opposition-controlled congresses than when their party controls the legislature. Based on the congressional anticipations framework, to avoid defeat, presidents can refrain from submitting proposals that they expect to be highly likely to be defeated. This leads to the prediction that presidential agendas will be smaller during divided than unified government. This hypothesis differs from the sincerity one, which predicts no effect of party control on the size of the president's legislative agenda.

There is scattered evidence in the literature of the party control–agenda size hypothesis. Eshbaugh-Soha (2005, p. 265) finds for the period from 1949 to 2000 that presidents make six fewer legislative proposals during divided than united government.[17] Cameron and Park (2008), although they do not inspect the effect of divided government on the size of the president's agenda, find that the agenda grows as presidents sense that Congress is in a mood to legislate. Finally, Marshall and Prins (2007), in looking at presidential positions on roll calls, find that presidents are 9% more likely to take positions during united compared with divided government. All of these studies employ theoretical models similar to the one proposed here,

the president to acquire those resources that would improve his bargaining situation with Congress, for instance, mobilizing public support.

[17] For a proposal to make it into Eshbaugh-Soha's list, the president must make a public statement about the proposal twice, once in the SUA and again in another public statement. The number of presidential proposals in his sample varies from 1 to 40, with an average of 14.5, and a standard deviation of 9 (calculated from the data presented on pp. 266–267). Thus the effect of divided government is quite substantial.

that presidents are sensitive to the congressional environment and that this sensitivity affects presidential proposing and position-taking behavior.

The Moderation Hypothesis

Another prediction of the congressional anticipations hypothesis is that presidents can moderate their policy stances in anticipation of legislative defeat. The logic of the hypothesis is quite straightforward: The closer the presidential proposal is in a policy space to the critical decision maker in Congress, such as the median or the pivot, the higher are the odds of enactment. Presidents can reduce the policy distance between their proposals and the congressional "decider" by amending the proposal, moving it closer to the preference of the congressional "decider." Because the policy distance between the president and Congress is wider during divided than united government, presidents have a stronger incentive to alter or moderate their policy proposals during divided than united government. Thus we can hypothesize that presidents will be more moderate during divided than unified government.

There is little research that directly bears on this strategic moderation hypothesis. Much of the literature on presidential-congressional relations suggests that presidents and Congress "negotiate" over policy, often trying to find a compromise acceptable to both. In that literature, however, such negotiation occurs after the president has staked out a policy position, whereas my congressional anticipations hypothesis suggests presidential moderation also occurs as presidents build their legislative agendas.

Wood (2009a) presents some relevant evidence in support of the divided government-presidential moderation hypothesis. He measures presidential policy liberalism from the late 1940s to early 2000s from the president's public rhetoric. His analysis indicates that presidents are rhetorically more centrist during split government configurations (p. 115); however, his data are rhetorical and not policy proposals. There might be differences in presidential behavior between the two types of policy behaviors. In addition, Wood looks only at modern presidential behavior, compared with this study's longer historical perspective, but his results are consistent with the divided government-presidential moderation hypothesis.

The Presidential "Blame Game" Hypothesis

Sometimes presidents, facing an opposition-controlled Congress, will "flood" the legislature with proposals that have little chance for enactment. Consider Harry Truman (Hartmann, 1971; Peterson, 1990, p. 43; Rudalevige, 2002, p. 118). With the 79th Congress (1945–1946) under Democratic control, Truman submitted 137 legislative recommendations.[18] Party control changed hands with the 80th Congress (1947–1948). Assuming that in two years the public mood did not change markedly, the congressional anticipations-divided government hypothesis predicts a decline in the number of presidential proposals, but Truman steeply increased the number of legislative proposals to 231. Rudalevige (2002, p. 188) reports similar behavior for George H. W. Bush and Bill Clinton, both minority presidents, as their reelection contests neared. Such proposing behavior seems contrary to the congressional anticipations-divided government hypothesis.

Peterson (1990, p. 43) argues that the Truman example provides evidence of sincere presidential behavior. Rudalevige (2002, p. 118) provides a different account: "[P]residents . . . may calculate that the issue is more valuable than the bill, that political success accrues from legislative failure. . . . " In effect, minority presidents play a "blame game" when up for reelection. Blame games lead minority presidents in reelection periods to submit large agendas to Congress. The logic of the presidential blame game accounts for the seemingly anomalous proposing behavior of minority presidents in reelection periods.[19]

In the presidential blame game, presidents submit numerous "popular" legislative proposals to Congress, expecting them to be defeated. Because these proposals are popular with the public, the president can criticize or "blame" the opposition-controlled Congress for its failure to enact them, saying that Congress is out of step with the public. Additionally, the president will ask voters to replace the opposition in

---

[18] This count is based on the presidential proposal database used in this study, as detailed later.

[19] In Groseclose and McCarty's (2001) congressional blame game, opposition-controlled congresses possess incentives to present the president with legislation that it knows he will veto. Congress can *blame* the president for vetoing the legislation, contending the president is out of step with the public because he opposed "popular" legislation. They find that congressional blame games lead to drops in presidential approval.

Congress with the president's party. This charge and request becomes the crux of the president's campaign theme. Historical accounts suggest that Truman used such a strategy successfully in 1948 (Hartmann, 1971). The presidential blame game leads to the hypothesized interaction between minority status and the reelection cycle, predicting larger agendas during minority–reelection congresses. To my knowledge, other than Groseclose and McCarty's (2001) related congressional blame game, there is no similar hypothesis in the literature on presidential-congressional relations. Thus, we cannot point to evidence other than the anecdotal type reviewed here.

The Agenda Size-Legislative Success Hypothesis

The sincerity perspective suggests higher defeat rates for presidents confronted with divided as opposed to unified government. This hypothesis is based on the logic that presidents will submit all proposals that they support, irrespective of the proposal's prospects for congressional support. As policy agreement between the president and Congress declines from unified to divided government, we should see a higher rate of presidential defeat with divided than with united government. A large body of empirical literature, reviewed earlier, presents evidence supporting the divided government-high defeat rate hypothesis.

If presidents behave more in accord with the congressional anticipations than the sincerity perspective, however, we should not find such a large effect of divided government on success as found in the literature. This is because presidents, under the congressional anticipations scenario, strip from their legislative agendas those proposals with a high risk of defeat. The resulting presidential agenda is smaller for divided than united government, but the odds of enactment for proposals under the two party control configurations should be similar – whether government is divided or united, presidents will submit only those proposals with strong prospects for enactment.

This is not an argument that divided government has no effect on the president's legislative agenda, but that the effect of divided government is felt on the composition of the agenda rather than at the congressional roll call stage. Past research on presidential success with Congress has overstated the direct effect of divided government on success rates because of underspecified empirical models. We must include agenda size as a predictor variable. Thus, we should find a smaller effect for divided government on presidential success on estimations that include the size of the agenda as a variable than estimations without the agenda size variable. The congressional anticipations perspective also predicts a positive relationship between the size of the president's agenda and success with Congress. According to the congressional anticipations perspective, presidents will submit all legislative proposals to Congress that have a strong likelihood of enactment.

Rivers and Rose (1985) argue in contrast that there should be a negative relationship between agenda size and presidential success in Congress. They argue first that large presidential agendas are ambitious, "large programs – as measured by the sheer quantity of presidential legislative requests – are likely to be ambitious ones . . ." (p. 186). A large agenda can be composed of many small and incremental changes to existing policy, however, whereas a numerically small agenda could be ambitious in terms of scope and innovativeness. For example, Ronald Reagan is often characterized as having an ambitious legislative agenda on assuming office in 1981, focusing on a few top priorities – tax cuts, regulation reduction, defense increases. Bill Clinton, especially after his failed attempt at health care reform, is characterized as submitting a large agenda composed of small policies (Light, 2000). Second, Rivers and Rose argue, "[W]hen a president offers a large number of policy proposals the likelihood on Congress approving a specific proposal, if only because of time constraints, falls" (p. 186).[20]

There are several limitations to the Rivers and Rose study. One, their data from the CQ box score spans a short period, 1954 to 1974. As we will see, this is a period of extraordinarily high presidential proposal rates. Two, the CQ box scores are themselves problematic.

---

[20] Another possibility is that as presidents dig deeper into their agenda, they will wind up submitting proposals that have decreasing prospects for enactment. This assumes that presidents give higher priority to proposals that have better success prospects. Adding these weaker proposals onto his legislative agenda will decrease the percentage that will be enacted. If this type of logic is true, then we should witness a negative relationship between the size of the president's agenda and success.

The CQ box score calculates success within calendar year units; that is, a proposal is scored a success if Congress enacted it in the year in which it was proposed. Congressional sessions last two years, however. Proposals made in Year One of a session may be passed in Year Two. If a proposal made in Year One is not enacted that year, it counts in the box score as a failure, although it might in fact be enacted in Year Two. Rivers and Rose never explain how they handle this issue.

Finally, Rivers and Rose use a simultaneous equation system for estimating both presidential success and the size of the presidential agenda. Their equation for estimating agenda size includes a variable for the past year's success in Congress, arguing that presidents who were more successful in the past year will have larger agendas in the current year. This modeling decision is problematic for several reasons. Again, using annual time units violates the biennial congressional session structure. Why would presidential success in the previous congress necessarily affect the size of their agenda in the next congress when conditions between the two congresses can vary so greatly, such as a shift from united to divided control (or vice versa)? Moreover, why would a president look to his predecessor's success rate in a previous congress to fashion his agenda? These issues are not addressed in their estimation strategy. The instrumental variable for agenda size in their success estimation depends on the equation for estimating agenda size. Because their estimation strategy could be problematic for the several reasons noted earlier, the resulting instrument too may be questionable. Rivers and Rose (1985) are important for taking seriously the endogenous relationship between proposal and success, however.

A handful of other studies also bear on the relationship between the size of the president's agenda and success with Congress. In a time series analysis using monthly data from 1953 to 1980, Ostrom and Simon (1985) find a negative relationship between the number of congressional roll call votes presidents take a position on and success with Congress. They rely first on Mueller's (1970, 1973) coalition of minorities concept to explain their finding. Mueller's argument is that as presidents take positions and make decisions, some voters will disagree with the president's action and withdraw their approval of the president. The more decisions that presidents make, the larger the number of voters who defect from the president's public support coalition. Ostrom and Simon extend the effects of declining public support to success in Congress. Because public support is one resource that presidents can employ to rally support in Congress, as approval rates decline, support in Congress should also fall. For our purposes, there are issues with Ostrom and Simon's study. First, it covers only the modern period and relies on presidential roll call positions, not presidential proposals for legislation. Also, there are issues with the construction of their congressional success variable, which cumulates presidential success in Congress from one month to the next during a year, and they include only roll calls on domestic policy.

In contrast, several studies argue for a positive relationship between presidential position taking or proposing and legislative success. First, using two-stage least squares estimation on annual data from 1953 to 1988, Brace and Hinckley find a positive relationship between the number of presidential roll call positions and presidential success. They also find, however, that the number of roll call positions is negatively related to approval, and approval is positively associated with congressional success. Thus, position taking has positive direct effects but negative indirect effects through approval on success. Again, this study looks at roll call behavior and is restricted to the modern era, unlike my study, which looks a presidential proposing and the entire history of the presidency.

Light's interview evidence also supports the positive relationship between size and success, "The main factor contributing to variations in agenda size is capital: as presidential capital contracts, so does the President's domestic agenda" (1991, p. 57). To Light, capital includes party support (including majority control of Congress), public support (approval), reputation, and election margin (pp. 25–33).

Furthermore, Cameron and Park's (2008) burden-sharing model implies a positive relationship between agenda size and presidential success. They find that the president's agenda is larger when presidents sense a mood in Congress to legislate. When Congress is in a mood to be legislative, the prospects that Congress will enact presidential proposals also should rise. Hence, the Cameron-Park model should also lead to a positive relationship between agenda size and success, but Cameron and Park do not present any evidence in support of that hypothesis.

There is also anecdotal evidence in support of the positive relationship between success and agenda size. Upon assuming office on March 4, 1933, Franklin Roosevelt called Congress into a special legislative session. Within two weeks, Congress enacted three major pieces of legislation that FDR asked for, including legislation to address the banking crisis, cuts in federal expenditures (called the Economy Act), and a amendment to the Volstead Prohibition Act, which made 3.2 percent beer and wine legal. According to Simon (2012), in his history of the New Deal, FDR had planned to terminate the special congressional session after these three bills were enacted, but "his success emboldened him to press forward" (p. 246). In relatively short order, FDR submitted legislation to Congress that led to the enactment of other major legislation, including the Agricultural Adjustment Act (AAA), the Civilian Conservation Corps (CCC), the Tennessee Valley Authority (TVA), the Federal Emergency Relief Administration (FERA), the Home Owners' Loan Corporation (HOLC), and the Federal Securities Act, which established the Securities and Exchange Commission. This second set of proposals was enacted by mid-June, giving rise to the one hundred day label, the standard for legislative accomplishment that would be used to measure all succeeding presidents upon taking office. Overall then only a small number of studies investigate the relationship between presidents' legislative activity levels and success, and those studies present contrasting findings.

The Moderation-Success Hypothesis

The divided government-moderation hypothesis predicts that presidents will moderate their policy stances when confronting opposition-controlled congresses. Underlying this hypothesis, based on the congressional anticipations perspective, is the idea that presidents want to reduce how often they are defeated. By moving their proposals from their most preferred position closer to the preference of the key congressional "decider," like the median or the pivot, the chances of enactment for the proposal will rise. The distance between the president and the key congressional decider is small during united versus divided government. Presidents do not need to move much during united government but might have to move a considerable distance during divided government. Thus, the moderation-success hypothesis suggests an interaction effect between presidential moderation and divided government: During divided government, the more moderate the president, the higher the president's success with Congress.

Modern Presidents and Agenda Building

The modern presidency puzzle presented previously asks why modern presidents submit such large legislative agendas, compared with traditional presidents, when they can expect such a difficult time in getting their proposals through Congress. Again, why do modern presidents allow themselves to be defeated so often? For the divided government puzzle, the congressional anticipations perspective leads to hypotheses regarding both presidential proposing behavior and sources of presidential success with Congress. The modern presidency puzzle, in contrast, begins with an observation regarding presidential proposing. The congressional anticipations perspective also begins with that observation, leading to several hypotheses regarding presidential success with Congress.

The Modern President-Success Hypothesis

What are the implications of the modern office on presidential success with Congress?[21] There is scant research on this question. Cohen's two analyses (1982a, 1982b) are the only studies to raise this question using quantitative data. He finds that modern and traditional presidents have similar success rates on average but that the factors affecting success vary between the two periods.

The congressional anticipations perspective suggests that presidents can do several things when they expect to be defeated by Congress. The large body of literature on presidential-congressional relations leads Krutz, Fleisher, and Bond (2000) to argue that there is a "presumption

---

[21] The modern presidency is a frequently used idea for explaining the development of the office and the behavior of its occupants. The idea is not without its critics. Some argue that other concepts, such as political time, better explain presidential behavior (Skowronek, 1993, 2009). Debate also exists over when the modern presidency emerged (e.g., Tulis, 1987 v. Greenstein, 1978, 1988), leading Woolley (2005) to argue that instead of trying to pinpoint the timing of the emergence of the office, we need to explain what gave rise to it.

of failure" for most presidential proposals and roll call positions. Facing this expectation of defeat, the congressional anticipations perspective argues that modern presidents have engaged in the third method for reducing the incidence of defeat – they have sought resources that would strengthen their bargaining situation with Congress.

One of the important differences between the modern and traditional presidencies is the level of institutional resources provided to the modern executive (Greenstein, 1978, 1988).[22] From the late 1930s, the office of the presidency has accumulated institutional resources, including formalized authority, staff, and decision-making processes. As argued here, the legislative clearance process, fully realized in 1949, became an important resource that would enhance the presidential bargaining relationship with Congress.[23] Legislative clearance allowed the president to harness the expertise of the bureaucracy, to restrict congressional access to that expertise, and to regulate the transmission of that expertise to Congress to the furtherance of presidential policy goals.

The annual legislative clearance process culminates with the presentation of the president's legislative program to Congress (Larocca, 2006; Neustadt, 1954, 1955; Rudalevige, 2002; Wayne, 1978). In building the legislative program, Bureau of the Budget (BoB, later Office of Management and Budget [OMB]) staff would review all proposals from the bureaucracy (and other sources, like White House staff) for inclusion in the program. Proposals deemed inconsistent

---

[22] Another resource that might differentiate modern from traditional presidents is public support. Considerable debate exists over whether public support, measured typically as approval, influences congressional support for the president. The literature on this debate is huge. See the review in Edwards (2009).

[23] The seeds of the legislative clearance process date to 1921, with the enactment of the Budget and Accounting Act, which created the Bureau of the Budget (BoB), to be located in the Treasury Department. Under Coolidge, the BoB began clearing all legislation that required appropriations, but BoB comments were restricted to fiscal, not policy, implications of these bills. Frustrated by learning of agency legislative recommendations from newspapers and other unofficial channels, in 1935 FDR expanded clearance to all legislation, requiring inclusion of a statement that indicated whether the bill was consistent with the president's program. Soon after his election in 1948, Truman instructed all agencies to submit their legislative proposals for clearance, beginning the formalized, exhaustive legislative clearance process. Larocca (2006, pp. 34–35, 49–51) provides a concise historical summary of the development of the legislative clearance process.

with the president's policy priorities would be excluded from the program and prohibited from being presented to Congress. Those proposals consistent with presidential policies are then classified according to priority, high versus lower-priority proposals. High-priority proposals gain a slot on the president's program and are labeled *presidential priorities*. They will receive the most attention from the president. The other consistent proposals can be transmitted to Congress by the bureaucracy, but they lack the prestige of being elements of the president's program.

This process altered the relationships of the president and the bureaucracy with Congress. Although presidents always submitted legislative proposals to Congress, rarely did they attach bill drafts. Congress would at times react with hostility to traditional presidents who submitted bill drafts, arguing it was an encroachment on Congress's constitutional prerogatives and violated separation of power. Binkley (1947, p. 298), for example, reports such a reaction when Lincoln transmitted a bill draft to the legislature. Congress, in contrast, was more open to bill drafts from the bureaucracy. In the traditional era Congress had clear and direct access to the expertise of the bureaucracy through bill drafts and bureaucratic testimony to Congress. At times Congress requested drafts of bills from the bureaucracy.

Bureaucratic expertise can be important to the congressional policy-making process. In making public policy, members of Congress might be uncertain as to the policy and political effects of different courses of action. Policy knowledge can reduce the uncertainty over the effects of different policy directions. Members of Congress have only limited capacity to develop the necessary policy expertise on their own, however, especially as society has become more industrialized and complex. Thus, Congress delegates deep policy expertise to others, usually the bureaucracy. Before the advent of the modern presidency, the bureaucracy essentially served Congress in this regard.

The legislative clearance process severed the direct bureaucratic-congressional linkage that previously existed. Agencies could no longer submit proposals at variance with the president's policy aims or without presidential consent. Landy and Milkis (2000, p. 82) describe the relationship between Congress and the departments this way in the years prior to the establishment of the legislative clearance process: "[C]abinet members ignored the president's wishes and pursued their own departmental agendas through direct contact with Congress." Ties between cabinet members and Congress also strengthened once the committee system in Congress emerged in the early 1800s: "Cabinet-committee relationships became the principal 'medium of intercommunication' between the two branches of government" (Landy and Milkis, 2000, p. 82).

With the creation of the legislative clearance process, Congress could draw on bureaucratic expertise only through the presidency. Through the legislative clearance process, bureaucratic expertise was transformed into a presidential resource, to be used as the president desired. The president could now regulate the availability and type of bureaucratic expertise provided to Congress. This should provide modern presidents with an advantage over traditional presidents in dealing with Congress. Insofar as Congress needs or wants policy expertise to craft legislation, Congress relies or depends more on the modern executive than was the case during the era of traditional presidents. It might not be too much of a stretch to argue that modern presidents created the legislative clearance process with this type of effect in mind. This leads to the hypothesis that presidents of the legislative clearance era should be more successful in Congress than presidents serving before legislative clearance existed.

Modern Presidents, Size of Agenda, and Success

The limitation of the previous hypothesis is that it does not uniquely test the informational advantages hypothesized to result from the legislative clearance process. As stated, that hypothesis tests only for differences in success of the traditional and modern presidents. Because there are several differences between traditional and modern presidents besides the legislative clearance process (Greenstein, 1978, 1988), any of those other differences could account for the hypothesized higher success rate of modern presidents, assuming that modern presidents are more successful than traditional presidents.

The theory developed here focuses on the informational advantages that accrue to the president from the legislative clearance process, similar to Cameron and Park's (2008) burden-sharing and Larocca's

(2006) informational models.[24] Furthermore, the congressional anticipations theory offered here argues that presidents will refrain from
submitting or will modify their legislative proposals if they expect that
Congress will defeat their proposals. Earlier we hypothesized a positive relationship between agenda size and presidential success with
Congress.

If modern presidents possess bargaining advantages with Congress
that traditional presidents lack because of the legislative clearance
process, then there should also be an interaction effect between
modernity and agenda size with legislative success. In the modern
era, presidential proposals come to Congress through the legislative
clearance process, carrying within them the expertise from the bureaucracy. Proposals from traditional presidents do not possess this bureaucratic expertise characteristic, or if they do, Congress can still gather
expertise from the bureaucracy directly. We can model this interaction
effect as: *Legislative Success = Modern President + Agenda Size + (Modern
President × Agenda Size)*. The interaction hypothesis predicts a positive, statistically significant effect for the *Modern President × Agenda Size*
term.

Summary

The theory of congressional anticipations offers several novel hypotheses with predictions that differ from existing perspectives on the presidency and presidential-congressional relations. Because defeat can
be costly to presidents, chief executives would prefer to avoid or
minimize how often Congress defeats their legislative proposals. The
congressional anticipations theory argues that presidents can reduce
the incidence of congressional defeat by withholding proposals that
appear destined for defeat, by modifying proposals to make them more
appealing to Congress, and/or by gathering resources that improve
the president's bargaining position with Congress. These adaptations

---

[24] Larocca's (2006) theory primarily accounts for presidential influence over the congressional agenda, rather than legislative enactment, although he suggests that it
can be extended to explain enactment success: "[T]his informational advantage can
be used to bring policy closer to the president's ideal on a given issue, but I focus
instead on how the president uses this informational advantage to determine what
issues are considered by Congress" (p. 52).

to expectations of success/defeat in Congress are applied to two situations, divided versus unified government and modern versus traditional presidents.

Presidential agendas are complex documents. Factors besides the congressional context can affect presidential agenda-building decisions. To appreciate the utility of the congressional anticipations theory, we also must take in account rival perspectives on presidential agenda building. The rest of this chapter reviews some of the major rivals to the congressional context as influences on the president's legislative agenda.

ALTERNATIVE PERSPECTIVES ON PRESIDENTIAL AGENDA BUILDING

More than just expectations regarding congressional action on their proposals affects presidential agenda-building decisions. A complete theory of presidential agenda building incorporates these other factors in addition to the impact of these expectations of congressional action. Although the primary aim of this study is to assess the impact of congressional expectations on presidential agenda building, and then to assess the impact of that agenda on success with Congress, it is also useful to identify these other factors that might influence presidential agenda building. Doing so will help set a stage for further research. Inclusion of variables related to these other factors also serves another purpose, to determine whether the congressional factors remain statistically significant in the face of controls for other variables.

There are always more potential proposals than space, or *proposal berths*, on the president's legislative policy agenda.[25] Thus, the president's legislative policy agenda is a scarce resource. Potential proposals must compete with each other to secure one of the valued placements on the legislative policy agenda. Presidents need a way to rank or prioritize the potential proposals seeking entry onto their legislative policy agenda. In building their legislative policy agendas, presidents must balance multiple and often competing demands. The decision

---

[25] Presidential resources, such as staffing, time, and political capital, limit the size and other attributes of his agenda.

process for prioritizing among potential proposals is therefore complex. Three sets of factors in addition to the congressional context can affect presidential agenda-building decisions: 1) representational concerns, 2) administrative responsibilities, and 3) party differences.

Presidents, Representation, and Agenda Building

Two emerging research programs suggest the potential payoff of studying the president's legislative agenda from a representational perspective: 1) agendas as a representation process and 2) the presidential responsiveness literature. The idea that representational pressures could affect how presidents construct their legislative policy agendas integrates these two emerging research programs.

Bryan Jones and his colleagues (Jones and Baumgartner, 2004, 2005; Jones, Larsen-Price, and Wilkerson, 2009) provide the clearest statement of the agenda representation perspective. They argue that studies of representation focus almost exclusively on *positional* outcomes, that is, whether the policy outcomes of government match the policy preferences of the public. This, they argue, presents an incomplete picture of the degree of governmental representation of the public in policy making. Although government outputs, its policies, might match voters' preferences, those government policies might not represent the public's policy *priorities*. This would be the case if government failed to produce policies on issues of importance to the public and instead produced policies of lesser concern to voters. The agenda representation perspective argues that besides the position of government on policies produced, we also need to know about the degree of match between the *issue priorities* of voters and government policy production to gain a fuller portrait of the representational qualities of the political system. This perspective argues that to be fully representative, there should be a high degree of match for both the policy priorities and positions of the public and the government.[26]

---

[26] The intellectual seeds of viewing agenda setting from a representational perspective can be found in Cobb and Elder (1972) and Cobb, Ross, and Ross (1976). Cobb and Elder make the distinction between the systemic or public agenda with the institutional or governmental agenda. Although they do not articulate fully the relationship between the two agendas, Cobb, Ross, and Ross (1976) begin to do so with their comparative agenda-building perspective. They identify three models of agenda building: outside initiative, mobilization, and the inside access model. The outside initiative model, in which an issue moves from the systemic agenda to the

Another research program asks whether representational pressures or concerns affect presidential policy making. In saying that representational concerns influence presidential agenda building, I mean that presidents take into account the public, its policy preferences, and likely or estimated reactions to presidential decisions when building their legislative agendas and taking other policy stances. Although a long-held concern dating to the debates over ratification of the Constitution (Canes-Wrone, 2006, p. 4), theoretical and empirical work on the representational character on the presidency is relatively recent.[27] Most of the research on presidents and representation looks at the policy positions of the president and the public. That research at times reports presidential responsiveness to public opinion (e.g., Erikson, MacKuen, Stimson, 2002); other studies fail to detect such presidential responsiveness (Cohen, 1998; Eshbaugh-Soha, 2005). A third group of studies (Canes-Wrone, 2006; Rottinghaus, 2006) argues that presidential responsiveness is conditional. The few studies that look at agenda setting find relatively strong presidential responsiveness to public opinion (Cohen, 1998; Jones, Larsen-Price, and Wilkerson, 2009).[28]

The primary mechanism that links the president's legislative agenda to public opinion is reelection.[29] From this perspective, presidents

---

governmental one, anticipates the agenda representation perspective. In contrast, the mobilization model suggests that leaders mobilize support in the public for their policy priorities; that is, issues move from the governmental to the systemic/public agenda. Finally, the inside access model limits all policy making, including agenda setting, to governmental settings, outside or hidden from public view. At this early stage in their research, Jones and colleagues merely demonstrate the correlation between the public and governmental agendas but have not determined the casual direction to account for the correlation. They recognize the theoretical possibilities using language somewhat different from that of Cobb, Ross, and Ross.

[27] See Cohen, 1998; Hill, 1999; Canes-Wrone, 2006; Erikson, MacKuen, and Stimson, 2002; Eshbaugh-Soha, 2005; Rottinghaus, 2008; Wood, 2010; Yates and Whitford, 2005; for reviews of the literature on representation and policy making more generally, see Burstein, 2003, 2005 and Manza and Cook, 2002.

[28] See Eshbaugh-Soha, 2005, who finds that the number of major and total proposals increase as presidential approval rises, but the effects are marginally significant.

[29] Role theory, in particular when presidents assume or adopt an "instructed delegate" perspective, can offer an alternative or complementary mechanism for linking public opinion to the president's program. Very little research on the presidency has looked at whether representational roles (i.e., trustee v. delegate) affect presidential behavior. The only study that I know of that explicitly analyses a president from that perspective is Hargrove's study of Jimmy Carter (1988).

select policies for their legislative agenda because of their popularity or anticipated popularity with the public. Because of the policy's popularity, presidents expect voters will be more likely to vote for the president (and/or members of his party) than if he placed less popular policies on his legislative agenda.[30] Light's interviews with White House staffers suggest that electoral calculations often weigh heavily in building the president's legislative agenda (1991, pp. 64–66).

The electoral connection can operate either retrospectively or prospectively. For example, presidents might have found certain issues to be popular with the electorate and credited their election to the popularity of those issues. Consequently, presidents might then decide to repay voters for their electoral support by placing those issues on their legislative agendas, or they may assume that if an issue played well with the public during the campaign, it would continue to do so once in office. Congress might be more willing to enact legislation on issues popular with the public than issues with less public support. By submitting proposals on popular issues, with the president's policy alternative aligned with public preferences, he increases the odds of congressional enactment, which can burnish his leadership image. Submitting popular issues to Congress can also help to maintain public support of the president and convert his electoral support into job approval.[31] Rather than being merely reactive, however, presidents can anticipate the public reaction to their proposals, going with items that they think will resonate more positively with the public, while deciding against proposals that they think the public will react negatively to (Edwards, 2010, pp. 344–347).

Although we might expect the electoral linkage with presidential legislative agenda building to weaken in the second term, Light (1991, p. 66) suggests that the electoral connection can stay strong in the second term for several reasons. Presidents can remain attuned to public preferences in building their second-term agendas because it served them well during the first term: Such sensitivity to public opinion leading to enactments, high popularity, and reelection in

---

[30] This dynamic resembles Canes-Wrone's (2001, 2006) strategic going public model.

[31] This, however, begins to blend the electoral connection-representation model to the congressional context one, developed above. Conceptually we should keep these two perspectives distinct, but they can interact.

the first term. They also might keep a close ear on public sentiment in their second term to improve their party's prospects of retaining the White House and/or to have some say in their party's choice of whom to succeed them. A president is also more likely to leave a long-lasting policy legacy to the nation if his party remains in government. Reversals of the policy course that an incumbent president took in office are more likely to be overturned if the opposition party gains control of the elected branches of government.

Somewhat jadedly, this discussion suggests that presidents might pander to the public when building their legislative agendas (but see Jacobs and Shapiro, 2000, who argue otherwise). Geer (1996) contends that the rise of polling since the mid-twentieth century has provided politicians with more precise information about the public's preferences.[32] With this better information, politicians can fine-tune their policy stances to align with the public to a greater degree than in the days without such polls. In other words, Geer suggests a secular trend toward pandering with the advent of polling. Jacobs and Shapiro (2000) counter that politicians, including presidents, do not use polls to pander but to find ways to craft their appeals to the public. Rather than pandering, polls could allow politicians to manipulate (or lead) the public. Canes-Wrone (2006) presents a conditional theory that argues that "pandering" is most likely to occur for presidents of medium popularity, as opposed to both very popular or unpopular popular presidents, in periods nearing reelection.

To sort through these complex causal linkages between the public and the president's agenda requires data that simply do not exist – poll data covering a long period of history across a variety of presidential proposals. Useful public opinion data exist from only the late 1940s or early 1950s, about the time that the president's program appeared,

---

[32] Numerous studies have documented the institutional of polling operations in the White House and presidential use of polls in policy making. There is some debate in this literature over whether polls constrict president policy choice or allow greater policy latitude, with the better information that polls provide enabling presidents to manipulate the public. See Druckman and Jacobs (2006), Druckman, Jacobs, and Ostermier (2004), Eisinger (2003), Geer and Goorha (2003), Hall (2002), Heith (1998, 2004), Jacobs and Burns (2004), Jacobs and Shapiro (1994, 1995/1996), Murray (2006), Murray and Howard (2002), Rottinghaus (2003), and Shapiro and Jacobs (2001).

making it impossible to test for presidential responsiveness to public opinion for earlier periods.

Thus, the analysis here uses an indirect method to gauge the degree of presidential responsiveness to the public by starting with the assumption that across most of U.S. history, the public has held the president accountable for the overall state of the nation. In justifying this assumption, it is important to note that even during the early days of the republic, the competing parties (or pre-party factions, the Federalists and Jeffersonian Democrats) saw the presidency as an important office to control (Milkis and Nelson, 2008). The presidency held the veto power, and with it the potential to shape public policy (McCarty, 2009). Moreover, as a unitary office, the occupant symbolized and personified his party. The visibility of the president also meant that the public would to some degree hold him accountable for the health of the government and the nation. For example, despite the relatively weak economic policy instruments under his control, Martin Van Buren lost reelection in 1840 because of the panic (depression) of 1837 (Forsimano, 1993).

Objective conditions provide an indication of the state of the nation and the potential political implications of those conditions. By political implications, I mean whether the condition or problem is likely to become an issue that could affect the outcome of the upcoming election. In the absence of (or in conjunction with) public opinion data, presidents will look at these objective conditions for signals or information about the state of the nation and potential political-electoral ramifications.[33] They might pay particular attention to deterioration in objective conditions, such as rising unemployment, inflation, or other economic indicators, fearing or anticipating that such events and conditions will rile and disquiet the public, and that voters might blame the administration for the souring state of affairs. When faced with deterioration in objective conditions, we should expect presidents to act to preserve their standing with the public and to minimize the

---

[33] Presidents also can use newspapers for information about sentiment regarding the state of the nation. Herbst (1998) argues that politicians often define public opinion by what they see in news reports. Prior to public opinion polls, politicians seemed to rely heavily on newspapers and magazines as barometers of public sentiment. On the importance of newspapers to the early presidency see Laracey (2002).

political damage that such conditions could do. For instance, a president probably will make public announcements about those problems, hoping to reassure the public that he is aware of the problem and is attending to it, a form of *agenda responsiveness* (Cohen, 1998; Jones, Larsen-Price; Wilkerson, 2009). Presidents also might take more substantive action, for example, by submitting legislation to Congress to address the problem.

Research on the public's agenda finds that matters of war and peace and the economy tower over other policy areas in importance. Jones and Baumgartner (2004, p. 5) show that these two policy areas dominated the public's "most important problem" designation for the years from 1946 onward, when such data existed. Cohen (1998) argues the public holds the president accountable for these two policy areas in particular, and the vast research on presidential approval indicates that presidential approval rises and falls with the state of the economy, wars, and other threatening international events (for a review see Gronke and Newman, 2003). Although we do not have as much systematic information about the political implications of war and the economy for earlier periods, the historical record suggests the defining implications of war and the economy for presidents from the pre-polling era as well (Milkis and Nelson, 2008).

The analysis presented in the following chapters uses indicators of the economy and war as independent variables to measure important objective conditions, hypothesizing characteristics of the president's legislative agenda will covary with these objective indicators. Still, I must point out that this provides only an indirect test of presidential legislative agenda responsiveness to the public. As detailed earlier, in using objective conditions, I am making several assumptions about the linkages between those conditions and voter reactions. It might also be the case that presidents react to changes in objective conditions for other reasons, such that they feel a responsibility to take care of problems or that they want a legacy of having left the nation better off at the end of their term than when they took office. As will be become clearer in the empirical chapters to follow, however, we face enormous data limitations that frustrate analysis, which cautions us not to "overinterpret" the empirical findings.

Administrative Responsibilities and the President's Agenda

Generally, research on presidential agenda choice emphasizes presidential discretion in selecting items for their legislative agendas (e.g., Light, 1991). An alternative perspective, however, contends that presidents possess much less discretion in their choice of policies and issues for their agenda than commonly assumed, because there is a set of policies and issues to which presidents *must* attend. These issues tend not to be new, novel, or departures from the status quo but represent the existing activities, policies, and programs of government. As Charles O. Jones argues, presidents make agenda decisions within the context of the ongoing activities of government. "Normally he [the president] chooses from among a set of issues that are familiar because they are continuous. Many of these issues are directly traceable to programs already on the books" (1994, p. 168).[34] In other words, there is a class or set of issues that presidents put on the agenda not because they want to, although they might, but because they *have* to. Why do presidents so feel compelled to concern themselves with these types of issues?

First, the Constitution holds the president accountable for the performance of government, and we can argue that presidents take this responsibility seriously. Two clauses in the Constitution outline the president's administrative responsibilities. Article II, Section 3 reads that the president "shall take Care that the Laws be faithfully executed." Article II, Section 2, creates lines of authority and responsibility from the ranks of the bureaucracy to the president: The president "may require the Opinion, in writing, of the principal Officer in each of the executive Departments, upon any subject relating to the Duties of their respective Offices." The Constitution also grants the president important appointment powers. Although Congress must confirm nominations of "Ambassadors, other public Ministers and Consuls, Judges of the supreme Court, and all other Officers of the United States, whose Appointments are not herein otherwise provided

---

[34] Neustadt (1960, p. 34) puts the matter of lack of presidential discretion this way: "What Presidents do every day is make decisions that are mostly thrust upon them, the deadlines all too often outside their control, on options mostly framed by others, about issues crammed with technical complexities and uncertain outcomes." I want to thank Matthew Holden for pointing out this quote to me.

for" (Article II, Section 2), "Congress may by Law vest the Appointment of such inferior Officers, as they think proper, in the President alone" (Article II, Section 2). Presidential appointees not subject to congressional confirmation now number several thousand. These constitutional provisions hold the president responsible for the personnel of the executive branch, for their actions and performance, and the reporting language of Article II, Section 2 gives the president a system for making these appointees answerable and accountable to the president.

Partly from this constitutional foundation, the rest of the political system, Congress, the courts, and the citizenry view the president as responsible and accountable for the performance of the programs and policies administered through the executive branch, and more generally, the actions and behaviors of the individuals who populate the bureaucracy and executive branch. Bureaucratic failures become presidential failures. Poorly working, ineffective, and costly government programs are viewed as problems of presidential leadership and reflect on the president's administrative competence.

This all provides a rationale for why presidents would be concerned with the operations and performance of the bureaucracy and the effectiveness and efficiency of government programs and policies, but not why the president would privilege such issues when building his legislative policy agenda. Why would issues related to the existing programs and policies of government often have an easier route onto the president's agenda than other issues?

First, the legislative calendar can dictate presidential attention if he wants to have any input into congressional action on these matters. Adler and Wilkerson (2005) make an important point, that Congress often takes formal action only when a deadline approaches, for instance, if a program needs to be reauthorized or money for a program is running out, hence requiring an appropriation to continue the program. Such deadlines force Congress to make a decision on a program, such as whether to continue it, and if so, how it will be continued. The president also might feel this deadline pressure, especially for policies that require legislative action and for which the president wants to have some say or input. In this sense, the president and Congress share an agenda, the ongoing policies and programs of government. The more that government does and the larger government is, the more issues and problems will make it onto the president's desk because of deadlines that force making a decision on an issue.

Two other factors also could give ongoing government programs and policies advantages in gaining access to the president's legislative agenda, namely bureaucratic and interest group support. The expertise and information that the bureaucracy possesses provides it with important resources or advantages in identifying problems, issues, and solutions to the president and in gaining presidential attention to these issues. Light stresses the limited informational and expertise resources of the president and the White House staff (1991, pp. 18–23). The president and the White House thus must rely on others to identify problems and suggest solutions to those problems. Despite the often tense relations between the president and the bureaucracy (e.g., Aberbach and Rockman, 2000; Cronin, 1975; Cronin and Genovese, 1998; Lewis, 2008, 2009; Randall, 1979), Light's interviewees frequently mention the bureaucracy as a major source of ideas or issues for the president's legislative agenda.[35] Why is the federal bureaucracy such a major source of ideas? Presidents turn so much to the bureaucracy as a source of agenda ideas primarily because of its resources, size, and expertise, something that the president and White House cannot match.

Moreover, the bureaucracy can strongly influence the policy direction that the president takes to address the problem. Lack of time and expertise place constraints on the presidential agenda-building process. Presidents and their White House staffs generally lack the technical expertise to study a problem and devise an approach or solution to the problem. Time pressures further constrain the president, often forcing the administration to select an "available alternative" (Light, 1991, p. 147). The president thus often selects alternatives

[35] The executive branch (e.g., federal bureaucracy) ranked third, just behind Congress and events as a source of ideas for the president's agenda (1991, pp. 86, 91). Of Light's respondents, 46% cited the executive branch as a source of agenda ideas, compared with 52% and 51% for Congress and events. Public opinion ranked fourth at a distant 27% and the president's own campaign, which ranked fifth, was mentioned by only 20% of respondents.

developed in the departments and agencies of the executive branch. Those departments and agencies might already have been working on policy solutions to a problem and therefore can easily provide the president with a policy solution (Light, 1991, p. 147).

When policy expertise is the primary foundation of bureaucratic influence on the president's agenda, the political resources of interest groups can also advantage ongoing government policy and program access to the president's agenda. The creation of government programs usually forges tangible ties between government and elements of society that benefit from those policies. Those societal elements or sectors often organize into political interest groups to gain, protect, maintain, and enhance the benefits that they receive from these government programs. Sometimes existing interest groups mobilize for enactment of policies beneficial to its members. Other times, the creation of new policies leads to the establishment of new interest groups, to ensure that its members continue to receive the benefits of the government policy (Walker, 1991).

Interest groups possess ties and potential allies throughout the political system, for example in Congress and the bureaucracy, forming the famous policy subsystems, iron triangles, and issue networks that characterize so much of American politics (Baumgartner et al., 2009). An interest group also can have direct ties to the administration, for example, through the Office of Public Liaison (OPL). The OPL can coordinate administration and interest group activities on policy initiatives; such interest groups can be viewed as presidential allies and targets for presidential mobilization of political resources (Peterson, 1992; Loomis, 2009). Especially since the reforms of the presidential campaign finance and nomination system in the 1970s, interest groups have become critical for the nomination of presidential candidates through their endorsements, campaign contributions, and mobilization of voters. Through these direct and indirect channels, interest groups can apply pressure on the presidential agenda-building process.

Thus, for various reasons, constitutional rationale, deadlines, bureaucratic expertise, and interest group political strength, the ongoing activities of government can be advantaged over issues emanating from other political quarters in gaining placement on the president's legislative policy agenda.

Partisanship and Presidential Agendas

Party differences have been found to be important in explaining a wide range of political behaviors and phenomena. At the mass level, party identification informs the vote choice, positions on issues, and evaluations of the president (e.g., Bartels, 2000; Bond and Fleisher, 2001; Newman and Siegle, 2010). The party is also a primary factor in congressional roll call voting. Across numerous issues, Democratic and Republican members of Congress often divide into relatively homogenous party camps opposed to one another (Poole and Rosenthal, 1997). Political economy studies have found that governments pursue different economic policies dependent on the party in power: Where Democratic administrations tend to pursue policies to ease unemployment, Republican administrations seem more likely to combat inflation (Hibbs, 1977; Alesina and Rosenthal, 1995). Even studies of judicial decision making find that party of the judge or justice is an important statistical predictor (Gates and Cohen, 1988).

Party can also influence presidential agenda-building decisions. First, the U.S. parties have traditionally held different governing philosophies. For example, the Republicans have opposed large government, government regulation of and intrusion into the economy, instead preferring market solutions to governmental ones for economic and social problems. In contrast, Democrats prefer a bigger, more activist approach to governing. Furthermore, Democrats are more disposed to using government agencies and policies for social ends, such as reducing economic and other forms of inequality (Gerring, 1998). This difference in governing orientation should lead Democrats to offer larger legislative agendas than Republican presidents.

Second, the parties have often competed over policy priorities, often claiming ownership on the issue that the party ranks most highly (Petrocik, 1996). Historically, Republicans claim ownership on foreign policy issues, with the Democrats "owning" many domestic issues. Thus, we are likely to find Republicans submitting a larger number of foreign policy proposals to Congress than Democrats, whereas Democrats submit more domestic policy proposals than Republicans. Party can influence the overall size of the presidential agenda as well as its substantive composition.

Party influences on presidential agenda decision making can operate through several mechanisms. First, presidents generally receive greater support in Congress from members of their party than the opposition. They might find it easier then to build legislative support for their agenda if they offer an agenda consistent with the policy preferences of their congressional co-partisans. Second, the intraparty recruitment process for presidential candidates is likely to be biased for candidates loyal to the party's policy aims rather than those who might challenge what the party has traditionally stood for. Finally, as the major representative of the party, presidents might feel a duty or obligation to promote the party's policy goals. Because of these mechanisms, we are likely to find presidents building legislative agendas that closely resemble their party's policy preferences and aims.

Summary

This chapter offered a theory of presidential legislative policy agenda building. That theory assumes that the president's agenda is a scarce resource. More issues vie for a place on the president's agenda than placements exist. As a consequence, presidents must prioritize among the competing issues in deciding which to put on their legislative agenda.

Although numerous factors influence presidential agenda choice, the theory proposed in this chapter argues that presidential anticipation of success with Congress has a strong influence on which proposals the president decides to submit to Congress for legislative consideration. Everything else being equal, this theory hypothesizes that presidents are more likely to submit proposals that have a higher chance for enactment than those unlikely to be enacted. From this simple anticipatory calculation, this chapter develops a series of hypotheses about the size of the president's legislative agenda and the factors that condition presidential success in Congress. Because greater support is to be expected from congressional co-partisans than out-party members of Congress, the presidential agenda should be larger with majority than minority control. Furthermore, because agenda size is an indicator of expected success, agenda size should be positively associated with success. Once agenda size is controlled for, divided government should not be as potent a direct influence on success as found in the extant literature on presidential-congressional relations. This theory then offers a novel prediction at odds with much of the existing literature on presidential success in Congress.

This chapter also introduced a series of other factors that can influence presidential agenda choice: representational pressures and concerns, administrative responsibilities, and the president's party. Although less time will be spent on these factors compared with the congressional context, a full theory of presidential agenda building must recognize the multiple influences on this presidential decision process. Adding these factors into the discussion takes a first step in that direction and also allows us to test whether the congressional context theory holds up as a significant influence on presidential agenda building in the face of controls for these other factors. The next chapter begins the empirical test of the theory of anticipated reactions by looking at the size of the president's agenda.

CHAPTER 4

The Size of the President's Agenda, 1789–2002

This chapter looks at perhaps the most basic characteristic of the president's legislative agenda, the number of legislative proposals that the president submits to Congress, what Cameron and Park (2008) term *legislative activism*. The conventional wisdom holds that modern presidents, those from FDR onward, have been more active in the legislative policy-making process than their predecessors. Theories of the modern presidency often cite increased presidential involvement in the legislative process as a characteristic that distinguishes modern presidents from traditional ones (Greenstein, 1988; Pfiffner, 2008; Shaw, 1987; Wayne, 1978).

Thus, it is no surprise, as documented later in this chapter, that presidents are more legislatively active in the modern era than before. The legislative proposal database allows us to pinpoint the timing of the increase in presidential activism. That takeoff in legislative activism did not come during the FDR administration, but with Harry Truman after the end of the Second World War. As we shall see, this is consistent with the theory of congressional anticipations, which argues that presidents submit larger legislative agendas when they expect greater success with Congress. The creation of the legislative program and central clearance allowed the president to regulate the provision of bureaucratic expertise to Congress. Insofar as that expertise is useful to Congress in building legislation, control over this resource potentially strengthened the president's bargaining position with Congress. Thus, we should find the surge in legislative activism occurring in the late 1940s, rather than with Franklin Roosevelt's presidency, the more common view derived from the modern presidency perspective.

From George Washington until the 1940s, there was also a slow, steady increase in the number of presidential proposals submitted to Congress. Traditional presidents were not as legislatively inactive, in terms of submitting proposals for legislation to Congress, as conventional wisdom portrays. These proposal data, spanning nearly the entire history of the office and the nation, lead us to revise our understanding of the presidency with regard to legislative activism. The first part of this chapter details the trends in presidential legislative activism.

Although precisely describing trends in legislative activism is important, more important is identifying the factors that affect presidential activism over both the long and the short haul. This chapter raises the following questions: Why the long-term secular increase in proposals across the first 150 years of presidential history? Why the abrupt surge in legislative proposing in the late 1940s? Why has that higher rate of legislative proposing persisted to the present? Why does presidential legislative activism rise and fall in the short run, from congress to congress? The second half of this chapter uses the theory of congressional anticipations outlined in Chapter 3 to explain variation in presidential legislative activism. Although the analysis looks at a variety of factors, that theory focuses in particular on divided government and the establishment of the presidential program and central clearance, hypothesizing that presidents will submit larger agendas to Congress under united than divided government and once the presidential program and central clearance are established.

TRENDS IN PRESIDENTIAL PROPOSAL ACTIVITY: THE LONG VIEW

Figure 4.1 plots the number of presidential requests for legislation by Congress from the first Congress (1789–1790) through the 107th (2001–2002). I use "congress" as the temporal unit for several reasons. First, the two calendar years that make up each congress is the legislature's natural time unit. Proposals submitted by any member[1]

---

[1] The president cannot formally submit legislation directly to Congress; this must be done by a member of Congress.

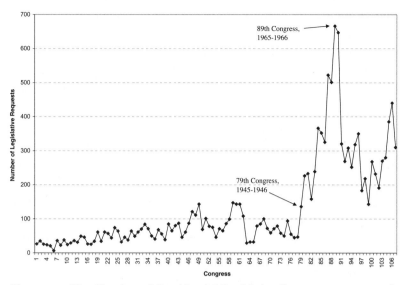

Figure 4.1. The Number of Presidential Legislative Requests, 1st to 107th Congresses (1789–2002).

during the congress remain alive until the end of that congress, when all bills that Congress did not enact and the president did not sign into law die. Someone must reintroduce those bills in the next congress to keep them on the legislative agenda. Presidents are obviously aware of this temporal structure.

Rethinking the Modern Presidency

Figure 4.1 illustrates the conventional wisdom of the higher legislative activism of modern compared with traditional presidents. There is a remarkable surge in presidential proposing beginning in the mid-twentieth century. Given the importance of Franklin Roosevelt in establishing the modern presidency (Greenstein, 1988), we might expect to see the upsurge in proposal activity during his term of office; however, it might take time for the executive branch to acquire the institutional support and foundation necessary to sustain a high level of legislative proposing. Although FDR might have set the seeds for presidential modernity during his tenure, to submit a large volume of legislative proposals to Congress would require staff resources that would take time to accumulate and to organize behind such a task. Thus we might expect the surge in legislative proposing to begin sometime after the establishment of the Executive Office of the Presidency (EOP) in 1939. With the EOP came the recognition that the presidency had fundamentally transformed, and that the office would need to be reorganized and staffed in accord with that transformation. The EOP would provide the institutional platform for the modern presidency.

The proposal data support neither of these hypotheses, the first that we should see a great rise in legislative activism early in FDR's term, the second that the upsurge should commence soon after the establishment of the EOP in 1939. Rather, the steep rise in presidential proposal activity does not begin until the end of the Second World War, during the Truman administration. The big jump in proposal activity begins with the 79th Congress (1947–1948) and continued with the 80th. During the 78th Congress (1943–1944), in the midst of war, FDR submitted forty-six legislative proposals to Congress. The next Congress, the 79th (1945–1946), the last year of war and first postyear, FDR and Truman together submitted 137 proposals. Proposal activity continued to climb steeply during the 80th Congress (1947–1948), with 225 submissions. Thereafter proposal activity leveled off until the mid-to-late 1950s and 1960s, another period when presidential submissions to Congress rose dramatically.

The 79th and 80th Congresses (1945–1948) mark a transition period in legislative activism. During these four years, presidential submission rates to Congress rose steeply, and subsequent presidents maintained that high level of proposal activity to the present. The high rate of proposing for the 79th and 80th Congresses is not a short-term spike in legislative activism but began a new period of presidential legislative activity. From the 68th to the 77th Congresses (1923–1944), presidents submitted on average 69.7 proposals, somewhat higher than the 46 of the 78th Congress. Truman's proposal rate during the 79th Congress is twice as high as the average for the 68th to the 77th Congresses. His proposal rate for the 80th Congress is nearly three times the rate for presidents from the 68th to 77th Congresses. What accounts for this abrupt and sustained change in presidential proposal activity beginning with the 79th and 80th Congresses?

Two conventional answers for Truman's unprecedented degree of legislative proposing consider the impact of the Second World War and political conditions in Congress during the 80th Congress (1947–1948). First, the Second World War might have constrained the amount of presidential proposal activity as the president and the nation focused more on the war effort.[2] Once the war ended, pent-up demand from several years of a restricted agenda and limited governmental resources to handle anything other than war-related matters might have led to the increase in presidential proposal activity. Proposal rates during the war years do appear slightly lower than for the late New Deal, but not by much. The war constraint–pent-up demand hypothesis predicts an uptick in proposal activity soon after the cessation of the Second World War, and this is basically what we see.

Secondly, political conditions during the next Congress (80th, 1947–1948) might have also spurred the increase in Truman's proposal activity. Republicans controlled the 80th Congress, blocking numerous policy initiatives from the Truman administration. Looking weak to voters because of these defeats in Congress, Truman decided to try to back the Republican Congress into a corner, submitting proposals for legislation that he knew would be defeated but that were popular with voters. This legislative strategy allowed him to build a campaign theme to run against the Republicans in the 1948 presidential elections (Hartmann, 1971; Rudalevige, 2002, p. 118), a strategy that proved effective. Not only was he reelected, but voters turned out the Republicans in Congress, giving Truman Democratic majorities for the 81st Congress (1949–1950).

Both of these impulses toward greater presidential proposal activity must also be understood in the context of a more institutionally resourceful presidency. Although postwar pent-up demand and a resistant Congress might have led Truman in the short term to submit large legislative agendas to Congress, to sustain that level of proposing required both the means (e.g., staff resources) and the motivations to do so.

---

[2]　One hypothesis that we entertain later is that war constrains the agenda to policies directly relevant to the war effort. This war effect would have implications for several attributes of the president's legislative agenda, including its size.

The motivation for presidential legislative leadership comes primarily from a change in the nation's public philosophy (Beer, 1978), allowing for a larger federal government and public expectations for presidential leadership of this enlarged governmental establishment. These legislative proposal data lead us to reinterpret the transformation of the presidency into its modern form, at least as it pertains to the legislative presidency. Several elements needed to come together. As is often mentioned in the modern presidency literature, the political culture needed to change. In this new political culture, presidents would be expected to be policy leaders, and the public would also expect greater effort on the part of the federal government to handle national problems.

Second, for the president to be a legislative activist would also require staff and other institutional resources. It would take the FDR administration some time to learn the importance of additional staffing for modern presidential leadership. These cultural-institutional factors alone would have probably led to an increase in presidential activism but do not adequately account for the timing of the upsurge in legislative activism. The Second World War also might have dampened presidential legislative activism. Soon after the war ended, we see an upturn in the number of presidential proposals. Finally, the political circumstances associated with the 80th Congress interacted with the cultural expectations for presidential leadership and the stronger institutional presidency to spike presidential activism in 1947/1948. Truman's successful reelection strategy, along with expectations for presidential leadership and a strong presidential institution, provided the incentive for continued high levels of legislative activism by presidents.

To maintain that high level of activism would require presidential resources devoted to that task, however. As the theory of congressional anticipations argues, presidents look to the likelihood that Congress will enact their proposals in deciding what to submit for legislative consideration. The greater their expectation of success with Congress, the larger the legislative agenda is. Central clearance and the presidential program gave the president control over an important resource that could affect his bargaining situation with Congress, bureaucratic expertise. Prior to the creation of these processes, Congress could solicit input from the bureaucracy directly, whenever its members thought that they needed the bureaucracy's expertise to inform the crafting of legislation.

With central clearance procedures in place, the president could regulate all bureaucratic contact with Congress. Presidents could deny the provision of bureaucratic expertise to Congress and perhaps more crucially could bias the type of information that the bureaucracy would pass along to Congress – providing Congress with only the expertise supportive of the president's policy goals. Inasmuch as bureaucratic expertise is important to Congress for policy making, the presidential bargaining situation with Congress is strengthened by the establishment of central clearance. The rise of presidential activism in the postwar years therefore must be seen as both the presidential response to demands for legislative and policy leadership and the acquisition of resources that enhance the president's ability to bargain successfully with Congress.[3]

Rethinking the Legislative Activism of Traditional Presidents

Figure 4.1 obscures as much as it reveals because the level of proposal activity in the post-War World Two era dwarfs that of the previous years, visually compressing the variability in proposal activity from 1789 to 1944. There are a few notable short-term spikes in legislative activity prior to 1946 (e.g., 49th Congress, 1885–1886; 59th–61st, 1905–1910). There also appears to be an upward slope in proposal activity across these first 150 years of the presidency. The data on Figure 4.1 are so compressed, however, that one cannot see clearly what is going on. To give a clearer picture of the trend in proposal activity before the great postwar upsurge, Figure 4.2 plots just the years from 1789 to 1944, the 1st to the 78th Congresses.

---

[3] Congress would come to realize the bias in bureaucratic information coming to it once central clearance was in place; still, there would be times when Congress would rely on such biased information. Congress can to some degree offset this presidential advantage by building its own expertise, as it has done for instance with the Congressional Budget Office (CBO). Congress cannot match the expertise of the executive branch – the bureaucracy is just too large. Moreover, presidents can also respond to congressional attempts to narrow the expertise gap between the branches (Epstein and O'Halloran, 1999; Krause, 2002).

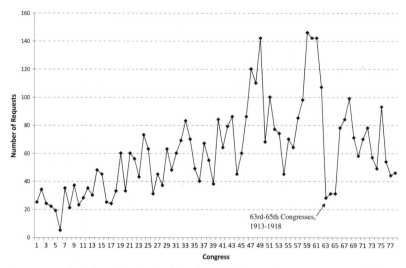

Figure 4.2. The Number of Presidential Legislative Requests, 1st to 78th Congresses (1789–1944).

First, Figure 4.2 reveals that early presidents might have been more legislatively active, in the sense of submitting requests to Congress, than conventional understandings of the early presidency suggest. George Washington, for instance, submitted on average twenty-six requests per Congress, ranging from twenty-two to thirty-four. His volume of request activity might be a function of his being the first president and the problems that had mounted during the Articles of Confederation period. The inability of the government under the Articles of Confederation to produce necessary legislation (e.g., policy) to handle issues such as defense, western uprisings, and economic distress provided the major rationale for the Philadelphia Constitutional convention. With this as a backdrop, a major task of the first president and the earliest congresses was to address problems that had been festering and worsening during the Confederation period. The first president and early congresses confronted a large problem stream (Kingdon, 1995).

The early presidents after Washington, except for John Adams, showed no signs of reducing the number of proposals, however. Although John Adams averaged only 12 proposals per Congress, about half of Washington's rate, Jefferson averaged 29 per Congress,

Madison 35, Monroe 32, and John Quincy Adams 46.5. Even the supposedly "do-nothing" Monroe submitted legislative proposals at the rate equal to these other early presidents. Admittedly these totals pale when compared with those of twentieth-century presidents, who average more than 200 requests per Congress, but these numbers are far from trivial.[4]

These figures should lead us to rethink the legislative activity of early presidents. Accounts of presidential-congressional interactions in the early period generally stress two points: presidential fidelity to separation of powers and that presidents tended to refrain from becoming heavily involved in the legislative policy-making process. Most early presidents were not as involved in legislative processes as are modern presidents (Greenstein, 2009; McCarty, 2009). George Washington usually sat on the sidelines after making legislative requests to Congress (Chernow, 2010). His Treasury Secretary, Alexander Hamilton, spearheaded the administration's legislative efforts, sometimes directing legislative strategies and coordinating them with friendly members of Congress (McDonald, 1974). Jefferson too was sometimes deeply involved in legislative matters, although he too tended to work with and through the party leadership in Congress, rather than publicly (McDonald, 1976).

Figure 4.2 also shows that presidential request levels steadily climbed from the First until the 78th Congress (1943–1944). Where Washington through John Quincy Adams proposed on average thirty requests per Congress, presidents of the 1890s submitted on average sixty-six proposals, twice the rate of the earliest presidents. The supposedly inactive, restrained Republican presidents of the 1920s and early 1930s (i.e., Harding, Coolidge, and Hoover) proposed on average seventy-seven items, again a marked increased from late nineteenth-century presidents, and surprisingly more than Franklin Roosevelt from 1933 to 1944, who averaged only fifty-seven. Even if we exclude the war years from FDR's totals and look only at the congresses from 1933 to 1940 (73rd–77th), FDR merely issued sixty-three proposals per congress, lower than the Republican presidents who preceded him. If FDR altered the relationship between the president

---

[4] For a reinterpretation of the leadership of the early presidents see Greenstein, 2009.

and Congress, it is not because he made more legislative proposals to Congress than his predecessors.

Furthermore, Figure 4.2 reveals several spikes in proposal activity across the first seventy-eight congresses. One spike occurs with the 49th Congress (1885–1886), the first two years of Grover Cleveland's first term of office. Cleveland's election was the first time that a Democrat sat in the Oval Office since James Buchanan (1857–1860). Perhaps the spike in Cleveland's proposal activity is a function of Democrats being out of the presidency for such a long time (Welch, 1988). Not only is Cleveland at times a "high-rate proposer," but he is also a "low-rate proposer," as is the case for his very low proposal rate during the 54th Congress (1895–1896), the last two years of his second term. The economic panic of those years and strong Republican control of both houses of Congress might have dampened Cleveland's proposal activity rate compared with his other years in office.

Another spike in activity occurs during the 56th to the 61st Congresses (1905–1910), the last four years of Theodore Roosevelt's administration and the first two for his successor, Taft. Although Roosevelt's activity here could be predicted from his stewardship conception of the presidency, Taft, famously associated with the clerkship perspective on the presidency, appears more active than expected (Korzi, 2003). Soon after, however, from 1913 to 1918 (63rd–65th Congresses), the first six Wilson years, we see a sharp decline in proposal activity, despite Wilson's reputation as a legislative leader with an expansive agenda. These figures somewhat belie conventional views of Wilson as an activist and progressive, but other accounts suggest that Wilson's legislative agenda was not large in terms of the number of proposals, although it was bold and innovative in terms of policy ambition (Macmahon, 1956).

Post-World War Two Proposal Activity: A Closer Look

As noted, legislative activism surges with Harry Truman in the postwar years and continues to the present. From Truman's initial full Congress, the 79th (1945–1946) through the 89th (1965–1966), LBJ's remarkably productive Congress, there is a massive and steady increase in presidential proposal activity. Truman averaged 187 proposals per Congress, three times the rate of FDR. Republican

Eisenhower not only maintained Truman's rate but also increased it to 320 per Congress, 70% higher than for Truman. Kennedy and Johnson from 1961 to 1964 submitted even more, 511 on average. The peak in proposal activity came with LBJ's two full congresses (1965–1968) with 665 proposals in 1965/1966 and 646 in 1967/1968, a tenfold increase compared with FDR. The approximately twenty years from 1947 through 1968 represents, at least with regard to presidential legislative activism, a remarkable transformation of the presidency.

High levels of legislative activism persist to the present, although not at LBJ's remarkably high levels. Proposal activity drops off steeply with LBJ's Republican successors, Nixon and Ford, whose activity levels of 286 proposals on average between them compare somewhat with Eisenhower. The post-LBJ decline in proposal activity is not just a Republican phenomenon, however. Democrat Jimmy Carter averaged 333, closer to Nixon and Ford than LBJ. Republicans Reagan and the first Bush scaled back their proposing levels to about Truman's level, 202 and 210. Clinton increased the average number of proposals to Carter's level, 342, still a far cry from LBJ, and during his first congress, George W. Bush made 309 proposals, more in line with the post-LBJ Democrats than Republicans. Compared with LBJ, these presidents look modest in their legislative activism, but they still appear highly active when compared to the pre-Truman presidents, with a proposal rate about five times as high as the most legislatively active premodern presidents.

The post-World War Two trend shows high proposal activity for both Democrats and Republicans, although Republicans appear to propose legislation at lower rates than Democrats. Democrats averaged 366 proposals per congress to 264 for Republicans. A simple regression analysis for the postwar years, with a dummy for presidential party and controls for a linear time trend and a square of the linear trend (to account for the decline in activity after LBJ), indicates a significant difference in partisan proposal activity. The regression results suggest that Democrats issue about 140 more proposals per congress than Republicans.[5]

---

[5] The regression results (SE) are: Proposal Level = 90.0 (83.6) Constant + 139.6 (46.2) Democrat + 28.6 (11.4) Time − 0.9 (0.4) Time Squared; R^2 = 0.32, n = 29. All independent variables are statistically significant at the 0.01 level or better.

A "big bang" did occur in presidential legislative activism, but it commenced more than a decade after the beginning of FDR's presidency, with Truman in the late 1940s. Legislative activism is only one aspect of presidential legislative leadership, however. Other aspects, such as active lobbying of Congress and focusing congressional and public attention on the president's legislative priorities, might have begun earlier, during FDR's tenure, as historical accounts suggest. The "big bang" in legislative activism is not simply a story of presidential activity rates jumping to a higher level under Truman and settling at that level. For the twenty years after Truman, the level of presidential activism grew at a rapid pace, peaking with LBJ, whose activity rate was more than three times greater than Truman's. After LBJ, presidential activism receded to about one-half of Johnson's rate, still quite high by historical standards.

Comparisons with Congressional Bill Introduction Activity

How does presidential proposal activity compare with congressional bill introductions, another form of legislative activism? To some degree presidential requests and congressional bills introductions are analogous – presidents and members of Congress, through these activities, are asking Congress to produce legislation, and thus both may be seeking to influence the congressional policy-making agenda.

Members of Congress engage in many activities, not only for legislative output but also to improve their electoral odds, for instance, by position taking and constituent service (Mayhew, 1974). Bill introductions can represent one type of constituency service. Members of Congress introduce bills to signal service to their constituents, even if there is little chance for enactment. Bill introductions also can be viewed as a form of position taking and could be useful to members especially when the odds of enactment are small. Thus, bill introductions have utility for members of Congress even when enactment appears unlikely. Presidents can also engage in similar symbolic behaviors when submitting legislative requests to Congress.

Figure 4.3 plots the number of presidential requests and the number of congressional bill introductions. The two series correlate ($r = 0.34$, $p = 0.000$), but they do not track very closely. Congressional bill introductions peaked in the Progressive era of the early twentieth

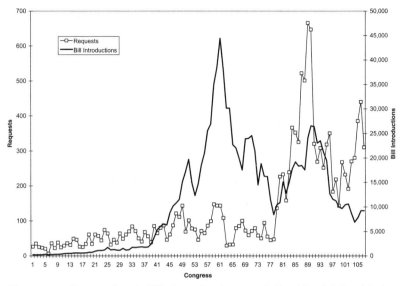

Figure 4.3. Congressional Bill Introductions and Presidential Legislative Requests, 1st to 107th Congresses (1789–2002).

century, a half-century before the peak in presidential request activity. After the high point in 1909 and 1910 (61st Congress), congressional bill introductions slide steeply through the 78th Congress (1943–1944). Like the presidential request series, congressional bill introductions began to grow again with the end of World War Two, but not at the rate of the increase for presidential requests. Still, paralleling presidential behavior, congressional bill introductions reach a modern peak in the late 1960s, then began to recede steadily through the rest of the series, unlike presidential proposals, which show an uptick with the 100th Congress (1987–1988).

To some degree presidential proposing is incorporated into the congressional bill introduction series. Presidents need a member of Congress to introduce their proposals for formal congressional consideration. We lack data on which presidential proposals secured a congressional sponsor and which did not, although it is likely that the overwhelming number of presidential proposals in the modern age found a sponsor (Edwards and Barrett, 2000). The difference between the presidential proposal and congressional introduction series during the second half of the nineteenth century and the Progressive era also suggests that Congress might have been the center of legislative activity then, but that presidents became more central to the legislative process from the second half of the twentieth century onward.

Summary

There are two major periods of presidential proposal activity. For the first 150 years or so of the nation's history, the 1st to the 78th Congresses, presidential proposal activity levels increased steadily but incrementally. Although there are several surges in presidential activity, such as the 49th Congress (1885–1886) and the 59th to the 61st Congresses (1905–1910), these peaks are short-lived, reverting to the long-term trend line. Thus, there is both a secular trend of incrementally increasing rates as well as short-term oscillations.

Beginning with the 79th Congress (1945–1946), the presidency entered a new era of much higher proposal rates. There are also long-term secular patterns to postwar proposal levels. Proposals rates climbed steadily and steeply from Truman through LBJ. After LBJ, presidential proposing recedes, but the post-LBJ presidents still propose at a rate several multiples higher than pre-Truman presidents. There are also short-term oscillations in the proposal activity levels of the modern presidents. The historical trend in presidential proposal activity suggests that at least this aspect of presidential-congressional interactions came not during FDR's tenure, usually identified as the time when the modern presidency emerged, but with Truman, about the time that the presidential program was invented and the presidency was accumulating and rationalizing executive branch resources.

ACCOUNTING FOR TRENDS IN PRESIDENTIAL PROPOSAL ACTIVITY: VARIABLES USED IN THE ANALYSIS

The theory of congressional anticipations argues that before submitting a legislative proposal to Congress, presidents calculate the odds that Congress will enact the proposal. For a variety of reasons (detailed in Chapter 3), presidents want to avoid congressional defeat of their legislative proposals. If a president thinks that a proposal will be defeated, he can either decide not to submit the proposal or he can modify it to make it more acceptable to Congress. The partisan makeup of Congress gives presidents an easy way to predict the odds of enactment: Presidents can expect more support when their party controls Congress than when the opposition party does. Thus, when confronting opposition-controlled congresses, presidents either will submit fewer proposals to Congress or will moderate their proposals compared with when their party controls Congress. This chapter tests the divided government-agenda size hypothesis. Chapter 6 tests the divided government-moderation hypothesis. For this analysis, we measure divided government as 1 when the opposition party controls one or both house of Congress; 0 denotes when the president's party controls both houses. The divided government-agenda size hypothesis suggests that the president's agenda should be smaller under divided than united government; that is, there is a negative relationship between divided government and the size of the president's legislative agenda.

This chapter also tests the presidential blame game hypothesis. That hypothesis is a special condition of the congressional anticipations theory. Presidents can use congressional defeats of their proposals to their political advantage in particular circumstances. The hypothesis predicts that in reelection years, when the opposition party controls Congress, presidents will flood the legislature with proposals that have a high probability of being defeated but that are popular with voters. Presidents can then use these legislative defeats to make a reelection case before voters, for instance, that Congress is out of touch with voters and thus voters should reelect the president and a congress controlled by the president's party. To measure the presidential blame game, I interact divided government with presidential reelection congresses, coded 1 for divided government and 0 otherwise, and 1 for presidential reelection congresses and 0 otherwise. The presidential blame game hypothesis predicts a positive relationship between the interaction term (divided government during reelection congresses) and the size of the president's agenda.

Chapter 3 outlines several other influences on the size of the president's agenda. These perspectives serve two purposes. One is to provide a fuller view of the influences on presidential agenda building. The other is to serve as statistical controls on the key congressional anticipations variables. Our confidence in the divided government and blame game hypotheses will be bolstered if they remain statistically significant and substantively influential influences on the size of the president's agenda with these controls in place. The following section lists these additional control variables.

CONTROL VARIABLES

Party Polarization

Polarization between the parties can affect the president's ability to forge winning coalitions. As polarization between the parties widens, presidents might find it increasingly difficult to attract opposition party members into their support coalition. The inability to attract opposition members might not affect the prospects for legislative success of majority presidents, who can build winning coalitions composed primarily of their co-partisans in Congress. In contrast, party polarization can affect the legislative success of minority presidents. By definition, minority presidents require some opposition support for their proposals to see congressional enactment, but wide polarization creates a barrier to finding such support from across the aisle. Modest to minimal levels of party polarization might not impose such a high barrier for minority presidents to lure some opposition members to support at least parts of their legislative agenda. As polarization between the parties spreads, however, the barrier to finding opposition support heightens, and prospects for success of minority presidents will fall. As prospects for success fall, the logic of the theory of congressional anticipations suggests that the size of the agenda will recede. This suggests an interaction between polarization and divided government. To test this hypothesis, I create an interaction term that multiplies the divided government dummy (1 = divided government, 0 = otherwise) times party polarization.[6] We expect a negative sign for the interaction – as polarization increases under minority presidents, proposal rates should fall.

[6] To create the polarization variable, I use the distance in the first DW-Nominate dimension between the medians of two largest parties, calculating separate polarization scores for the House and Senate. I then use the average of the House and Senate polarization scores for the measure of overall congressional polarization. The House and Senate polarization scores correlate at very high rates, 0.95+, and therefore it makes little difference if I use the Congress, Senate, or House versions of polarization.

Administrative Responsibilities

Administrative responsibilities also can affect the size of the president's legislative agenda. As Chapter 3 argues, in building their legislative agendas, presidents could privilege (give higher priority to) issues relating to the ongoing activities of government for several reasons, such as their constitutional duties, congressional and public expectations that hold the president responsible for bureaucratic and government performance, the informational advantages of the bureaucracy, and interest groups that mobilize in support of policies from which their members receive benefits.

For these reasons, the ongoing activities of government and the bureaucratic establishment can influence presidential legislative agenda decisions. This leads to the hypothesis that the larger the size of government, the greater the number of proposals that the president will submit to Congress. The size of government indicates the volume of ongoing government activity, as well as the size of the bureaucracy. In other words, the more that the government is doing, the more administrative things exist that presidents must handle.

Two types of data can be used to test this hypothesis: the size of government relative to the economy and the number of bureaucrats. I use government outlays as a percentage of GDP instead of government employment, because budgetary data exist across nearly the entirety of U.S. history. In contrast, we have federal employment data since only 1817. Using employment data would lose the first fourteen congresses. Moreover, annual federal employment data exist from only 1909. From 1817 to 1908, federal employment data exist only for every decade.[7] Finally, the correlation between government outlays and federal employment (as a percentage of population, a measure of relative size) from 1817 to 2002 is 0.96 ($p = 0.000$).[8] Given the longer outlay series, the analysis uses outlays rather than employment to measure the size of government. Everything being equal, the larger

---

[7] Furthermore, government has often relied on contractors for implementation of programs. Without accurate counts of such contractors, we will understate government employment. See Light, 1999b.

[8] Because we possess annual government outlay data, I create an outlay figure for each Congress by taking the average of the outlays of both years of each Congress. When annual data exist for federal employment, I do the same.

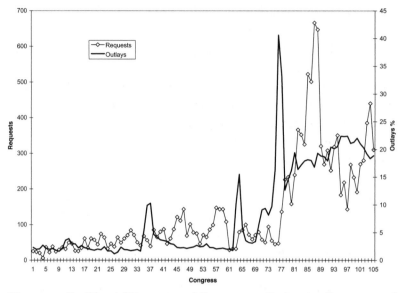

Figure 4.4. Presidential Requests and Government Outlays as a Percentage of GDP, 1st to 107th Congresses (1789–2002).

the size of government, the larger is the president's legislative policy agenda.

Figure 4.4 plots both the government outlay and presidential request series. Both lines grow over time, which produces a strong correlation of $r = 0.65$ ($p = 0.000$), but the two series also deviate at times. Peaks in government spending occur during major wars, such as the 37th to the 39th Congresses of the Civil War, the 65th and 66th Congresses of the First World War, and the 77th to the 79th Congresses of the Second World War. We do not see major surges in presidential proposal activity during those war years, however. Moreover, presidential proposal activity grows at an accelerated rate in the twenty years after the end of World War Two, but we do not see a comparable increase in government outlays, which, after falling in the immediate postwar years, begins to grow again but at a slower and steadier pace than presidential requests.

Representational Concerns
The representational perspective suggests that presidents take the public into account in building their legislative policy agendas. The

specter of future vote and/or approval losses creates incentives for presidents to pay attention to the public, an "electoral-approval" connection from the public to the president. To stem expected congressional seat and approval losses, presidents can react to the public's demands concerning policy or try to anticipate the public's concerns.

It is not always clear whether a change in this environment will lead to larger or smaller presidential agendas. To illustrate how environmental changes could stimulate larger agendas, consider the Obama administration's placing major health care reform at the top of its policy agenda in 2009, during a deep recession. Rahm Emanuel, then Obama's chief of staff, was quoted as saying, "You never want a serious crisis to go to waste."[9] From this perspective, crises create an atmosphere of urgency and a host of lingering problems can be resold or reframed as urgent and thus can be tied to the larger crisis. In other words, crises create policy windows, which presidents can exploit by attaching or "coupling" other policy initiatives to them that without the crisis setting would not appear to have strong prospects for public support or enactment (Kingdon, 1995). This crisis-policy window dynamic suggests these hypotheses: Wars and increased economic stress lead to an increase in presidential proposals.

Changes in the environment can also lead to smaller presidential agendas, however. During periods of extreme environmental stress, presidents might focus their attention on those problems at the expense of other problems. Problems not directly related to the environmental problem at hand are put on the back burner, to be solved at a later time.

Many events and trends can distress the public, but over the course of U.S. history, two stand out in importance because of the special responsibility that the public places on the president, the international situation and the economy.[10] There are two possible ways for changes in the international and economic environment to affect the size of

[9] Quoted in Gerald F. Seib, "In Crisis, Opportunity for Obama," *Wall Street Journal*, November 21, 2008, http://online.wsj.com/article/SB122721278056345271.html.
[10] These and similar disquieting events, like civil disturbances, can also present the president with opportunities to offer leadership and to consolidate power and authority in the presidency. The potential for enhanced leadership and a stronger presidential institution can provide a further incentive for the president to exploit such situations.

the president's agenda. First, international and economic change can trigger a public reaction, to which the president responds. By this account, the international and economic environment affect the president's agenda only much as those factors affect public opinion. Alternatively, change in the international and economic environment can directly affect the president's agenda. We need public opinion data to sort out whether environmental change directly affects the president's agenda or does so indirectly, through public opinion. Such data do not exist, except since the mid-1950s and thereafter. Still, we can test whether presidential agendas respond directly to change in the international and economic situations.

To measure the international environment, I use a dummy variable for whether the United States was engaged in a major war, defined as the War of 1812; the Mexican-American, Civil, and Spanish-American Wars; the first and second World Wars ; and the Korean and Vietnam Wars. Obviously, other international tensions exist that could color public opinion and affect the president's agenda, but war should have a great effect on mass political psychology and administration behavior. If war fails to affect the president's agenda, then other types of international events are unlikely to affect the president's agenda. War therefore provides a "best case" for finding international event impacts on the president's agenda. Based on the previous discussion, it is not clear whether war will lead to smaller or larger presidential agendas.

Change in the economy can also affect the size of the president's agenda. The analysis uses these economic variables to test for the effects of the economy on the size of the president's agenda: interest rates, inflation rates, and a dummy variable for whether the United States was in a recession. Economists have measured interest and inflation rates for most of U.S. history.[11] Unemployment data,

---

[11] The interest rate data come from EH.Net, maintained by Miami University and Wake Forest University at http://eh.net/hmit/. Again, as the interest rate data are presented in annual units, I average them for the two years of each Congress. EH.Net also allows one to recover inflation rate (Consumer Price Index) data. In the analysis for this book, I also experimented with CPI inflation rates, but it never emerged as a significant factor, even if I dropped interest rates from the estimations. Interest and inflation rates are mildly correlated over time ($r = 0.23$, $p = 0.02$). As EH.Net discusses, there are issues with building a CPI series over such a long time, which might account for the weak performance of this variable in the estimations. Since

another important macroeconomic factor, have been collected only since 1890, and these data are really reliable only after 1946. Using the available unemployment data would entail losing approximately one-half of our cases.[12] Again, based on the previous discussion, it is unclear whether changes in economic factors will lead to larger or smaller presidential agendas.

Presidential Party Differences

To capture the impact of party on presidential agendas, I use two dummy variables, Democrat = 1 (otherwise 0) and Republican = 1 (otherwise 0). The analysis then compares the behavior of Democratic and Republican presidents to presidents from the other parties, Federalists, Jeffersonians (Democratic-Republicans), and Whigs. Statistically comparing the coefficients for the Democratic and Republican variables allows us to test whether the agenda behavior of Democrats and Republicans differs. Based on the governing philosophies of the two parties, we expect presidential agendas to be smaller under Republican but larger under Democratic presidents.

Estimation Issues

The first estimation issue concerns the functional form of the dependent variable and selecting the appropriate estimation technique. As the presidential request series is a count, it would be natural to turn to event count models like Poisson regression. As the number of events per unit increases, however, the Poisson and normal distribution converge. Poisson regression is most appropriate when the number of events per unit remains relatively small and when events are relatively rare. The presidential request series ranges from 5 to 665, averaging 129 requests per congress. Because presidential requests to Congress are not rare events, we can justify using linear regression, which assumes a normal distribution of the dependent variable.

doing this analysis, the data on eh.net have moved to a new Web site, Measuring Worth, at http://www.measuringworth.com. For the timing of recessions, I use the NBER dates, reported in Dolan et al. (2007). NBER dates recessions starting in 1857. I add two other dates, 1812 and 1837, based on Copeland's (1983) list of earlier recessions and economic panics.

[12] The *Historical Statistics of the United States* reports unemployment data from 1890 in Table Ba470–477 – Labor force, employment, and unemployment: 1890–1990.

TABLE 4.1. *Dickey-Fuller Unit Root Tests for Variables Used in the Analysis of Total Presidential Requests to Congress, 1789–2002*

	Test Statistic		
Variable	Levels	Changes	Critical Value at .01
President's Legislative Requests	−1.71*	−10.57	−3.51
War Dummy	−5.60	−12.03	−3.51
Congressional Polarization	−1.91*	−7.57	−3.51
Minority President × Congressional Polarization	−7.32	−16.29	−3.51
Interest Rates	−1.66*	−7.83	−3.51
Inflation	−8.34	−14.57	−3.51
Deficit % of GDP	−5.08	−9.55	−3.51
Minority President	−6.86	−13.72	−3.51
Minority President × Term 2	−14.29	−31.68	−3.51
Recession Dummy	−6.82	−17.23	−3.51
Dem. Pres. Dummy	−4.88	−9.96	−3.51
Rep. Pres. Dummy	−4.66	−9.95	−3.51
Govt. Outlays % GDP	−0.15*	−8.53	−3.51

* Indicates the series is nonstationary.
Source: President's Legislative Policy Agenda Database, see text for details.

A second reason for using regression is that it allows us to take into account time dependency issues better.[13] For instance, nonstationarity and serial correlation can undermine confidence in statistical analysis of time series. Visual inspection of the series on Figure 4.1 suggests the presence of nonstationarity processes owing to the explosive growth in presidential submissions, commencing with the 79th Congress. Even though growth in submissions peaks with the 90th Congress (1967–1968), subsequent years still exhibit much higher levels than for the 1st to the 78th Congresses. Formal diagnosis of the presidential submission series with Dickey-Fuller tests, reported on Table 4.1, confirms nonstationarity in the presidential proposal series with a test statistic of −1.71, compared with a critical value of −3.51.[14]

---

[13] A class of event count models exist that allow one to correct for autocorrelation, such as arpois in STATA. As I discuss later, however, autocorrelation is less an issue in this analysis than cointegration, and well-established regression techniques exist to handle cointegration issues.

[14] The Dickey-Fuller tests are conducted for the 5th to the 106th Congresses, the years for which we have complete data on all variables.

Furthermore, several of the independent variables, interest rates, government outlays, and congressional polarization also exhibit nonstationarity. When nonstationarity exists in the dependent variable and one or more of the independent variables, the possibility exists for cointegration, that the variables share a common trend. This common trend can produce a statistical correlation between the trending variables, which in turn can lead to faulty causal inferences, for instance, that the independent variable(s) affect(s) the dependent variable, when the relationship between the variables is spurious. First differencing, an accepted approach to correct for nonstationarity, succeeds in producing stationary series for each of these variables, as shown on Table 4.1. In each case, the first differenced form of all the stationary variables now has a test statistic much lower than the critical value of -3.51. First differencing the dependent variable has another nice property – it turns a skewed variable in levels to a normally distributed variable in changes.

The accepted approach for dealing with cointegration is an error correction model. The error correction model used here, the Bardsen transformation, takes this form:[15]

$$dY_t = a_0 + b_1 Y_{t-1} + b_2 dX_t + b_3 X_{t-1} + \varepsilon$$

where dY_t is the dependent variable in first differences or changes,[16] a_0 is the constant, bs are regression coefficients, Y_{t-1} is the dependent variable in levels lagged one period (congress), dX_t is the independent variable in first difference form, X_{t-1} is the independent variable in levels lagged one period (congress), and ε is the error term.

Error correction models identify both long-term and short-term (or dynamic) influences on changes in the dependent variable. Lagged variables in levels provide information on long-term trend effects of the variable on the dependent variable. The first differenced variables,

---

[15] Error correction models can take several forms, but all present the same information. For a discussion of the variety of Error correction models see De Boef and Keele (2008).

[16] First differences are calculated as $dY_t = Y_t - Y_{t-1}$.

the difference of the value of the variable in the current and past period, provide information on the effect of short-term change on the dependent variable.

A common approach to estimating error correction models is to create an error correction mechanism (ECM). To calculate ECM, the dependent variable is regressed on itself lagged one period, plus the independent variables in levels. The resulting residuals, lagged one period, constitute the ECM mechanism. Error correction models that employ this ECM method combine all long-term factors into one variable. Substantive analysis thus emphasizes the impact of the short-term (first differenced) variables on the dependent variable.

A single-equation error correction model, which contains all the independent variables in lagged and first differenced form, provides an alternative approach (Durr, 1993; De Boef and Keele, 2008). The single-equation error correction model provides information on the short- and long-term impacts of each variable, but given the number of parameters, it consumes degrees of freedom. Because little theory or empirical work exist on the president's legislative agenda, we have little guidance as to whether any of the hypothesized variables will affect proposals rates in the short and/or long term. Thus, I have opted for the single-equation error correction model, despite the consumption of degrees of freedom. As the next analysis shows, several of the variables have both short- and/or long-term impacts on presidential proposal rates.

ANALYSIS

Table 4.2 presents results of two estimations, one that includes all of the variables mentioned previously, and a second reduced-form estimation that excludes the inflation and congressional polarization variables. Inflation never achieves statistical significance but is positively correlated with interest rates, as one would expect ($r = 0.20$, $p = 0.03$). Congressional polarization also never attains statistical significance, although its interaction with minority presidents nearly reaches such levels but points in the wrong direction. Because the substantive findings otherwise are quite similar across the two estimations, the discussion focuses on the reduced form estimation.

TABLE 4.2. *Congressional, Administrative, Representational, and Partisan Impacts on the Number of Presidential Legislative Proposals, 1789–2002 (Single-equation Error Correction Estimation)*

Variable	Full Model			Reduced Form Model		
	b	SE	p	b	SE	p
Requests-Lag	−0.31	0.08	0.000	−0.30	0.08	0.000
Minority Pres.-lag	−177.51	94.08	0.03	−47.87	28.64	0.05
Minority Pres.-changes	−162.74	74.35	0.02	−56.27	18.88	0.002
Re-election Congress	−5.41	15.04	0.72	−8.28	14.88	0.58
Minority Pres. × Reelection Congress-lag	73.63	46.70	0.06	78.07	44.82	0.04
Minority Pres. × Reelection Congress-changes	45.46	27.61	0.05	51.45	26.33	0.03
Congress Polarization-lag	18.76	64.37	0.77			
Congress Polarization-changes	91.56	98.70	0.36			
Polarization × Min. Pres.-lag	188.49	129.48	0.08			
Polarization × Min. Pres.-changes	156.56	101.70	0.07			
Govt. Outlays % GDP-lag	8.37	1.96	0.000	6.80	1.71	0.000
Govt. Outlays % GDP-changes	−4.39	6.66	0.26	0.56	5.96	0.93
War-lag	.65	20.80	0.98	−0.31	18.84	0.99
War-changes	−12.23	19.51	0.53	−6.24	18.54	0.74
Interest rates-lag	−10.44	3.89	0.01	−8.42	3.39	0.01
Interest rates-changes	2.30	11.01	0.84	−0.78	9.54	0.94
Inflation-lag	−0.31	1.70	0.86			
Inflation-changes	0.01	1.14	0.99			
Deficit % GDP-lag	8.75	3.99	0.02	9.16	3.86	0.01
Deficit % GDP-changes	−2.87	8.57	0.74	3.82	7.75	0.62
Recession-lag	−49.76	19.41	0.01	−47.62	18.39	0.01
Recession-changes	−23.54	15.27	0.06	−23.30	14.44	0.01
Democrat-lag	−13.14	23.76	0.58	14.07	19.76	0.48
Democrat-changes	−28.43	27.97	0.31	−21.26	26.80	0.43
Republican-lag	8.14	22.97	0.72	27.37	20.79	0.19
Republican-changes	−45.54	29.50	0.07	−46.17	29.38	0.06
Constant	63.39	51.83	0.22	55.30	25.12	0.03
R^2/Adj. R^2	0.48	0.30		0.44	0.29	
Breusch-Godfrey LM-lag 1	1.55		0.21	1.66		0.20
Breusch-Godfrey LM-lag 2	3.20		0.20	4.04		0.13
Breusch-Godfrey LM-lag 3	3.30		0.35	4.31		0.23
Breusch-Godfrey LM-lag 4	4.65		0.33	6.08		0.19
n	100			100		

Source: President's Legislative Policy Agenda Database, see text for details.

Overall, the equation fits the data well, accounting for 44% of the variance.[17] Numerous variables affect presidential request behavior as hypothesized. First, the lagged dependent variable is negative and statistically significant, indicating equilibrium between the past level of presidential submission and changes in submissions. Higher past levels lead to smaller changes in submission rates, whereas lower past levels lead to increases in proposal activity. In change models, the lagged dependent variable indicates the rate of error correction, or how quickly the dependent variable returns to its equilibrium level after a shock from an independent variable. The small coefficient, −0.30, suggests that it takes a long time for the series to revert to equilibrium.[18]

There is also strong support for the divided government and presidential blame game hypotheses. Being a minority president has both long- and short-term statistically significant effects on presidential request totals. In the short term, losing majority control of Congress leads to fifty-six fewer presidential proposals to Congress. Becoming a minority president has longer-lasting effects on request totals, with a cumulative drop of forty-eight proposals, 30% or fourteen in the next congress. Substantively the effects of minority status are meaningful, equal to about 41% and 36% of the standard deviation (135) for presidential requests for short- and long-term effects, respectively.

As the presidential blame game hypothesizes, minority presidents during reelection congresses submit more, not fewer, requests to Congress. In the short term, minority presidents will submit fifty-one more proposals in reelection congresses. This nearly offsets the drop in proposals from becoming a minority president such that this subset of minority presidents has proposal rates similar to that of majority presidents. The long-term effect is an additional seventy-eight proposals. These findings suggest a strategic element to the president's agenda, in which the chief executive adjusts his legislative agenda to

---

[17] The adjusted R^2, which takes into account the large number of variables, is 0.28.

[18] After the shocks to the system from the independent variables, presidential requests return to equilibrium at a rate of only 30% in the first period (congress), another 15% in the second period, and so on. At this rate, after eight congresses, presidential requests have returned only 60% of the distance to the equilibrium.

partisan control of Congress, providing us with initial support for the theory of congressional anticipations developed in Chapter 3.[19]

Administrative responsibilities, measured as government outlays as a percentage of the economy, also strongly affect presidential legislative proposal activity, but the effect is entirely long term. It makes some sense that government size would have a long-term but not a short-term effect on presidential proposal rates. Turning to the coefficients, we find a 1% increment in the size of government leads to an increase of nearly seven presidential proposals. Government outlays vary from less than 1% of GDP to more than 40%, averaging slightly more than 8%. Comparing presidents during different spending epochs reveals the magnitude of government size on the president's legislative agenda. Being president during an era of large government, say 35%, leads to 168 more proposals than a president during an era of average-sized government (8%), and 231 more proposals than a president during an era of small government (2%). The growth in government accounts for much of the secular rise in presidential proposals in the postwar era.

War and economic variables measure representational pressures on the president's agenda. Surprisingly, war does not affect the size of the president's agenda, but interest rates and recessions do. Higher interest rates reduce the size of the president's agenda, but changes in interest rates do not. Thus, the interest rate effect is entirely long term. Each 1% increment in interest rates leads to an immediate decrease

---

[19] Besides party control and polarization, I also looked at whether other aspects of the congressional environment affected presidential proposal rates. Taking a lead from Cameron and Park (2008), who argue that presidents look to whether Congress is in a legislating mood, I asked whether the number of congressional bill submissions would provide the president with that type of information, and thus affect his proposal activity. Because members must submit presidential proposals before Congress can formally address them, congressional submissions contain information on presidential requests. To handle this complication, I created an instrumental version of the congressional bills variable, using patent totals as the instrument. Patents are statistically correlated with bills but not presidential proposals, making it a useful instrument. Thus I regress changes in bill introductions, on levels of bill introductions lagged, interest rates lagged, the log of patents lagged, and changes in the log of patents. Each of these variables significantly predicts changes in bill introductions, which produces an overall R^2 of 0.12. The predicted values of this equation become the instrumented bill introduction variable. Using the instrumented variable, bill introductions do not affect presidential requests.

of nearly ten presidential proposals. A one-standard deviation change in interest rates is 2.1. Using the average rate of 5% as a base, a one-standard deviation shift in interest rates corresponds to +/−55 requests. Interest rates produce substantively meaningful effects on presidential request totals.

As do recessions, which like increases in interest rates, depress presidential request rates. Recessions, unlike interest rates, have both long- and short-term effects, although the short-term effect does not reach the conventional 0.05 level. It is 0.055, just slightly above the 0.05 threshold. Substantively the short-term effect does not appear impressive, at about twenty-four requests, but the long-term effect is stronger at forty-eight. Both in the short and long term, recessions reduce presidential requests, affecting presidential proposal activity in much the same way as the other economic variable, interest rates. The depressing effect of interest rates and recession on the president's agenda runs counter to the crisis window of opportunity dynamic discussed earlier. It could be the case, however, that interest rates must become extraordinarily high and recessions very deep before policy makers and voters regard them as crises.

Both interest rates and recession show stronger long-term than short-term effects on the president's agenda. Why don't presidents seem to respond in their legislative agendas more quickly to these economic disturbances? First, economic change at the national level is a slow-moving process itself. It takes time before people notice that the nation has slipped into recession or that it has recovered and come out of recession. Recall that by the 1992 election, the recession had ended and recovery had begun, but people still thought the nation was mired in recession and voted against the incumbent George H. W. Bush (Hetherington, 1996). Economic factors have strong impacts on the president's agenda, but not in the short run. Before representational pressures kick in to affect presidential policy making, economic trends must become noticeable, and that takes time.

Finally, deficits affect the president's agenda, but only in the long run. Each 1% increase in the deficit leads to a long-term drop of nine presidential requests. Deficits/surpluses have varied widely across U.S. history, from being as high as 25% of GDP (mostly during war) to surpluses as high as 3%.[20] A one-standard deviation shift is about 3.5, which corresponds to a change of $+/-31$ presidential proposals, not a large amount but still a statistically significant influence on the size of the president's agenda. During wartime, however, with deficits more than 10%, the decline in proposal rates becomes substantively meaningful (a decline of 90 at a 10% deficit, but a decline of 216 at a deficit of 24%, as it was during the Second World War). Presidents seem to take into account available government resources in submitting legislative proposals to Congress. Contraction in governmental resources leads to a corresponding contraction in the president's agenda. Because war produces deficits, the lack of war effects on presidential requests might have to do with the fact that war produces large deficits.[21] To test this idea, I dropped the deficit variables from the estimation. War still failed to affect the president's agenda.

Finally, partisan differences hardly matter for the number of presidential requests submitted to Congress. Neither of the party dummies in levels affects request rates, nor does the Democratic change variable. The Republican change variable points to a possible effect, however: Change to a Republican administration corresponds to lower request rates, consistent with Republican preferences for smaller, less active government. When a Republican assumes office, the agenda contracts by forty-six proposals, but the effect does not quite attain statistical significance, with a p value < 0.10, less than the conventional 0.05 threshold. Consequently, we might not want to place much confidence in this finding.[22]

Overall, the results indicate systematic influences on the size of the president's legislative agenda from its early years into the early 2000s. Presidents adjust their legislative agendas to conditions in Congress (party control), to the overall size of government, and to environmental factors, especially the economy. In contrast, presidential policy

---

[20] Surpluses were more common in the nineteenth century, owing to small government and high tariffs.

[21] The correlation between war and deficits is 0.19, $p = 0.05$.

[22] An F test finds no differences in the coefficients comparing Democratic and Republican presidents (lagged) ($F = 0.72$, $p = 0.40$) or that between changes in Democratic and Republican presidents ($F = 2.24$, $p = 0.14$). The lack of significant difference in the effects of Democratic and Republican presidents is obviously a function that both are insignificant to begin with.

preferences that emanate from the doctrines toward governance of their parties do not seem to affect the size of the president's agenda.

Finally, the fact of an R^2 of 0.44 and an adjusted R^2 of 0.29 raises the question of the sensitivity or precision of the previous analysis. A considerable amount of variation in the size of the president's agenda is still left statistically unexplained.[23] One source of imprecision in accounting for variance could be the inclusion of all presidential requests from large important ones to many smaller ones. Smaller, less consequential proposals might be less subject to the types of considerations detailed earlier; however, it is also possible that the analysis left out some important factors that influence presidential decisions over the size of the legislative agenda. On the other hand, the dependent variable is measured in changes, which is harder to account for statistically than a variable measured in levels.

Inspection of residuals could help to sort through this issue. Figure 4.5 plots the residuals of the reduced form estimation from Table 4.2. Visually, it appears as if there are more large misses (residuals) later in the series than earlier on. Statistical tests suggest this is not the case. First, as displayed on Table 4.2, the Breusch-Godfrey LaGrange multiplier test at various lags suggests that the residuals are white noise. More to the point, the Breusch-Pagan test detects no heteroskedasticity; the series has a constant variance, which counters the notion of larger residuals later in the series.[24] Apparently the larger residuals in the later years is a function of the larger number of presidential proposals.[25]

---

[23] There is some debate over the utility of the R^2 statistic. King (1990) argues that more emphasis should be in model testing, that is, focusing on significance tests of specific variables, whereas Lewis-Beck and Skalaban (1990a, 1990b) argue that the R^2 provides important information about overall model fit that could be useful in refining theory. Because we know so little about the factors that affect presidential agenda building, the R^2 provides useful information about how well we are statistically accounting for variation in the size of the president's agenda.

[24] The test has a Chi-square of 0.15 and a p value of 0.70.

[25] To demonstrate this I took the absolute size of the residuals for each congress, then divided it by the total number of requests for the corresponding congress. For the first 20 congresses, this ratio is 0.43; it is 0.39 for the 21th to the 40th Congresses, 0.27 for the 41st to the 60th Congresses, 0.61 for the 61st to the 80th Congresses, but only 0.19 for the 81st and all subsequent Congresses. The residuals are proportionately smaller in the modern era, indicating greater statistical precision then, too.

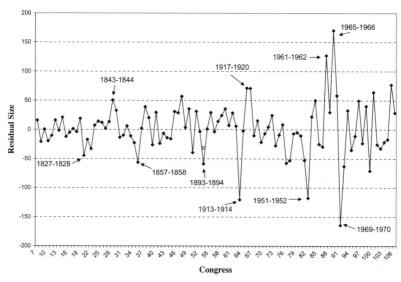

Figure 4.5. Residuals for Analysis of the Size of the President's Agenda from Table 4.2, Reduced Form Estimation.

MODERN PRESIDENTS AND LEGISLATIVE ACTIVISM

There are several limitations to the preceding analysis. For instance, the fact that modern (post-World War II) presidents clearly exhibit much higher rates of legislative proposal activity than their predecessors suggests the possibility that the causal factors that affect presidential proposal rates differ between the modern and the earlier era. Consistent with theories of the modern presidency (e.g., Greenstein, 1988), in the mid-twentieth century the presidency transformed; the rise of presidential legislative activism might be one consequence or behavioral manifestation of that transformation. Perhaps the relative weight of the factors affecting presidential agenda building changed as the president transformed, with some factors that did not weigh very heavily in the president's decision process carrying more weight in the modern period as opposed to the premodern era, or vice versa. For example, ongoing government activities might have counted less in building the president's agenda in the premodern era because government was so much smaller compared with the modern era. Public considerations might have grown in magnitude and force over presidential agenda decisions in the modern period as the president's public image grew, making the president a more central figure and focus of the public's political attentions.

Furthermore, the R^2 is modest, suggesting that the model estimated on Table 4.2 is underspecified. In particular, there is no measure of public opinion. Third, inspection of Figure 4.1 shows remarkably high proposal rates for Kennedy and Johnson during the 87th to the 90th Congresses, which deserve explanation. During those congresses, Kennedy and Johnson submitted from 500 to 665 requests per congress, averaging 583. In contrast, Eisenhower submitted from 238 to 365 per congress, averaging 320, whereas Nixon and Ford submitted 251 to 319, averaging 286. Even the relatively prolific Bill Clinton issued far fewer legislative recommendations than Kennedy/Johnson, from 269 to 439, an average of 343, only marginally higher than Eisenhower. Kennedy and Johnson submitted proposals at rates 40% or higher compared with other modern presidents.

Statistically, the high activity rates of JFK and LBJ are so much higher than other presidents of the modern period that they might be in effect outliers, and might be affecting the substantive results reported in Table 4.2. We received a glimmer of the possible outlier status of these data points from the residual plot on Figure 4.5. To check this possibility, I entered dummy variables for lagged levels and changes for the four congresses of Kennedy and Johnson, while keeping all of the other variables used in the estimation presented on Table 4.2.[26] The R^2 improves markedly, from 0.44 to 0.70. Most importantly, however, the substantive results of Table 4.2 remain intact.[27] Although this additional analysis improves model fit in terms of R^2 and helps account statistically for the very high activity levels of Kennedy and Johnson, it does not provide a theoretical account for their high proposal levels.

Let us return to the possibility that the decision processes of modern versus premodern presidents differ and that the model estimated on Table 4.2 might be underspecified. As already noted, the model

[26] In other words, I created a dummy variable score 1 for the 87th to the 90th Congresses, 0 otherwise, and following the procedure for the single equation ECM entered this dummy in both lagged and changes form.

[27] Details of the analysis are not presented but are available from the author. The magnitudes of some regression coefficients and standard errors change but the substantive interpretations remain the same for all variables in the reduced form estimation on Table 4.2.

on Table 4.2 does not take into account public opinion directly. The 1960s, according to historical accounts, as well as James Stimson's public mood indicator, was one in which the public held decidedly liberal preferences on issues.[28] Mayhew's (2005, 2008) work on policy production also characterizes the 1960s (and early 1970s) as a liberal, activist period. From a different perspective, Cameron and Park (2008) argue that the 1960s was also an era in which liberal interests groups mobilized, either reflecting or adding to the liberal tenor of the times.

Kennedy's and Johnson's high rate of proposals might have been in response to the existing public mood, a hypothesis consistent with the representational perspective on agenda building proposed in Chapter 3 (and Cameron and Park's, 2008, burden-sharing model). Here the idea is that when the public is in a liberal mood, it has a larger appetite for governmental solutions to problems, for a larger government, and for governmental activism in general. Kennedy's and Johnson's high rate of legislative activism might be in response to (or anticipation of) this public mood. The analysis on Table 4.2, which covers the entire history of the presidency, however, does not include a direct measure of public opinion, nor could it. For a shorter, albeit still long period of time, however, we possess relevant public opinion data.

Figure 4.6 plots the number of presidential requests by year from 1951 through 2002, as well as Stimson's mood indicator. For the most part the two trends follow the same time path, with a correlation of 0.45 ($p < 0.000$). Moreover, just as public liberalism peaks in the early-mid 1960s, so does presidential legislative activism. Still, at times the two series diverge. In the late 1950s and again in early 1970s, a large gap separates the two series, with the public in a decidedly liberal mood and yet presidential proposing at a lower rate. Another gap between the president and the public appears in the 1980s. Even for the gaps of the 1950s, 1970s, and 1980s, the trends of the two variables generally move in the same direction. Only in the 1990s do the public mood and presidential legislative activism appear to move

---

[28] Stimson presents and regularly updates his mood indicator at http://www.unc.edu/~jstimson/.

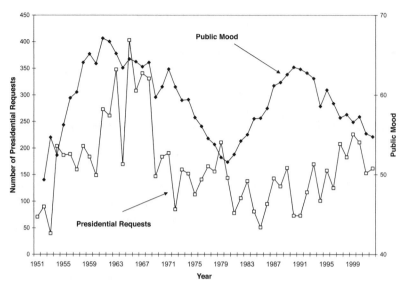

Figure 4.6. Presidential Requests to Congress and the Public Mood, by Year, 1951–2002.

in opposite directions, but they converge by the mid-1990s, thereafter hugging each other quite closely. In general, Republican presidents are in office during most of time when these president-public gaps appear, suggesting the possibility of some resistance on the part of Republican chief executives to liberal sentiment in the mass public.

Although large government should motivate presidents to submit higher numbers of proposals to Congress, as the administrative responsibility hypothesis predicts, once government reaches a certain level, then presidents and the public might want to scale down the size of government. When government reaches such a size or threshold, we may see presidents reducing their legislative activity levels, as they resist expansionary forces within government, and might even view reauthorizations and other deadlines as opportunities to kill programs. In the modern period, large government might be negatively associated with presidential proposal rates, although for the entire historical record, large government could motivate presidential request activity. At the same time, the smaller size of government in the premodern presidency might have fewer implications for the size of the president's agenda.

This leads to two additional hypotheses that we could not explore in the previous analysis. First, presidents will respond directly to the public mood. Greater public liberalism will be associated with greater presidential legislative activism. Second, presidents will respond negatively to the size of government in the modern era. As government gets larger, we will see lower levels of presidential legislative activism, the opposite of the hypothesis offered to explain presidential legislative activity over the entire course of U.S. history.

We can test these alternative hypotheses, but not on the full time series of data used for Table 4.2.[29] Stimson's public mood indicator starts with 1952, allowing us to test these hypotheses on data spanning from 1952 to 2002. In addition, rather than use congress as the time unit, to expand the number of cases I use years as the time unit. Table 4.3 presents two estimations, one with the full range of variables and a second with a reduced form estimation, again using the single equation ECM framework. One major problem with the full model estimation is the large number of parameters to cases. Whenever possible for the full model estimation, I tried to restrict the number of variables to preserve degrees of freedom but still remain as true to the theoretical model as possible. Thus, rather than separate variables for inflation and unemployment, I created a *misery index* that adds the two variables together.

The results on Table 4.3 are quite instructive, providing evidence of direct presidential responsiveness to public opinion, plus that size of government in the modern era might have the thermostatic, threshold implications as argued previously. First, overall model performance improves markedly over the longer historical analysis: The R^2 jumps from 0.44 to 0.77. We seem to do a better job of accounting for the size of the president's legislative agenda in the modern era than across the entire history of the presidency. Figure 4.7 presents the residual plot for the reduced form estimation. Although we notice a

---

[29] For all but the mood indicator it is possible to test the idea of differences between premodern and modern presidents, using for example a regime-switching regression. I attempted such an analysis, but the statistical solution never converged and so no results were produced. Splicing the data into two series (e.g., 1st–78th and 79th–109th) is also unsatisfactory. The different variances in the dependent variable across the two periods prohibit direct comparison of results.

TABLE 4.3. *Influences on the Size of Modern Presidential Legislative Agendas, 1951–2002 (Annual Data; Single-equation Error Correction Estimation)*

Variable	Full Model			Reduced Form Model		
	b	SE	p	b	SE	p
Requests-Lag	−0.98	0.22	0.000	−1.02	0.15	0.000
Minority Pres.-lag	−414.93	215.64	0.03	−33.52	21.14	0.06
Minority Pres.-changes	−369.51	231.61	0.06	−36.02	22.50	0.06
Year 4 of Pres. Term-lag	6.63	66.91	0.92			
Year 4 of Pres. Term-changes	19.96	39.85	0.62			
Minority Pres. × Year 4-lag	−11.20	82.27	0.89			
Minority Pres. × Year 4-changes	−37.50	47.40	0.44			
Congress Polarization-lag	−284.53	196.38	0.08			
Congress Polarization-changes	−899.69	487.00	0.04			
Polarization × Min. Pres.-lag	549.97[+]	309.64	0.09			
Polarization × Min. Pres.-changes	486.37[+]	328.29	0.15			
Govt. Outlays % GDP-lag	−18.79	7.84	0.01	−13.82	4.50	0.002
Govt. Outlays % GDP-changes	−18.29	14.96	0.12			
Korean War-lag	−283.23	120.20	0.01	−189.41	62.35	0.002
Korean War-changes	−261.03	92.12	0.001	−290.07	76.37	0.001
Vietnam War-lag	28.12	21.39	0.10	38.76	18.31	0.02
Vietnam War-changes	−8.13	53.58	0.88	81.04	34.16	0.01
Misery Index-lag	−0.90	5.01	0.43			
Misery Index-changes	−8.12	5.13	0.06			
LBJ Dummy-lag	0.01	0.05	0.46			
LBJ dummy-changes	−0.07[+]	0.03	0.04			
Public Mood-lag	2.93	2.70	0.14	3.43	1.86	0.04
Public Mood-changes	13.00	5.68	0.02	13.98	4.56	0.002
Democrat-lag	3.08	43.64	0.47	71.60	20.27	0.001
Democrat-changes	−9.37[+]	43.07	0.83	47.94	24.02	0.03
Constant	593.21	301.89	0.06	223.96	150.05	0.14
R^2/Adj. R^2	0.86	0.71		0.77	0.69	
Breusch-Godfrey LM-lag 1	1.73		0.19	2.32		0.13
Breusch-Godfrey LM-lag 2	6.69		0.04	2.36		0.31
Breusch-Godfrey LM-lag 3	10.73		0.01	4.22		0.24
Breusch-Godfrey LM-lag 4	11.77		0.02	5.50		0.24
n	50			50		

[+] Wrong sign; thus two-tailed test is reported. One-tailed tests for all other variables.
Source: President's Legislative Policy Agenda Database, see text for details.

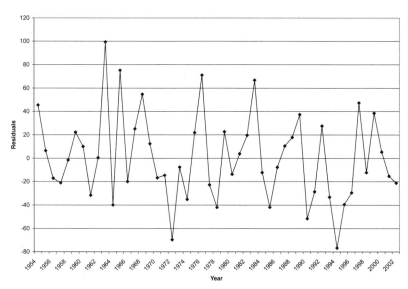

Figure 4.7. Residuals for Reduced Form Estimation, Annual Results, from Table 4.3.

few relatively large residuals, the residuals are white noise based on the Breusch-Godfrey test (see Table 4.3).[30]

This analysis again provides support for the divided government hypothesis. Minority presidents, those serving during divided government, submit fewer proposals to Congress than do majority presidents. The minority status variables, however, do not quite reach the 0.05 statistical significance threshold but at 0.06 appear close enough to warrant attention, providing additional support for the divided government hypothesis. Minority status has both long- and short-term effects on proposal activity, with reductions of about thirty-three and thirty-six proposals in the long and short run.

The strong correlation between presidential party and divided government obscures the effect of being a minority president on the size of the agenda. For instance, Republicans held the presidency for thirty of the fifty years in this analysis. They were in the minority for all but four of those years. Likewise, the Democrats were usually majority presidents, the case for fourteen of the twenty years that

---

[30] In fact, residuals of the full estimation indicate some autocorrelation after lag 1, which is corrected with the reduced form model estimation.

they held the Oval Office during this period. In other words, there is some multicollinearity between divided government and presidential party.[31]

The statistical effect of divided government increases markedly if we drop the presidential party variables from the analysis. Now both minority status variables easily reach statistical significance, with the p value less than 0.01 in both cases. Plus the regression coefficients grow to -58.7 for the change variable and -66.7 for the lagged variable, about twice the effect as in the estimation that included the presidential party variables. Given the high correlation between divided government and presidential party, it is remarkable that divided government nearly reached conventional significance levels in the estimation with the party variables.[32]

There is little support for the hypothesized presidential blame game in this analysis, however. Again, a statistical issue is the culprit here: There are only three majority congress presidents/parties in office in reelection years in this series (1964, 1968, and 1980), which limits the variation on this variable. As for the longer historical analysis, congressional polarization does not affect proposal rates.

Unlike the long historical analysis, economic factors do not seem to contribute directly to the president's agenda in the modern era, and in another reversal, we see war's effects on the president's agenda. The effect of war appears only if we distinguish between the Korean and Vietnam Wars, which exhibit different but substantively meaningful impacts on the size of the president's agenda. Where the Korean War is associated with a drop in presidential activism, the Vietnam War is associated with an increase in legislative activism. The effects of Korea on presidential proposal rates are massive in both the short and long run (-290 and -189). In contrast, during the Vietnam War, we see both short- and long-term boosts in presidential proposal activity (81 and 38).

---

[31] The correlation between presidential party and divided government is 0.66, $p =$ 0.000.

[32] Dropping the party variable leads to a lower R^2, to 0.68 from 0.77, indicating that party adds to our understanding of presidential proposing and that party has effects that are independent from divided government.

Presidents during the Korean conflict behaved consistently with the hypothesis that war should constrict the president's agenda as attention turns to the war; however, Johnson in particular pursued a "guns-and-butter" approach to legislative leadership (Bernstein, 1996). We might interpret Johnson as being conscious of the possible implications of war for his domestic agenda and that he resisted the constricting and narrowing effects of war on his legislative agenda. If such an interpretation is correct, then we have indirect evidence in support of the war hypothesis but also a glimmer of the effects of a president's personal preferences in agenda building.

The results on Table 4.3 also reveal differences in the proposal activity of Democrats and Republicans. Consistent with common understandings of the two parties, Democrats submit proposals to Congress at a higher rate than Republicans. Party differences have both short- (forty-eight) and long- (seventy-two) term implications on proposal activity. Why did we not detect these differences between Democrats and Republicans in the longer historical analysis? One possibility is that over the long course of U.S. history, the governing philosophies of the two parties changed, in effect switching positions on issues relating to the size of government. This might be more apparent for the Democrats than the Republicans.

The governing philosophy of nineteenth- and early twentieth-century Democrats can be traced to the Jeffersonians, their critique of the Constitution, and their opposition to Federalist policies, which they viewed as too centered on the executive and national government.[33] Beginning with Andrew Jackson and extending until Franklin Roosevelt, Democrats tended to prefer local control and states rights. We see this in Jackson's battle with the National Bank and the eventual decentralization of the banking system toward state banks during his tenure. Southern Democrats resisted national government attempts to intervene in the region, first to protect slavery, and then Jim Crow and segregationist policies after the Civil War. The pre-FDR (perhaps pre-Wilson?) Democrats look quite different

---

[33] For a discussion of the governing philosophies or ideologies of the parties across U.S. history, see Gerring (1998) and Di Salvo (2007).

in their orientation toward government than Democrats from FDR to the present.

Republicans, although not quite a large government party from the Civil War era through the early 1900s, did not appear loath to use the power of the federal government for national projects, such as settlement of the west, building a transportation infrastructure (e.g., railroads), and regulation of business. Although not aimed at government control of the economy, building an environment conducive to large-scale business enterprises appeared to be one goal of Republicans until perhaps the mid-twentieth century. To some degree, late nineteenth- and early twentieth-century Republicanism bears a streak of Hamiltonianism.

These presidential request data conform to this interpretation of the political history of the two parties. Overall, Democrats submit only slightly more proposals to Congress than do Republicans (166 on average per congress, versus 152), reconfirming the lack of long-term historical distinction between the presidents of the two parties. In the modern era (1947–2002), Democrats clearly outpace Republicans in submitting legislation (383 to 264), as the results in Table 4.3 also demonstrate. Democrats in office prior to 1947 submit *fewer* proposals on average than Republicans, however, sixty-one to eighty-seven. Even if we include only Democrats from the Civil War era (1861) through 1946, they still submit fewer proposals than Republicans (sixty-five to eighty-seven).[34]

Turning to the two major hypotheses that motivated this part of the analysis, we find strong support for the public mood and government size hypotheses. First, the more liberal the public, the more legislatively active is the president. The public mood has both short- and long-term effects on presidential activism. Specifically a 1% shift in the level or change in the public mood corresponds to an increase of three and fourteen presidential proposals in the long and short term,

[34] A regression of changes in requests on lagged requests plus changes and lags for Republicans for 1861 to 1946 shows a modest increase in the short run when Republicans are in office ($b = 16$, $p = 0.06$). Although not statistically significant, these results almost meet the 0.05 threshold, but more important, they point in the direction consistent with the historical interpretation of greater government activism of premodern Republicans.

respectively. A one-standard deviation increase in the level (4.2) and change (1.9) in the public liberalism corresponds to an additional 12 to 13 and 27 to 28 presidential proposals. From this comparison, presidents seem somewhat more sensitive to changes in the public mood than its actual level.

The effect of mood swings on presidential activism appears paltry compared with the actual level of presidential submissions in the modern era, however. Compare a president in the most liberal (sixty-three) to the most conservative (forty-nine) mood eras. A president during a liberal period would submit about 42 (14 × 3) more proposals to Congress than a president during a conservative period. Moreover the largest year-to-year change in the public mood, 5.3 points, would correspond to an additional 74 (5.3 × 14) proposals. Viewed this way, the public mood appears to have pronounced substantive implications for presidential proposal activity.

Finally, as far as the impact of government size, unlike the long-term historical analysis, in which large government led to higher proposal rates, in the modern era larger government leads to decreases in presidential submissions. The effect here is purely long term, suggesting that presidents are responding to the long-term context of big government and not to short-term changes in the size of government. Each one-percentage point increase in the size of government leads to 13.8 fewer presidential proposals. During this fifty-year period, the federal government averaged about 20% of GDP, ranging from a low of about 14 to a high of around 24 (with a standard deviation of 2). Thus, a standard deviation increase in the relative size of government outlays will lead to a drop of about twenty-seven or twenty-eight presidential proposals. Using another calculation, we can see that presidents during the period of largest government will have about fifty-six fewer proposals than average presidents, and average presidents will have about eighty-four fewer proposals than presidents in office during "small" government. Finally, large government presidents will have about 138 fewer proposals than small government presidents. (Recall that during the modern era, presidents submit 166 proposals per year on average, with a standard deviation of 78, and a range of 39 to 402.) Changes in the size of government in the modern era have nontrivial impacts on the size of the president's agenda.[35]

CONCLUSION

The theory of congressional anticipations argues that in building their legislative agendas, presidents take into account expectations for success versus failure in Congress. When presidents expect Congress to defeat a proposal, they will be less inclined to submit that proposal to the legislature. Because presidents receive less support when the opposition party controls Congress than when their party does, this theory predicts that presidential agendas will be smaller during divided government than united government. Furthermore, at times presidents can use expected defeats to their political advantage. For instance, during presidential reelection years, presidents might flood Congress with proposals that are popular with the public but sure to be defeated. Presidents can present the public with the argument that Congress is out of step with the public and voters should replace the sitting party in Congress with the president's party, creating united party control over both branches of government.

Using data on the size of the president's agenda from 1789 to 2002, the analysis in this chapter finds strong support for both of these hypotheses. Being a minority president leads to meaningfully smaller legislative agendas, and minority presidents play a blame game during presidential reelection periods. Moreover, these results hold with controls for the size of government, environmental conditions (war and the economy), and presidential party. Unlike past research, which has argued that presidents are sincere in submitting proposals to Congress for legislative consideration and that expectations for success/defeat

---

[35] Finally I tried to test this hypothesis by including quadratic terms for government outlays into the long historical analysis, in an attempt to pick up the impact of very large government. That analysis did not uncover any statistically significant effects, in levels or changes, even if I restricted the quadratic term to the post-1946 congresses. Across the broad sweep of history, growth in government leads to growth in presidential activism that swamps any modern era effects of very large government. Perhaps a regime-switching model, if it could be implemented with these data, would detect the change in presidential response to large government in the two eras, but as noted earlier, I was unable to get such a model to estimate.

in Congress do not enter into the presidential agenda-building process, the results in this chapter argue that presidents are very sensitive to the congressional context. The next chapter peers more deeply into the presidential agenda-building process by asking whether the congressional context affects presidential proposing across policy types.

CHAPTER 5

The Substantive Content of
Presidential Agendas

This chapter has two tasks. First, Chapter 4 presented strong support for the theory of congressional anticipations. As hypothesized, the president's agenda is smaller under divided than united government. During reelection years, however, minority presidents increase the size of their agendas, knowing that Congress will defeat their proposals, using those legislative defeats as a reelection campaign theme, the presidential blame game hypothesis. The analysis in Chapter 4 lumps all presidential proposals together. This chapter asks whether congressional anticipations affect presidential agenda decisions across policy types or are such presidential calculations specific to certain types of policies, such as domestic as opposed to foreign policies.

To address that question requires classifying each proposal by policy type. The second task of this chapter does this. Classifying proposals by policy type allows us to trace presidential attention to different policies across U.S. history. To date, no one has tried to track or describe presidential attention to different policies or issues across a long time. A major contribution of this chapter is providing such a description, which allows us to address an unexplored, yet important question – how does presidential attention to one policy area affect attention to other areas? Do policy areas compete for placement on the president's agenda? If one policy area attracts presidential attention, does that mean that other policy areas will have a harder time gaining the attention of the president?

Rather than develop a unique policy typology for this research, I classify each presidential proposal using Katznelson and Lapinski's (2006) scheme. Clinton and Lapinski (2006, 2008) and Lapinski

(2008) have used that scheme to study congressional law production from the 1870s to the present. By using the Katznelson-Lapinski
policy scheme, we can compare presidential and congressional policy
attention, something rarely done, but necessary given our separation
of powers system and the importance of the president to the policy-
making process since at least the 1930s.

POLICY TYPOLOGIES AND THE PRESIDENT'S AGENDA

Can we classify policies or issues into general types? There is a long
tradition in policy studies doing so, arguing that substantive differences across policies are important. Theodore Lowi's (1964) famous
policy typology hypothesized that different types of policy (e.g., dis-
tributive, redistributive, regulatory, and constituent) result in different
policy-making processes and patterns. Using a different policy typology, Aage Clausen (1973, also Clausen and Van Horn, 1977; Clausen
and Wilcox, 1991) also suggested that different factors affect congressional policy making across policy areas (also Brady and Stewart, 1982;
Sinclair, 1977).

This venerable tradition, which emphasized the importance of
policy substance to understand the policy-making process and outcomes, came under question with the work of Poole and Rosenthal
(1997). They argued that all policy areas can be arrayed along one
liberal-conservative dimension. Differences across substantive policies
become less important from the Poole-Rosenthal unidimensional policy space perspective; the only relevant difference across policies is
their location on that liberal-conservative dimension.[1]

More recently, Katznelson and Lapinski (2006) and Baumgartner
and Jones (1993, 2009; Jones and Baumgartner, 2005; Jones et al.,
2009) have resurrected the policy typology approach. Past typologies
of public policies, such as Lowi's and Clausen's, fell out of favor for a
variety of reasons. For instance, some found Lowi's highly conceptual
typology hard to operationalize and replicate, and others criticized the
Claussen policy domain framework as overly general (Smith, 2002).

---

[1] Poole and Rosenthal do find at times across U.S. history that a second policy dimension, civil rights, is also important, although it rarely rivals the power of the first
dimension, liberalism-conservatism, in structuring voting alignments in Congress.

The Katznelson-Lapinski and Baumgartner-Jones typologies are ambitious and more comprehensive than previous attempts at classifying substantive policy differences. Rather than offering only a handful of broad policy categories, these typologies make relatively refined substantive distinctions across policies. For instance, in their most disaggregated form, the Baumgartner and Jones typology contains 225 subtopics, whereas the Katznelson-Lapinski scheme has 69. Although the designers of these two policy typologies, which are substantively quite similar, suggest that the refined categories can be aggregated in broader categories, researchers can combine and recombine the disaggregated categories in whichever way or combination that suits their purposes.

Both the Baumgartner-Jones and Katznelson-Lapinski policy typologies have spawned important empirical research. For example, Lapinski (2008) found varying factors account for congressional production of important legislation across four major policy domains, lending some credence to the policy differences approach.[2] Aside from the many studies that have employed the Baumgartner-Jones category, and equally importantly, their data collection in studying U.S. policy making, Jones and colleagues (2009) offer one of the first cross-national policy comparison using a common typology of substantive policy areas. This cross-national study finds certain similarities in the policy-making process across nations, despite obvious differences across nations and political arrangements.

Studying the president's agenda segmented into substantive policy areas might help to resolve one nagging nonfinding from the previous chapter, the lack of effect of war on the president's agenda. A large literature has detailed the effect of war on society and government. Political sociologists, such as Charles Tilly (1985), identify war as critical in building the modern state, transforming government, and enhancing the power of the state to penetrate society and extract resources from it. Quite commonly, the executive branch reaped the greatest "benefit" from war, since government power and authority increasingly was

[2] The policy differences (e.g., Katznelson and Lapinski, Baumgartner and Jones) and the underlying unidimensional (e.g., Poole and Rosenthal) approaches need not be contradictory. It is possible for all policies to align across one liberal-conservative dimension, but different factors lead to the production of policy across policy areas.

centralized in the executive branch. Critics of the "imperial" presidency cite war and national security as rationales for the expansion of presidential power, criticizing such accretion of power in the executive as threatening democratic institutions and processes (Rudalevige, 2005; Schlesinger, 2004).

Although the analysis in this book does not bear on the question of executive power directly, war might lead presidents to increase their attention to international relations and defense policies, while reducing their attention to other policy concerns. This might result in no net shift in the overall size of the president's legislative policy agenda, but a major shift in presidential policy emphasis and orientation. By this argument, war shifts the composition of the president's legislative agenda but not necessarily its overall size. Comparing presidential legislative agenda attention across substantive policies allows us to test this hypothesis and perhaps resolve the nagging finding of the last chapter, that war seemed not to affect the president's agenda.

Following from this point, congressional anticipations might not affect presidential agenda-building decisions for all types of policies. Perhaps foreign policy differs from domestic issues in this regard, because national security and international conditions and not expectations for success with Congress motivate presidential proposals for foreign policy. Expectations for success with Congress might apply only to domestic policy. The two-presidencies thesis (Wildavsky, 1966; Shull, 1991; Canes-Wrone et al., 2008), which argues that presidents have advantages in foreign as opposed to domestic policy, offers a rationale for this idea: Presidents do not have to worry as much about success with Congress for foreign as opposed to domestic policy, because they can expect relatively high rates of congressional support for their foreign policies under all types of conditions (i.e., whether government is divided or not).

CLASSIFYING PRESIDENTIAL REQUESTS INTO POLICY AREAS

I use the Katznelson-Lapinski (2006, hereafter KL) scheme for classifying presidential proposals to Congress. Although they developed their scheme to analyze congressional policy making, Katznelson and

Lapinski grounded their scheme in theory with an eye on using it across time and place. Their scheme can also be used for comparing institutions, although they do not mention doing so.

Baumgartner and Jones (BJ) also have developed an alternative and useful scheme, but their scheme was developed explicitly for the United States in the post-World War Two era. Some issues of importance to American political debate prior to that war do not appear on the postwar agenda, such as Indian-Native American removal, national boundaries, and admission of states to the Union.[3] Using the Baumgartner-Jones scheme would require adding policy categories for such policy areas. Still there is considerable overlap between the Baumgartner-Jones and Katznelson-Lapinski schemes and for the most part one can move back and forth between them, even if the organization of their specific categories differs.

Furthermore, in categorizing each presidential proposal, I found the 19 major topic codes from Baumgartner and Jones too crude for my purposes, but resource limitations prohibited me from classifying 14,000+ proposals using the 225 subtopic codes. The sixty-nine categories from the Katznelson-Lapinski scheme offered a middle ground of many refined categories. Plus, I selected the Katznelson-Lapinski scheme because of Lapinski's (2008) recently published work on the history of congressional production of legislation, with the aim of eventually comparing congressional production and presidential proposing.

The KL scheme is arranged into three tiers, representing different degrees of aggregation. Table 5.1 presents their scheme. Four Tier 1 policy distinctions comprise the most general and highest level of policy aggregation – national sovereignty, government organization and scope, international relations, and domestic policy. For purposes here, I relabel Tier 1 as *Policy domains*, the Tier 2 designations is called *Policy clusters*, and the Tier 3 classifications is called *Policy areas*.

---

[3] Alaska and Hawaii were admitted to the Union after the Second World War. In the nineteenth and early twentieth centuries, admission of states to the Union was a major issue. For instance, prior to the Civil War, such admission could disrupt the balance between slave and free states. Although some political controversy arose with the admission of Alaska and Hawaii, it was minor compared to the debates over admission of states in the nineteenth century.

TABLE 5.1. *The Katznelson-Lapinski Policy Coding Scheme*

Tier 1	Tier 2	Tier 3
Sovereignty	Liberty	Loyalty and Expression; Religion; Privacy
	Membership and Nation	Commemorations and National Culture Immigration and Naturalization
	Civil Rights	African Americans; Native Americans; Other Minorities; Women; Voting Rights
	Boundaries	Frontier Settlement; Indian Removal and Compensation; State Admission/Union Composition; Territories and Colonies
Organization and Scope	Government Organization	Congressional Organization and Administration; Executive Org. and Admin.; Impeachment/Misconduct; Judicial Org. and Admin.
	Representation	Census/Apportionment; Elections; Groups and Interests
	Constitutional Amendments	Federalism and Terms of Office; Political Participation and Rights; Other
International Affairs	Defense	Air Force Organization and Deployment; Army Org. and Deploy.; Conscription and Enlistment; Militias; Naval Org. and Deploy.; General Military Org; Military Installations; Civil/Homeland Defense
	Geopolitics	Diplomacy/Intelligence; Foreign Aid; International Orgs.
	International Political Economy	Maritime; Trade/Tariffs; Economic International Orgs.
Domestic Affairs	Agriculture and Food	Agricultural Technology; Farmers/Farming Support; Fishing and Livestock
	Planning and Resources	Corporatism; Environment; Infrastructure and Public Works; Natural Resources; Social Knowledge; Post Office; Transportation; Wage and Price Controls; Interstate Compacts/Federalism; Urban, Rural, Regional Development
	Political Economy	Appropriations; Multiple Agency; Business/Capital Markets; Fiscal/Taxation; Labor Markets/Unions; Monetary; Economic Regulation
	Social Policy	Children/Youth; Crime; Disaster; Education; Handicapped/Disabilities; Health (Civilian); Housing; Military Pensions, Benefits; Public Works; Volunteer Employment; Regulation-Social; Social Insurance; Transfers/Poverty

Source: Katznelson and Lapinski, 2006.

The *National sovereignty* domain concerns matters relating to the existence of the state, its national borders and boundaries, and definitions of citizenship. *Government organization and scope*, the second domain, refers to the operation and administration of the branches and agencies of government, reform of those offices and the Constitution itself, and matters of representation and citizen participation in political and governmental affairs. The third policy domain, *International relations*, concerns the diplomatic, military, economic, and other relationships between the United States and other nations and international organizations. The fourth domain, *Domestic policy*, refers to relationships between the government with the economy and the welfare of the citizenry.

Each presidential legislative request was coded into one of the sixty-nine Tier 3 *policy areas*, the most refined coding level. One can easily aggregate from this level into the higher order levels (policy clusters or domains) depending on the question at hand. Coding each presidential request is generally straightforward, but some requests could potentially fall into more than one policy area. For instance, grants to the states for education have both federalism and educational policy aspects. If a proposal could legitimately and reasonably fall into several substantive policy areas, the proposal was coded for a primary and secondary policy area. To determine the primary policy area, coders relied on the way that the president packaged the proposal. Usually the document conveying the proposal to Congress provides sufficient information on how the president defines the primary purpose of the proposal. For instance, if the president issued a request to support school funding efforts in the states in an education message or if it were included with other education requests as part of a set of education initiatives, the proposal would be classified primarily as education and secondarily as federalism. In contrast, if the educational aid proposal were contained in a federalism message or with other policies directed at the states, federalism would be designated as the primary policy area and education as the secondary policy area.

After initially training a graduate student assistant, I double coded a random sample of 200 requests, with coding agreement of 94%. There were two main sources of coding disagreement, 1) whether the code was the primary or secondary code and 2) the interpretation of one of the KL issue areas, corporatism. The coding procedures were then clarified for the other coders. Afterwards, I also coded each request independently, achieving 99% agreement with the other coders.[4]

TRENDS IN THE POLICY SCOPE OF THE PRESIDENT'S LEGISLATIVE POLICY AGENDA

As in the previous chapter, counting the number of presidential requests gives us one measure of presidential legislative activism or leadership. Another way to measure presidential legislative leadership looks at the policy scope of the president's legislative agenda, whether it is broad or narrow. *Policy scope* refers to the number of policy areas in which the president issued a request. The president's agenda is broad in scope when his proposals for legislation spread across numerous policy areas, but the agenda is considered narrow in scope if the president concentrates his proposals across a small number of policy areas.

Combining these two dimensions, activity and scope, leads to a four-fold configuration to describe the president's legislative policy agenda and the type of legislative policy leadership that the president aims to supply. When presidents submit a large number of proposals across numerous policy areas, their agenda is broad and activist. A broad but restrained agenda exists when presidents spread a small number of proposals across a wide range of policy areas. A narrow, activist agenda consists of a large number of proposals concentrated in a limited number of proposals, whereas a narrow, restrained agenda consists of a small number of proposals concentrated in a small number of policy areas. Figure 5.1 plots how many of the sixty-nine policy areas contained at least one presidential proposal per congress.

In some important respects, the plot on Figure 5.1 resembles Figure 4.1, which traced the total number of discrete presidential requests. First, like Figure 4.1, Figure 5.1 shows an increase in the number of policy areas that make it onto the president's agenda over time.

---

[4] I also classified each proposal into one of the nineteen Baumgartner and Jones major topic codes, and when possible aggregated the sixty-nine Katznelson-Lapinski Tier 3 policy area codes into the BJ major topics independent of the Baumgartner-Jones coding of proposals. I then compared the two codings, producing almost identical classification of proposals into policy areas.

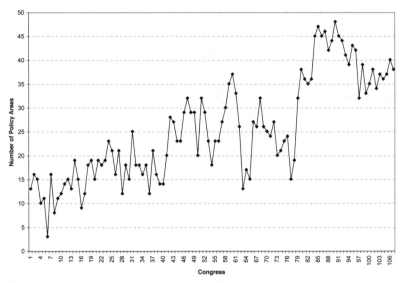

Figure 5.1. Number of Policy Areas in Which the President Made at Least One Legislative Request, 1789–2002 (1st to 107th Congresses).

The two series correlate highly ($r = 0.85$, $p = 0.000$), confirming the similarity between the two trend lines. Activism and breadth of legislative leadership, in general, go together.

In contrast to the trend in proposals, the number of issue areas does not exhibit the explosive growth in the post-World War Two years observed for the number of discrete requests. Two factors account for this difference. First, there are only sixty-nine policy areas. Although a considerable number of policy areas can appear on the president's agenda, this number falls well short of the number of discrete proposals, which often tally into the several hundreds. Thus, there is a limit to the amount of congress-to-congress change that we can expect when looking at policy areas, as opposed to discrete proposals, which can change markedly in a short time span. Second, the number of policy areas on the president's legislative agenda has incrementally increased from the earliest days of the Republic to the present. As I discuss in more detail later, however, early presidents spread their proposals across a fairly wide range of policy areas, suggesting that early presidents exhibited a pattern of restraint but breadth in their legislative policy agendas.

There is, however, a increase in the number of policy areas on the president's agenda that begins with the end of World War Two and continues into the mid-1960s, like that observed for discrete proposals. For instance, during the 77th Congress (1941–1942), the number of policy areas drops to a low level for modern presidents at fifteen. The number in the next Congress (78th) is only slightly higher, at nineteen,[5] but there are thirty-two policy areas on the president's legislative agenda for the 79th Congress (1945–1946), rising to a peak in 1967/1968 (90th Congress), at forty-eight. Thereafter, similar to discrete requests, the number of policy areas falls to an average of thirty-eight from the 91st to 107th Congresses.

Similar to the discrete request series, the policy area series suggests that Franklin Roosevelt was not as legislatively active across policy areas as historical accounts suggest. Roosevelt did not expand the scope of the legislative agenda compared with his immediate predecessors. In fact, these data indicate a modest contraction in the scope of the legislative agenda that FDR pursued compared with the three Republicans who served before him. The Republican presidents from 1921 to 1932 on average placed 26.7 policy areas on their legislative agendas. In comparison, FDR made requests on average for twenty-two policy areas during the pre-War years (1933–1940).

What differentiates FDR's New Deal legislative agenda in the prewar years from the Republicans who came before him is the substance, not the size or scope of the legislative agenda. FDR consistently turned his attention to policy areas that rarely made it onto the legislative policy agenda of his Republican predecessors. In other words, the *policy composition* of the agenda changed under FDR. The Republican presidents from 1921 to 1932 placed sixteen policy areas in at least five of the six presidential agendas of that period:[6] immigration, executive organization, judicial organization, military organization, diplomacy, international organization, maritime policy, farmers, public works, natural resources, transportation, business, fiscal matters, economic regulation, veterans, and social knowledge. FDR dropped seven of

---

[5] The lowest totals for twentieth-century presidents occurred in the 63rd to the 65th Congresses (1913–1918) of Woodrow Wilson at 13, 17, and 15 policy areas.

[6] Here a "presidential agenda" consists of all proposals submitted during a natural, two-year congress.

these issues areas, nearly one-half, in his four agendas of 1933 to 1940 (using the standard that the issue area had to appear on at least three of the four agendas). The dropped areas include immigration, judicial organization, military organization, international organizations, farmers, veterans, and social knowledge.

FDR also added three issues areas that never appeared consistently on the agendas of his Republican predecessors: labor policy, volunteer employment (like WPA), and social insurance. Circulation of policy areas should occur in realigning periods. We see the stark policy departure of FDR's New Deal from the Republican policy emphasis of the 1920s, as FDR dropped nearly one-half of their policy areas from his agenda, as well as adding labor, volunteer employment, and social insurance, areas not on their agenda but consistent elements on his.

From this perspective, the New Deal represents both a foray into policy areas not previously on the agenda and the elimination of numerous issues from previous presidential agendas.[7] At the same time, FDR's legislative agenda does not appear larger in either terms of discrete proposals (activism) or policy areas (scope) than his Republican predecessors. Substantive policy change, not greater presidential legislative leadership in terms of the size and breadth of the agenda, characterizes FDR's legislative agenda and the realignment associated with the New Deal. The expansion in leadership associated with the size and scope of the president's legislative agenda comes later, with Truman, after the conclusion of the Second World War.

Deleting and adding new issue areas from the president's agenda have important policy and political implications. First, deleting an issue area lessens the political power of the groups and interests associated with that policy area. Replacing the deleted policy area with a new one, or even just advancing a new issue area onto the president's agenda, enhances the political influence of groups associated with the newly arrived issue area. Access to the president's agenda is an important political resource. In the competition of groups for policy benefits, those with access to the presidency have acquired one type of resource that they might use to their advantage compared with groups

---

[7] Similar findings of changes in the substance of the agenda from the 1921–1932 Republicans to FDR can be found in Sinclair (1977) and Brady and Stewart (1982) studies of Congress.

that do not have access to the presidency and the president's policy agenda.

The circulation of issue areas onto and off of the president's legislative agenda potentially restructures the political landscape and recalibrates the political resources and power of affected groups. As these data suggest, the major impact of the New Deal with regard to the president's agenda was a restructuring of group and political access to the presidency through the substantive composition of the president's legislative agenda. Some groups that once had access to the presidency lost that access with FDR's presidency. At the same time, groups that had a difficult time gaining the attention of the presidency before Roosevelt found a friend in FDR, who placed their concerns on his legislative agenda.

These data also suggest a revised interpretation of the New Deal. By looking solely at the president's legislative agenda, FDR's New Deal *narrowed* presidential attention to matters most closely associated with combating the Depression and addressing the concerns of interests aligned with the Democratic Party. The policy novelty of the New Deal, compared with the Republican presidents of the 1920s, rests with its emphasis on policies for the less-well-off workers, unemployed, young people (WPA), and the elderly (social insurance), groups absent from the Republican presidential agendas of the 1920s and very early 1930s.[8]

Returning to Figure 5.1, we see that the early presidents also appear more legislatively active across a range of policy areas than our conventional picture of them, which portrays them as inactive and concerned with a narrow band of policy areas. Admittedly, early presidents submitted requests in fewer policy areas than the twenty-five policy areas on the average presidential agenda. The average from George Washington through John Quincy Adams is thirteen policy areas, ranging from three for John Adams (6th Congress, 1799–1800) to nineteen for James Madison (14th Congress, 1815–1816). Notably, Washington asked for legislation on average for 13.5 policy areas, a somewhat surprisingly large number of policy areas given our notion of limited

---

[8] This is similar to what Sinclair (1977) found in her study of the congressional agenda during these years.

government and limited presidential leadership in the early decades of the republic. Again, these data lead to us to revise our understanding of the early American presidents. They tended to have a relatively broad range of policy concerns on their legislative agendas despite their modest activity levels (e.g., number of discrete proposals) compared with more contemporary presidents.

POLICY CONCENTRATION IN THE PRESIDENT'S LEGISLATIVE AGENDA

The comparison of FDR's agenda with that of the Republicans who preceded him illustrates the value of looking at the policy composition of the president's legislative agenda and not merely counting the number of proposals. Change in the substantive composition of the president's legislative policy agenda can occur through three dynamics: Policy areas can remain on the agenda, they can fall off of the agenda, and others can gain a place on the president's agenda.[9] The previous section looked at the number of policy areas on the president's policy agenda. This section considers the question of how much continuity and change across policy areas do we see in the president's agenda.

Table 5.2 provides a first look at this question by listing the three *most common policy areas* on the president's legislative agenda for sets of ten congresses from 1789 through 2002, eleven sets in all. Rather than count the number of proposals per policy area, here I use policy areas as the unit of analysis, distinguishing between the policy areas in which the president made at least one proposal to any congress with those in which the president failed to submit any legislative proposal. Such an aggregation provides us with a sense of how often a policy area appears on the president's agenda but not how much attention the president gives to that policy area compared with other policy areas.

The data on Table 5.2 suggest important continuities and also changes in the substantive policy composition of the president's agenda over the course of U.S. history. First, diplomatic relations with

---

9 Of course, some policy areas might never make it onto the president's legislative agenda.

TABLE 5.2. *Presidential Legislative Requests: Three Most Important Policy Areas by Congresses*

Congress	Year	First	Second	Third
1–10	1789–1808	Indian Removal	Diplomacy	Native Americans and Naval (tied)
11–20	1809–1828	Indian Removal	Diplomacy	Military (General)
21–30	1829–1848	Diplomacy	Indian Removal	Monetary
31–40	1849–1868	Diplomacy	Indian Removal	Naval
41–50	1869–1888	Diplomacy	Monetary	Native Americans
51–60	1889–1908	Diplomacy	Natural Resources	Territories and Naval (tied)
61–70	1909–1928	Diplomacy	Natural Resources	Economic Regulation
71–80	1929–1948	Fiscal/Taxation	Executive Organization	Business/Capital Markets
81–90	1949–1968	Fiscal/Taxation	Health	Education
91–100	1969–1988	Diplomacy	Fiscal/Taxation	International Organizations and Natural Resources (tied)
101–107	1989–2002	Diplomacy	Health	Crime

Source: Presidential Legislative Request Database, 1789–2002. See text for details.

other nations is a near-constant presence on the president's agenda. For almost every set of congresses, diplomacy ranked as one of the top three concerns for the president. To a large degree, this makes sense and should not come as a surprise. The founders created the presidency in part to take the lead in foreign policy. The area of foreign relations is also a nondiscretionary policy concern. No matter the degree of entanglement with other nations, every nation needs a foreign policy and must communicate it to other nations. Even in eras of limited and restricted government, when presidents think that they should not be policy activists, other nations can behave in ways that require a response from the United States and from the president.

Although these data do not indicate whether the president actually led in foreign policy making, the data do indicate that foreign policy and relations with other nations consistently appears on the presidential agenda. Surprisingly, neither diplomacy nor any defense/foreign relations–related policy area made the list of top three for the sets of congresses from 1929 to 1968. This is understandable given the isolationist tendencies of the 1930s and the national preoccupation with the Depression. The 1920s, however, was also an era of isolationism, but diplomacy ranked highly among policy areas of presidential attention in the 1920s. It is also odd that during the Cold War, foreign relations do not appear more prominently on the president's legislative agenda. Perhaps presidents relied heavily on unilateral devices for making foreign policy during the Cold War (Schlesinger, 2004; Rudalevige, 2005); thus, they did not need to go to Congress as often with foreign policy matters during the Cold War.

These data also reveal the importance of matters relating to Native Americans for the presidency for the first 100 years of the Republic. Either Indian removal or Native American policies made the list of top three concerns for each of the first five sets of Congresses. By the late 1800s, the "Indian problem" had been solved. By then, the United States stretched across the continent, and all Native Americans had been relocated to reservations. Native American tribes and their affairs had ceased to be a military issue, instead becoming one that a civilian bureaucracy, the Bureau of Indian Affairs, was charged with managing.

Other than military-related matters also rising onto this list of top three during the pre-twentieth-century years, only one other matter, monetary policy, makes it onto this list during those years – the 1829-to-1848 and 1869-to-1888 sets. During the first of these sets, the Second Bank of the United States was a prime issue dividing Democrats from Whigs. Economic problems also plagued the United States in the 1840s, as it did again in the decades following the Civil War.

Overall, however, if we view Native American affairs as a type of foreign policy/national security issue, the president's agenda across the nineteenth century focused primarily on diplomatic and defense issues, which is consistent with the founders' intentions for the policy areas for which the president was to be responsible.

Military and defense issues remain important in the twentieth century, but other types of issues, notably economic and sundry domestic issues, also appear consistently on the president's legislative policy agenda. For the six sets of ten congresses from 1889 to 2002, diplomacy and defense issues occupied six of the eighteen slots (including two ties).[10] This compares with the same type of policies (including Native American issues) filling fourteen of sixteen slots for the first five sets of congresses. Oddly, as the United States became a world power, presidential attention to foreign policy and defense matters waned in relative importance on the legislative agenda. This does not mean that foreign and defense matters became less important to the president, but that presidential attention in the legislative agenda expanded to include other policy concerns. As speculated earlier, presidents might have felt a freer hand in making foreign policy without having to go to Congress as much.

Economic matters follow closely behind diplomacy/defense as the next most common presidential concern, appearing five times. Domestic policies appear four times, but presidents spread their attention across different domestic issues, with health appearing twice and education and crime once apiece. Finally, the issue of national resources occupies three of these slots, whereas executive branch reorganization and territorial expansion occur once apiece.

Compared with the nineteenth century, twentieth-century presidents not only emphasize a different set of policy areas in their legislative policy agendas but also spread their attention across a greater variety of policy areas. Fewer policy areas consistently appear on the legislative agendas of the twentieth century in contrast to nineteenth-century agendas, a finding that displays greater stability in presidential legislative policy attention.

TRENDS IN PRESIDENTIAL ATTENTION TO POLICY DOMAINS

Modern presidents submit more legislative requests to Congress than premodern presidents. They also submit proposals across more policy areas than do premodern presidents. The substantive composition of the president's legislative policy agenda has also changed, with somewhat greater attention to domestic policy in the modern era, less attention to sovereignty policies in the modern era, and relatively

---

[10] 3 policy areas × 6 congresses = 18 slots.

consistent presidential attention to international and defense policy across both periods.

This section peers more closely at the trends in presidential attention to the four policy domains, and at times to policy areas, looking at two attributes, *absolute* and *relative* attention. *Absolute attention* refers to the number of discrete requests for a policy area or domain. *Relative attention* assesses the percentage of a presidential agenda devoted to a particular policy domain or area. Absolute attention to a policy area can increase at the same time that relative attention to that policy area might have decreased, for example, because presidential attention to other policy areas has grown at a faster rate. As we shall see, relative attention to the international relations-defense policy domain has declined, although absolute attention has remained steady, if not increased. The explosive growth in post-World War Two presidential attention to domestic policy accounts for the seemingly contrary trends in presidential attention to international and defense policy. Comparing relative and absolute attention provides us with a more discriminating portrait of the substantive policy orientations of presidents and how their legislative agendas have changed over time. This section primarily explores absolute and relative attention to the four broad policy domains. Although it could be instructive to do the same for all sixty-nine tier 3 policy areas, the amount of information would be overwhelming to digest. Thus, I begin with the broadest level of policy categories, and when warranted, disaggregate into the policy clusters and policy areas.

Absolute Presidential Attention to Policy Domains

Table 5.3 presents basic descriptive information on presidential attention to the four policy domains. On average, presidents pay more attention to domestic policy than the other three policy domains. From 1789 to 2002, presidents allocated more than half of their legislative agendas to domestic policy (56.4%), compared with 26.3% to international affairs, 9.7% to national sovereignty, and 7.6% to government organization. Presidential attention to domestic policy also exhibits the greatest variability, with not only the largest standard deviation but also the widest range. During the 6th Congress, John Adams failed to submit a single domestic policy proposal to Congress, and on another twenty-four occasions, presidents sent ten or fewer domestic

TABLE 5.3. *Descriptive Statistics of Presidential Attention to the Four Policy Domains*

Policy Domain	Mean	sd	Min.	Max.
In Levels				
National Sovereignty	12.5	10.3	0	46
Government Organization	9.8	11.4	0	66
International Relations	33.9	24.0	3	118
Domestic Policy	72.8	105.1	0	506
Total Requests	129.0	134.8	5	665
In Changes				
National Sovereignty	−0.02	10.3	−33	32
Government Organization	0.1	8.3	−33	36
International Relations	0.7	14.7	−52	53
Domestic Policy	1.9	44.7	−268	207
Total Requests	2.7	59.1	−327	197

Source: Presidential Legislative Request Database, 1789–2002. See text for details.

proposals to Congress. In contrast, Lyndon Johnson submitted more than 500 domestic policy proposals in the mid-1960s.

Figures 5.2 to 5.5 plot absolute presidential attention to each of the four domains. The temporal pattern for domestic policy strongly

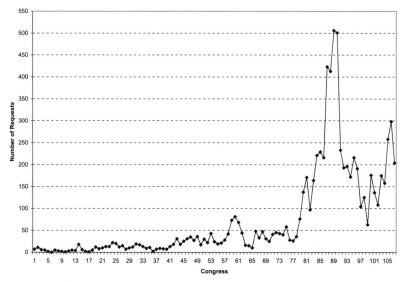

Figure 5.2. Number of Domestic Policy Presidential Legislative Requests, 1789–2002 (1st to 107th Congresses).

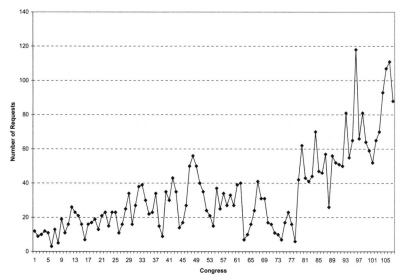

Figure 5.3. Number of International Relations Presidential Legislative Requests, 1789–2002 (1st to 107th Congresses).

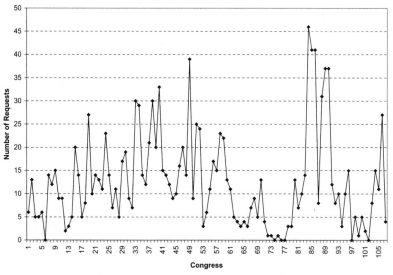

Figure 5.4. Number of National Sovereignty Presidential Legislative Requests, 1789–2002 (1st to 107th Congresses).

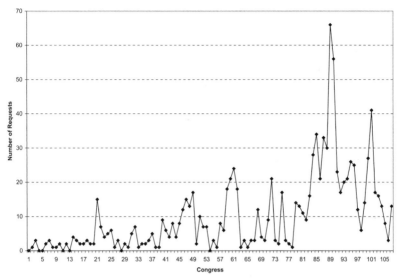

Figure 5.5. Number of Government Organization Presidential Legislative Requests, 1789–2002 (1st to 107th Congresses).

resembles that for presidential requests overall (Figure 5.2).[11] Across the first 78 congresses (1789–1946), presidents submitted comparatively few domestic policy proposals, with a peak occurring in the first decade of the 1900s. Even during that decade, the number of domestic policy proposals never reached 100. In contrast, in the post-World War Two era, there is a remarkable surge in domestic policy proposals, which peaks during the Johnson congresses (89th and 90th, 1965–1968). Only once in the post-World War Two era did a president ask for fewer than 100 pieces of domestic policy legislation, 97 for Truman in the 82nd Congress (1951–1952), his last two years in office. Even this figure tops almost all pre-World War Two congresses in terms of absolute presidential attention to domestic policy.

To some degree, absolute presidential attention to international relations resembles that for domestic policy (Figure 5.3), but at lower aggregate levels. Post-World War Two attention to international affairs definitely surpasses that of the prewar era, but presidents still paid considerable absolute attention to international affairs in the prewar era. Figure 5.3 indicates an incremental and long-term secular increase in

[11] The domestic policy and overall series correlate at 0.99, $p < 0.000$.

presidential attention to international affairs from the early Republic to 1880s, by which time presidents had submitted about fifty international affairs proposals per congress. After that absolute presidential attention to international affairs declines in fits and starts, bottoming in the 1930s and early 1940s. Prior to the conclusion of the Second World War, presidential attention to foreign affairs begins to rise. This rise occurs just before the upsurge in domestic policy attention, which commenced with the end of the war. Unlike presidential attention to domestic policy, in the post-World War Two era, presidential attention to foreign affairs builds steadily across the entire era and at a relatively steep rate. (Recall that attention to domestic policy rises until the mid-1960s, and then declines.) In absolute terms, however, presidents pay considerably less attention to international than domestic policy.[12] Rarely do post-World War Two presidents submit more than 100 international relations proposals to Congress. More commonly they submit about 65 international relations proposals per congress, compared with the 100+ for domestic policy.

Presidents never pay as much attention to national sovereignty policies as they do to either international or domestic policy (Figure 5.4). Still, sovereignty is an important part of the president's legislative agenda early in U.S. history. Absolute presidential attention to national sovereignty issues steadily increases until the 49th Congress (1885–1886), after which presidential attention to national sovereignty drops steadily, nearly falling off the president's agenda during the 1930s and early 1940s.

National sovereignty, in the Katznelson-Lapinski framework, pertains to matters such as immigration, definitions of citizenship, and civil and minority rights, as well as national borders, admission of states to the Union and Native American resettlement and removal. All were among the most contentious and persistent policy problems during the nation's first 100 years. By the late 1800s, however, Native American matters had been essentially resolved with resettlement onto reservations, and most of the states had entered the Union,

---

[12] As noted throughout, the legislative policy agenda might understate presidential attention to international relations policy. In that policy domain, presidents can make policy through unilateral powers more often than they can do in domestic policy, the latter more commonly requiring congressional production of legislation.

including the reentry of the secessionist states. By the late 1800s, numerous national sovereignty matters had been "resolved" such that they would not reemerge onto the national or the president's agenda.

New national sovereignty issues emerged in the mid-1900s, however, becoming quite contentious and gaining access to the president's agenda. The presidential agendas of the 84th to the 90th congresses (1955–1968) seem especially attentive to national sovereignty issues, compared with the presidential agendas of other modern congresses. Many of the national sovereignty matters that attracted presidential attention in the 1950s and 1960s concerned civil rights, especially for African Americans. Other than one Congress during this period (the 87th, Kennedy's first in office), presidents submitted about forty sovereignty measures, mostly civil rights measures, each congress. This flurry of civil rights attention quickly subsided; presidential attention to national sovereignty bottomed again, remaining modest for roughly the next twenty-five years (1969–1994; 91st–103rd Congresses). Thereafter attention to national sovereignty issues grew, although not to the heights seen during the civil rights years, with immigration and civil rights for non-black minorities appearing on these most recent presidential agendas.

The fourth policy domain, government organization and scope, tells a different story from the other three. Like national sovereignty, government organization rarely occupies much of the president's agenda in absolute terms, but like domestic and international relations, attention to government organization issues rises in the post-World War Two era. The trend line on Figure 5.5 indicates other periods of heightened presidential attention to government organization, like during the Progressive era years from 1905 to 1912, although the number of government organization proposals during these periods of heightened attention pales compared with that for domestic and international affairs.

In terms of absolute presidential attention, three policy domains, domestic policy, international relations, and government organization, all show increased presidential attention in the post-World War Two era, although the volume of attention to domestic matters swamps that of the other two. Absolute attention to national sovereignty displays a more variable historical story, with great attention in the

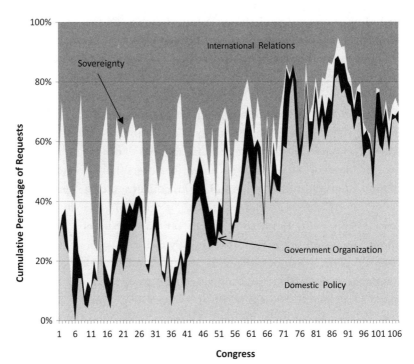

Figure 5.6. Proportion of the President's Legislative Policy Agenda Devoted to the Four Major Policy Domains, 1789–2002 (1st to 107th Congresses).

first 100 years, then falling attention but a resumption of presidential attention in the 1950s and 1960s, followed by less presidential attention through to the end of the century.

Relative Presidential Attention to Policy Domains

The relative perspective looks at the proportion of presidential attention to a policy area or domain at any point in time. Growth in the overall size of the presidential agenda does not imply that presidents have increased their relative attention to all policy areas or domains. One or a few policy areas can gain in relative attention at the expense of other policy areas. By looking at relatively attention, we can trace the substantive policy *emphasis* or *concentration* of presidential agendas. Relative attention gives us a sense of where presidents are focusing their legislative policy energies. Figure 5.6 plots the relative proportion (the percentage of proposals) for each of the four policy

TABLE 5.4. *Policy Domain Proportion by Congress, 1789–2002*

Congress	Sovereignty[a]	Govt. Org.[a]	International Relations[a]	Domestic Policy[a]	No. of Requests
1–10	34.69	5.31	42.86	17.14	245
11–20	28.53	5.54	48.20	17.73	361
21–30	25.82	8.48	39.88	25.82	519
31–40	33.33	5.85	44.23	16.59	615
41–50	18.37	10.35	42.09	29.19	860
51–60	17.65	8.99	30.85	42.51	901
61–70	8.78	9.88	35.12	46.23	729
71–80	3.06	9.99	24.68	62.28	851
81–90	6.80	7.60	12.05	73.54	3,999
91–100	2.63	7.29	26.35	63.73	2,619
101–107	3.19	5.28	27.89	63.64	2,101
All	9.72	7.58	26.25	56.45	13,800

[a] Figures in cells in the columns are the percentage of total requests in the policy domain.

Source: Presidential Legislative Policy Agenda Database, 1789–2002. See text for details.

domains for each presidential agenda during a single natural congress. Table 5.4 gives percentage breakdowns for sets of ten congresses.

In relative terms, national sovereignty (the white band on Figure 5.6), despite the low levels of discrete requests, commanded a considerable percentage of the president's legislative policy agenda for most of the first fifty congresses. Often national sovereignty matters occupied more space on the president's legislative agenda than domestic matters, which was the case for the first twenty congresses (1789–1828). It makes sense that early in a nation's history national sovereignty would consume so much of the president's and the government's relative energy and attention.

Applying a life cycle metaphor, a nation can age from childhood to adolescence to maturity. Across this maturation process, a nation develops and secures its identity. Early in that maturation process, a new nation, like the United States coming out of the revolutionary period, must devote resources to defining that identity, as well as building the governmental and societal institutions to secure that identity. To some degree we see this developmental process in the president's legislative agenda. Over time, less and less of the president's agenda concerned itself with national sovereignty and national identity issues. Once the United States was a matured nation, when national sovereignty issues arose, they concerned mostly the expansion or application of that national identity to new groups seeking a place in the political system, for instance, the push by minority groups in the 1950s and 1960s for their civil rights.

In contrast to the declining proportional attention to national sovereignty as the nation matured, government organization (the black band on Figure 5.6) appears to be a relatively stable fixture on the president's agenda, but it occupies only a relatively small fraction of presidential attention. Rarely do government organization issues capture more than one-tenth of the space on the president's legislative policy agenda. Despite this small quantity, government organization never falls off of the president's agenda for long. It is a persistent but not voluminous fixture on the president's legislative policy agenda. To a degree, the persistence of government organization follows from the constitutional requirements of the presidency, its executive duties and responsibilities. This persistence also might signify ever-present demands to reform the federal establishment, to bring it under the control of political authorities, and to express political demands through the organization and operation of federal agencies, among other factors. Although not the centerpiece of presidential policy attention, government organization is a mainstay on their legislative policy agendas.

The international affairs domain always occupies a significant and relatively large percentage of the president's legislative policy agenda (the dark gray band on Figure 5.6). For the first 100 years, until the late 1800s, international relations consumed proportionately more of the presidential agenda than any other policy domain. This presidential preoccupation with international affairs during the nation's first 100 years in part reflects the founders' intentions that the presidency would provide leadership in international affairs. Furthermore, unlike other policy areas, international affairs often requires a U.S. response to the actions of other nations, even during periods when the president, other political leaders, and voters prefer limited government. This second process also propels international affairs and defense issues onto the president's agenda.

By the turn of the twentieth century, international affairs' hold on the president's agenda began to recede in *relative terms*. Although we might expect this in the 1920s and 1930s, eras of isolationist sentiment, the decline in relative attention to international relations continues through the 90th Congress (1969–1970), that is, across much of the Cold War and Vietnam War eras. Beginning in the 1970s, relative presidential attention to international affairs increases, reaching a modern apex in 1985/1986, but still not occupying quite as much relative space as in the nineteenth century. With the end of the Cold War, relative attention to international relations fades somewhat, but remains about 10% higher than during the 1950s and 1960s.

The waxing and waning of relative presidential attention to international affairs seem to have more to do with the rise and fall of domestic policy than the Cold War or isolationist sentiment. Domestic policy had always attracted some presidential attention (the light gray band on Figure 5.6), but not until the turn of the twentieth century does domestic policy occupy more presidential attention than the other three policy domains. From 1901 onward, about 40% or more of the president's legislative agenda concerns domestic policy issues. In the 1960s, presidents seemed preoccupied with domestic policy compared with the other policy domains, with more than 70% of their legislative proposals pertaining to domestic policy. Ironically, this preoccupation with domestic policy during mid-century comes at the height of the Cold War and during the Vietnam War, when we might expect presidential attention to focus on international affairs.

After the peak of relative attention to the domestic policy domain in the 1960s, relative presidential attention to that policy domain falls, hitting a modern low in the mid-1980s, which also happens to be the modern peak of relative attention to international affairs. With government organization occupying a small place on the president's agenda and national sovereignty not being a large presence either, there appears to be an attention trade-off between domestic and international affairs in the modern era. Although there is a strong positive relationship for absolute presidential attention to domestic and international relations ($r = 0.63$, $p < 0.000$), the correlation between relative attention to these two policy domains is strongly negatively ($r = -0.78$, $p < 0.000$). As relative presidential attention to domestic policy increases, relative attention to international relations decreases, and vice versa. From this analysis, we cannot identify the causal mechanisms at work, whether attention to international affairs leads to less attention to domestic policy or the obverse, but descriptively we can say that across U.S. history, especially in the modern era, there is a trade-off in the relative presidential attention between domestic and international affairs.

DOMESTIC POLICY AND THE SIZE OF THE PRESIDENT'S LEGISLATIVE AGENDA

Domestic policy has profoundly affected the substantive orientation of the president's legislative policy agenda in both absolute and relative terms. The domestic policy domain subsumes a broad range of domestic policies. This section disaggregates the domestic policy domain into its components to learn if increased absolute and relative presidential attention to domestic policy concentrates on a subset of domestic policy topics.

Recall that shortly after the conclusion of the Second World War, the size of the president's legislative agenda began to grow at a steep rate until it reached a peak in the mid-to-late 1960s. Casual inspection of Figure 4.1 suggested two long historic periods to the president's legislative agenda overall, the pre-World War Two epoch, in which the size of the agenda rose incrementally and steadily, and the postwar epoch, in which it grew explosively, settling at a proposal rate much higher than for the prewar epoch.

Almost all of the surge in presidential submissions to Congress after World War Two can be attributed to domestic policy. We see this dramatically on Figure 5.7, which plots the number of domestic and nondomestic policy legislative submissions from 1789 through 2002. (The nondomestic proposals combine the number of proposals for the international affairs, government organization, and national sovereignty domains.) On that figure, the light gray band represents the number of nondomestic policy requests, the darker band, the number of domestic policy requests.

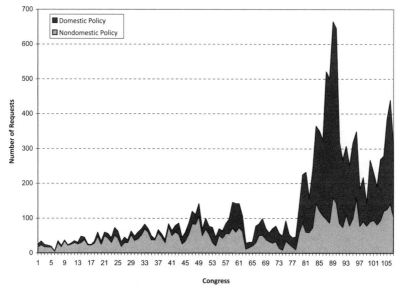

Figure 5.7. Comparing the Number of Presidential Proposals for Domestic and Nondomestic Policies, 1789–2002 (1st to 107th Congresses).

Looking just at the nondomestic requests, we notice an increase over time. On average, from the 1st to 78th Congresses, presidents submitted about 40 nondomestic proposals to congress, compared with about 101 per congress from the 79th to the 107th Congresses. By comparison, the average number of domestic policy proposals grew from an average of 21 across the first 78 congresses to an average of 212 for the 79th to 107th Congresses, a tenfold increase. From the 79th Congress onward, presidents submitted 9,079 legislative proposals to Congress; 6,160, or 68%, concerned domestic policy, leaving only 32% for the other three policy domains. The post-World War Two presidency is very much a domestic policy presidency in both absolute and relative terms.

The domestic policy domain contains a heterogeneous mix of policies. For instance, the Katznelson-Lapinski policy typology includes these *policy clusters*: agriculture, natural resources, political economy, and social policy. How much did each of these four *domestic policy clusters* contribute to the massive growth in presidential domestic policy proposals in the postwar era in both absolute and relative terms?

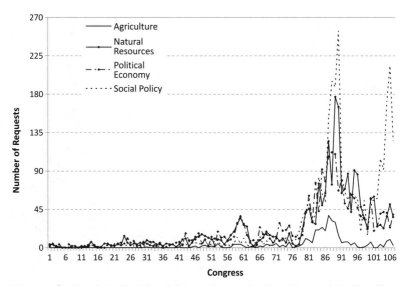

Figure 5.8. Trends in Presidential Attention to the Four Domestic Policy Clusters: Agriculture, Natural Resources, Political Economy, and Social Policy, 1789–2002 (1st to 107th Congresses).

Figure 5.8 plots the number of presidential proposals for each of these four policy clusters from 1789 through 2002. Each contributed to the rise of domestic policy on the president's legislative policy agenda, although with varying impact. Presidential attention to agriculture policy rises across the 1950s and 1960s, like the other three domestic policy clusters. During those years, presidents submitted roughly from twenty to forty agriculture proposals. After the late 1960s, however, agriculture virtually drops off of the president's legislative agenda, with only a modest uptick in attention during the late 1990s and early 2000s. Oddly, despite the importance of agriculture to national employment and the economy until the early 1900s, in the nineteenth century presidents rarely submitted agriculture recommendations to Congress.

In contrast, the natural resources cluster commanded presidential attention for a longer time and often at a higher rate than agriculture. Almost always a fixture on the president's legislative agenda, there is a rise in presidential attention to natural resources from the late 1870s into the mid-1890s. Then, from 1901 through 1912, the Roosevelt-Taft years, we see another and larger surge in attention to natural resources policy. After World War Two, however, comes the era of greatest presidential attention to natural resources policy, which peaks in the mid-to-late 1960s, similarly to the peak for domestic policy overall.

Political economy also exhibits increased presidential attention in the post-World War Two years, peaking in the 1960s, but presidents have paid attention to political economy for the entire history of the nation. Often presidential attention to the political economy appears to peak with economic panics and other major economic dislocations. For instance, in 1837, a year of great economic strife and distress, Martin Van Buren presented eleven political economy recommendations to Congress. Prior to that, presidents rarely made more than half a dozen such recommendations. Again in the 1870s and 1880s, also years of economic dislocations, turmoil, and divisions, we see an increase in the number of economic recommendations that presidents submitted to Congress. During the 1880s, the federal government began to increase its regulation of the economy, in part at the behest of Populist and Progressive movements.

A smaller peak of economic attention comes in the Theodore Roosevelt-Taft years, another period when the federal government assumed greater regulatory powers over the economy. Somewhat surprisingly, during the New Deal, FDR did not submit very many economic policy recommendations, especially compared with those of the Republican presidents of the 1920s. The height of presidential attention to economic concerns comes in the post-World War Two era, again peaking in the 1960s and subsiding somewhat thereafter.

Much of the increase in presidential attention regarding domestic policy in the post-World War Two era, however, was on social policy. Of the four domestic policy clusters, the social policy cluster accounts for 41% of all domestic policy proposals in the post-World War Two era, compared with 25% for economic policy, 29% for natural resources, and 5% for agriculture policy. Unlike each of the other domestic policy clusters, almost all presidential attention to social policy comes in the postwar era. Of the 2,861 social policy proposals that presidents submitted to Congress, 2,544, or 89%, were made in the post-World War Two era. In the prewar era, presidents submitted on average four domestic policy proposals per congress. During the postwar epoch the average rose to eighty-eight, a remarkable twenty-two-fold increase.

Like the other three domestic policy clusters, presidential attention to social policy rose dramatically in the two decades from the end of World War Two to the mid-1960s, and like those other domestic policy clusters, presidential attention to social policy waned for the next twenty-five years or so. In the 1990s, however, there is another increase in presidential attention to social policy, peaking in 1999 and 2000, Bill Clinton's last years in office, with 213 proposals, the second highest level of presidential proposing for social policy, just behind Lyndon Johnson's 254 in 1967/1968.

Summing Up

Franklin Roosevelt is often singled out as the first modern president (Greenstein, 1988). According to that theory, during FDR's term of office, all of the characteristics associated with the modern office coalesced to produce what we now recognize as the modern presidency. Greenstein identifies the following characteristics that distinguish the modern from the traditional (pre-FDR) presidencies: 1) the "greater formal and informal power to make decisions on their own initiative," 2) "chief agenda-setters in federal level policy-making," 3) "major staff and advisory capacity," and 4) "most visible actors in the political system" (1988, pp. 39).[13]

To some degree, the theory of the modern presidency has led to a stereotype that all pertinent changes that led to the modern presidency occurred during FDR's tenure, but seeds for the modern presidency can be located in the creation of the formal budget process in 1921 (Berman, 1979) and in the diffusion of the electronic media, especially radio, also in the decade preceding FDR (Cornwell, 1966). The budget process increased presidential influence over policy making and agenda setting, giving the president the first of several institutionally based staffs to draw on. Radio provided presidents with direct access to the mass public, expanding their public image and focusing public attention on the president as a personality, something less

---

[13] Greenstein is careful to point out the liabilities and costs of these developments on the presidency; also see Seligman (1956).

possible prior to radio. As is also sometimes forgotten, the modern presidency continued to develop in the years after FDR (Ragsdale and Theis, 1997). This is most apparent with the establishment of the president's legislative program and the legislative clearance process under Truman in the late 1940s (Neustadt, 1954, 1955; Wayne, 1987; Rudalevige, 2002).

The analysis in this and the previous chapter adds to our understanding of the development of the modern presidency. The president's legislative policy agenda is much larger for modern than traditional presidents, but this expansion began in the late 1940s, somewhat coincident with the creation of the legislative program, and it continued to grow until the mid-1960s. At the same time that we see the increase in legislative leadership, modern (post-World War Two) presidents offered legislative proposals across a larger range of policy areas than their earlier counterparts. Looking at substantive policy areas and not merely the total number of proposals provides a more refined picture of the policy orientation of modern presidents and the development of the presidency as a policy-making institution. The great rise in the number of proposals that presidents submitted to Congress from the late 1940s onward is due primarily to increased presidential attention to domestic policy, and to social domestic policy in particular. Without pushing the point too far, not only can we characterize the post-World War Two presidential legislative agenda as a domestic policy agenda, but we can also think of it as a heavily social policy agenda. This represents a remarkable transformation in the policy emphasis of the presidential legislative policy agenda.

ACCOUNTING FOR PRESIDENTIAL ATTENTION TO POLICY DOMAINS

Chapter 4 provided strong support for two key hypotheses of the theory of congressional anticipations, the divided government and presidential blame game hypotheses. The analysis in that chapter looked at the total number of presidential proposals. This chapter looks at the number of presidential proposals by policy domain. Does anticipation of success or failure with Congress affect presidential proposing similarly for all four major policy domains? For several reasons, anticipation of congressional action might not affect presidential proposals decisions for each policy domain.

First, analysis in Chapter 4 failed to detect any impact of war on presidential proposing behavior. It could be the case that war's effect on presidential proposing varies by type of policy. For instance, war could lead to increased proposing in international relations but a decline in proposing domestic policies, because war shifts presidential attention away from domestic concerns and toward international and defense issues. The contrary effects of war cancel out when foreign and domestic policies are combined, as in Chapter 4. Following this logic, the presidential decision process for foreign and domestic policies might differ. One difference might be that congressional anticipations play a larger role for domestic as opposed to foreign policy.

Analysis earlier in this chapter provides some evidence of differences in presidential attention across policy domains. For example, the topic of international affairs has always been a major component of presidential agendas, but domestic policy became an important part of the president's agenda only in the post-World War Two period. Moreover, other research suggests differences in policy-making processes across policy areas and domains. Lapinski (2008), using the same policy scheme as used here, finds that different factors affect congressional production of major laws across the four policy domains, something that might repeat here for the president's agenda.

Disaggregating presidential proposals by policy type raises another question, whether presidential attention to one policy domain affects attention to the other domains. From one perspective, presidential attention to one domain might undercut attention to other domains. Recall the assumption that presidents possess finite resources for legislative agenda building. Although there can be some elasticity with regard to resources (e.g., presidents can add or redeploy staff support to legislative agenda building), there are limits to the resources that presidents can gather in the short run for legislative agenda building. Consequently, there are limits to the number of policies, issues, and problems that the president can address at any point in time. In building their legislative policy agendas, presidents prioritize certain policies, issues, and problems over others. Those that rank higher in priority are placed on the president's agenda until presidential resources are exhausted and the president cannot handle an additional item for his legislative agenda. Thus, competition exists across policies, issues, and problems for presidential attention. Presidential attention to one item can limit or negate attention to another item.

At the same time, presidents can bundle legislative proposals as they try to build support coalitions in Congress. In other words, presidents, like legislators, may engage in logrolling but will do so at this early agenda-building stage of the legislative policy process. Some subsets of policies might not be in competition with each other. Through logrolling, their priority ranking rises, because the appearance of an item on the president's agenda not only enhances the enactment likelihood of other legislative proposals, but those other proposals' appearance improves the enactment prospects of this proposal. Comparing presidential attention across substantive policies allows us to address whether policy competition and logrolling affect agenda building.

STATISTICAL ESTIMATION ISSUES

From a statistical modeling perspective, presidential attention to one policy domain will not be independent of attention to another policy domain if policy competition and logrolling exist. For example, we could proceed as we did in Chapter 4, regressing presidential attention to each of the four policy domains on the variables used in that analysis in four separate estimations. Such an approach would provide us with valid estimates only if decision making about one policy domain had no implication for decision making on the other domains; that is, if policy competition and logrolling did not influence presidential decision making.

Seemingly unrelated regression (SUR) is an appropriate analytical technique for handling the issue of nonindependence across the four policy domains.[14] The analysis begins with the same independent

[14] I used the sureg command in STATA 10.0, which implements Zellner's (1962) seemingly unrelated regression. One issue arises in the use of regression techniques, like seemingly unrelated regression used here – the number of proposals for year. As the descriptive statistics on Table 5.3 and the trend plots (Figures 5.2 –5.5) indicate, presidential proposing rates for national sovereignty and government organization might be too low for linear techniques, calling instead for event count estimations. The event count models for modeling systems of equations, such as the nlsur command

TABLE 5.5. *Breusch-Pagan Test of Independence of Equations for the Seemingly Unrelated Regression (Estimation Results Presented in Table 5.6)*

	Correlations[a]			
	National Sovereignty	Government Operations	International Affairs	Domestic Policy
National Sovereignty	1.00			
Government Operations	0.21	1.00		
International Affairs	0.24	0.15	1.00	
Domestic Policy	0.24	0.55	0.21	1.00

Breusch-Pagan test of independence: $\chi^2(6) = 53.229$, $p = 0.0000$.
[a] All variables are in change form.

variables used in Chapter 4, again using the single-equation error correction form, but employing seemingly unrelated regression. Table 5.5 reports the results of the Breusch-Pagan test for independence of the four equations. That test indicates that the equations are not independent, providing support for using the SUR systems model.

Table 5.6 presents the results of reduced form of the SUR estimation that includes only statistically significant variables, or those required for estimating the interaction terms for each of the four policy domains.[15] Appendix Table 5.A presents the results of separate OLS estimations for each of the four policy domains. Those results differ from the SUR estimation presented on Table 5.6, adding to the case for a systems estimation. Although the SUR estimation cannot tell us whether policy competition and/or logrolling affects presidential agenda building, these results do inform us that a presidential decision to place an issue on his legislative agenda is not independent of decisions concerning other issues.

in STATA, cannot handle the time series operators used here, however. Because of the theoretical interest in the short- and long-term effects of variables, and to account for time series disturbances, like cointegration, I use the sureg regression estimation.

[15] Results of the full estimation with all variables is not presented but can be obtained from the author. The substantive conclusions remain the same with their inclusion. Furthermore, the differenced form of the dependent variables, presidential requests for each of the four policy domains, indicates no unit root. The Dickey-Fuller test statistic is -14.46 for national sovereignty, -11.44 for government operations, -13.934 for international affairs, and -10.569 for domestic policy against a critical value of -3.51 at the 0.001 level.

TABLE 5.6. *Congressional, Administrative, Representational, and Partisan Impacts on the Number of Presidential Legislative Proposals by Policy Domain, 1789–2002 (Seemingly Unrelated Regression, Single-equation Error Correction Estimation)*

	Policy Domain			
Variable	Sovereignty[a]	Government Operations[a]	International Affairs[a]	Domestic Policy[a]
Dependent Variable-lag	−0.57 (0.08)***	−0.39 (0.06)***	−0.61 (0.09)***	−0.32 (0.05)***
Minority Pres.-lag			−16.22 (11.28)	
Minority Pres.-change		−2.25 (1.21)*		−24.46 (7.93)**
Term				−2.14 (8.39)
Term × Min. Pres.-lag				
Term × Min. Pres.-change				11.98 (7.48)*
Congressional Polarization-lag			17.85 (10.26)#	
Polarization × Min. Pres.-lag			32.79 (16.46)*	
Govt. Outlays % GDP-lag		0.34 (0.10)***	1.82 (0.34)***	4.91 (0.95)***
Interest Rates-lag	−0.921(0.43)*	−0.82 (0.37)*		−6.26 (1.93)**
Deficit % GDP-lag			1.39 (0.61)*	
Deficit % GDP-change				4.85 (1.62)**
Recession-lag		−3.43 (1.34)**		
Recession-change				
Republican-lag		5.02 (1.39)***		
Republican-change				−41.95 (7.87)***
Constant	12.14 (2.85)***	5.33 (2.10)**	5.78 (7.34)	24.63 (10.60)*
R^2	0.28	0.32	0.39	0.37
n	101	101	101	101

[a] Cell entries are b (SE).

*** $p < 0.001$.

** $p < 0.01$.

* $p < 0.05$.

# $p < 0.10$.

Source: Presidential Legislative Request Database.

RESULTS BY POLICY DOMAIN

Results reported on Table 5.6 reveal similarities and differences in the factors that affect presidential proposal activity for each of the four policy domains. Before turning to the cross-domain comparisons, it is useful to review the findings for each domain separately.

National Sovereignty

First, very few factors affect national sovereignty proposing. Only past levels of national sovereignty proposals and lagged interest rates affect the current number of presidential national sovereignty proposals. Recall from the analysis in the last chapter that the lagged dependent variable in estimations like this refer to the rate of error correction, that is, how quickly the dependent variable returns to its equilibrium level after a shock from an independent variable. The negative sign on the lagged dependent variable indicates that higher past levels lead to smaller changes in current submission rates, whereas lower past levels lead to increases in proposal activity. The coefficient here, -0.57, suggests that national sovereignty proposing returns to equilibrium relatively quickly.[16] Lagged interest rates also affect proposing rates for national sovereignty. Each 1% rise in interest rates reduces by one the number of national sovereignty proposals. A one-standard deviation change in lagged interest rates, about 2.1, will result in a two-proposal shift in such proposals, a fairly minor substantive effect. Comparing a change from the maximum to minimum interest rate levels (14–2.6), however, will lead to a shift of about 11.4 proposals, a somewhat more substantial impact, but an implausible shift in interest rates over a such short period.

Although a different time frame is used, the general lack of variables that predict presidential proposal activity of national sovereignty resembles Lapinski's (2008) study of congressional production of major laws, where his analysis detected only one significant variable,

---

[16] In one congress, national sovereignty proposing returns 57% of the distance back to equilibrium. In the next congress, it reverts another 28.5%, or 85.5%. With the third congress, national sovereignty proposing has returned another 14.25%, essentially reaching equilibrium at this point.

polarization, that affected law production for this domain. He found that polarization boosted national sovereignty law production for his sample of 3,500 major laws, but not for his sample of 500 major laws. Both his analysis and this analysis point to the difficulty in explaining action on national sovereignty issues.

Government Operations

A larger number of variables affects government operations proposal rates. The equilibrium rate of return here is smaller than that for national sovereignty, at −0.39.[17] There is support in this analysis for the divided government hypothesis of the congressional anticipations theory. Changing the president from majority to minority status results in 2.25 fewer legislative proposals. This is a modest increment given the range (−33 to 32) and standard deviation (8.3) of changes in government operation proposals, but the effect is statistically significant at the 0.05 level.

All of the other effects on changes in government operations proposals are lagged, that is, long-term effects. For instance, recession in the previous congress leads to 3.4 fewer presidential proposals, but there are 5 more proposals after having a Republican in office during the previous congress. Interest rates also affect changes in government operations proposals. Each one-percentage point in the interest rate in the last congress is associated with a 0.82 change in government operations proposals. Interest rates average 5.2% across the entire time period, which converts into a shift of about 4.2 presidential proposals, again a small increment. Interest rates at times can be much higher, however, nearing 14% in these data. When interest rates are at their highest (14.0), presidents will submit eleven fewer proposals, which is greater than the standard deviation in changes in government operations proposals.

Past government outlay levels also affect changes in government operations legislative submissions. Higher government outlay levels lead presidents to increase the number of government operations

[17] After four congresses, the area of government operations has reverted only 71.5% of way back to the original equilibrium.

proposals submitted to Congress. Such an effect makes sense from the administrative responsibility perspective. Government outlays indicate the size of government and the range of its ongoing policy actions. As outlays grow, the number of ongoing government activities that require the president's attention also grows. Each 1% increment in government outlays as a percentage of GDP leads to a 0.34 increase in the number of government operations proposals. For an average Congress, when government outlays equal 8.4% of GDP, the president will submit about 2.9 more government operations proposals than during the previous congress. Again, this appears to be a small effect, but in modern times, government outlays equaled a much larger fraction of GDP, 33% in the post-1945 period. At this outlay rate, the number of governmental operations proposals will rise by about eleven compared with the previous Congress.

Changes in government operations proposals appear most sensitive, first to the size of government and second to the economy. As government grows, we see presidents paying more attention to government operations, which makes much more sense from an administrative responsibility standpoint. Economic distress, in contrast, diverts presidential attention away from government operations matters.

International Affairs

Like national sovereignty, presidential attention to international affairs reverts to equilibrium quickly, in as little as three congresses.[18] Shocks to independent variables have short-term effects on presidential attention to international affairs, and the effects of those shocks evaporate quickly. Again, the quick reversion to equilibrium makes sense for international affairs, a bundle of issues that has been a presidential priority across the nation's history.

Several political factors also affect presidential attention to international affairs. First, having a minority president in the previous congress reduces the number of international affairs proposals by sixteen, slightly more than one-standard deviation in changes in international affairs proposals (14.7). This finding is consistent with the

---

[18] In the first congress, attention reverts 61%, in the second, another 30.5%, and about halfway through the third congress reverts the final 8.5% back to equilibrium.

divided government hypothesis of the congressional anticipations theory.

The interaction between minority status and congressional polarization also affects presidential international affairs submissions, but this interaction seems to offset the reduction in international affairs proposals for minority presidents. Somewhat oddly, as polarization between the congressional parties widens, minority presidents submit more international affairs proposals to Congress. Normally, we should expect wide polarization in Congress to reduce prospects for legislative enactment for minority presidents. As policy differences between the parties grow, it can be harder for presidents to find support from the opposition party, but minority presidents increase their international affairs proposal rate as congressional polarization widens. What could account for this seemingly counterintuitive effect?

First, presidents tend to receive more support from Congress for their international affairs policies than domestic initiatives, the famous "two-presidencies" thesis (e.g., Canes-Wrone, Howell, and Lewis, 2008; Cohen, 1982b; Shull, 1991; Wildavsky, 1966). Second, the combination of minority status and polarization might doom the president's domestic policy initiatives. The thin prospects for domestic policy legislation might lead presidents to substitute international affairs for domestic policy proposals or at least increase their attention to international affairs, which generally has the advantage of gaining congressional support over domestic policy. Opposition party members during periods of extreme party polarization might have difficulty resisting or denying some of the president's international affairs proposals, especially when national security is at stake and the president has public backing for those proposals. These are mere speculations at this point, requiring more research, but the finding here suggests a complex interaction among policy type, presidential aims, and the congressional context.

While the economic context does not appear to affect presidential attention to international affairs, the government fiscal context does. Large government increases presidential attention to international affairs, but deficits depress the number of international affairs proposals. Each one-percent increment in the past level for government outlays leads to 1.8 more proposals, whereas a one-percent addition to the deficit leads to 1.4 fewer international affairs proposals. A one-standard deviation increment in government outlays (8.4) results in about fifteen additional international affairs proposals, whereas a one-standard deviation increment in the deficit (3.4) leads to about five fewer international affairs proposals.

Government outlays might affect international affairs proposals for the same administrative reasons offered before – when government is larger there are just more policies that require presidential attention. International relations policies and programs, especially those concerning defense (e.g., weapons systems, troop increases and deployments), can be costly. As budget pressures ease, we find that presidents ask Congress for more legislation in the international relations domain; as deficits mount, presidents submit fewer proposals to Congress concerning international affairs.

Oddly, war does not affect presidential proposing for this policy domain, as we initially hypothesized. Even when government expenditures and surpluses (deficits) are removed from the estimation, the war variables do not reach statistical significance. It could be that presidents pursue war policies through executive means more than legislative ones, or international relations and defense matters come to the top of the national agenda irrespective of whether the nation is at war. Finally, the estimated model does not contain any variable other than war that measures the international environment. The international environment could be the major factor affecting presidential agenda activity in international affairs, but it is not captured in the models estimated here.

Domestic Policy

A large range of variables affects presidential agenda activity in domestic policy. Many of the particular results mirror those found for overall presidential requests, which is far from surprising given the impact of domestic request activity on total presidential request activity, especially in the modern era.

The small coefficient on the lagged domestic proposals variable (−0.32) indicates that domestic policy only slowly reverts to equilibrium after shocks from the other independent variables. After four congresses, presidential domestic policy proposals have traveled only 60% back toward equilibrium.[19] Shocks emanating from the independent variables do not peter out in short order but seem to affect presidential domestic policy making permanently.

Several processes could account for this dynamic property of presidential domestic policy proposals. One, presidents might respond directly to these shocks, which in turn leads to the mobilization of interests that benefit from the president's domestic policy initiatives and/or want to see those initiatives enacted, protected, and continued, or the shocks themselves might lead to the mobilization of such interests and political forces, which then motivate a presidential policy response. These interests and forces become fixtures that presidents have to pay attention to, either because a policy has been enacted or because the president sees political benefits from promoting the interest's cause.

Similar to total presidential requests, there is strong support for congressional anticipations in proposing domestic policies. The shift from a majority to a minority president depresses the number of domestic policy requests, here by about 24.5 requests, slightly more than one-half of a standard deviation unit (44.7), a substantively significant effect. Consistent with the blame game hypothesis, minority presidents during reelection congresses submit more domestic policy proposals, about twelve additional proposals.

Government finances also affect presidential domestic policy submission rates. A one-percent increment in outlays during the previous congress leads to five additional proposals. For an average congress, with outlays equal to about 8.4% of GDP, we can expect about forty-one domestic policy submissions. During the post-1945 era, when government outlays averaged close to 20% of GDP, presidents would submit an additional 100 domestic proposals to Congress. Government size strongly affects the president's domestic policy program.

So also do government deficits and surpluses affect presidential attention to domestic policy. A one-percentage-point increase in the

---

[19] This is based on the calculation, 32% first congress + 16% second congress + 8% third congress + 4% fourth congress = 60%.

deficit leads presidents to submit approximately five fewer domestic policy proposals, nearly the same magnitude effect as government outlays. Other than during major wars, deficits rarely rise above 1% of GDP.[20] Consequently the effect of deficits in the aggregate might not equal that of large government, but as deficits and large government generally go together,[21] increases in the deficit put pressures on the president to reduce the size of his domestic policy program (Light, 1991, pp. 130–131).

One economic variable, past interest rates, also affects the president's domestic policy proposals. As interest rates rise, domestic proposing declines. The effect is quite strong – a one-percentage-point increase in interest rates leads to about six fewer domestic policy proposals. Interest rates average about 5%, which produces about thirty fewer proposals at that level. At times, however, interest rates have spiked much higher than the historical average, surpassing 10% for four congresses and once reaching 14%. At these rates, the domestic component of the president's agenda would contain thirty and fifty-four fewer proposals than when interest rates are at their historical average.

Why do domestic policy proposals fall in the face of high interest rates? High interest rates are one indication of inflationary pressures.[22] Domestic policies often cost money to implement, and increases in government spending can spur on further inflation pressures. Limiting the size and scope of the domestic agenda is one way to combat inflation or at least ease inflationary expectations. Wood (2007), for instance, finds that presidential rhetoric on the economy can affect economic performance. By pursuing a smaller domestic agenda when interest rates are high, presidents might be signaling to the economy their intention to combat high interest rates and related

[20] The average deficit as a percentage of GDP is about 0.9% during peacetime and 2.4% during wartime, but it can be much higher, mostly in years immediately following war.

[21] The correlation between government outlays and deficits is 0.66 ($p < 0.000$) for all years and 0.93 ($p < 0.000$) for the post-1945 period.

[22] In these data interest rates and inflation are correlated at $r = 0.23$ ($p = 0.02$). The hypothesized positive relationship between interest rates and inflation is called the *Fisher effect*, after economist Irving Fisher, who proposed the hypothesis, and has come under much scrutiny and criticism from economists.

economic ills, such as inflation. Furthermore, when interest rates are high, the cost of money to government also rises. The government budget might be unable to afford as many additional domestic policy programs when interest rates are high.[23] These fiscal pressures could also lead presidents to scale down their domestic policy aspirations when facing a high interest rate environment.

Finally, the analysis also detects partisan differences. The change to a Republican president will lead to forty-two fewer domestic policy proposals, a substantively consequential effect. This finding comports well with our understanding of party differences, with the Republicans preferring smaller government compared with presidents of the other parties.

COMPARISONS ACROSS POLICY DOMAINS

How does presidential proposing behavior compare across the policy domains, the key question of this chapter? The first point of comparison is that each policy domain travels back toward equilibrium, but at different rates. National sovereignty and international affairs seem only temporarily perturbed by shocks to equilibrium emanating from the other independent variables. Government operations and domestic policy revert back toward equilibrium much more slowly. Shocks to these policy domains show more lasting effects on the agenda.

Second, based on the SUR analysis, presidential decisions with regard to proposals from one domain are not independent from decisions about proposals from the other domains. We cannot say whether different policies compete with each other for presidential attention, or if presidents bundle them as a logroll to secure congressional support with the type of data used here. The important point is that a decision about one proposal is not made in isolation from considerations about other proposals. In this sense, the president's legislative agenda is more than a list of preferred policies but a package of interconnected policies.

---

[23] These fiscal effects could be especially important for the post-1945 era, when deficits were the norm.

Third, congressional anticipations affect presidential proposing for three of the four policy domains, national sovereignty being the unaffected domain. Several factors might account for the lack of impact of congressional anticipations on national sovereignty proposing. One, national sovereignty issues are most important in the early, identity-forming years of a nation. Presidents might think that they have to concern themselves with such issues during these early years. In this sense, at least during the formative years of a new nation, national sovereignty issues are not discretionary. Two, presidents rarely submit a large number of national sovereignty proposals. The combination of these two properties not only limits the impact of congressional anticipations on presidential proposing in this domain, but, as the analysis showed, few variables seem to affect the number of national sovereignty proposals.

In contrast, divided government affects the number of proposals for each of the other three domains. In each case, minority presidents scale down the number of proposals, consistent with the divided government hypothesis of the congressional anticipation theory. The only difference across the three domains is that divided government affects international proposals in the long term, where divided government only has short-term effects on government operations and domestic policy proposing.

Presidents, however, seem to play blame game politics with Congress only on domestic policy. Electoral politics motivate presidents to play the blame game with Congress. Minority presidents in reelection years will submit popular proposals, expecting Congress to defeat them. Presidents can then use congressional defeat to make the case that the opposition Congress is out of step with the public, and that voters should give the president's party control of both Capitol Hill and the White House. The key to blame game politics is that defeated proposals are important and popular enough to affect voting behavior in the upcoming election. Domestic policies are more likely to fit that bill consistently than government operations and international affairs. Government operations are often technical issues, which fail to capture public attention. Although at times international affairs do capture public attention, such as during wars, much of the time international affairs is a distant and unfamiliar set of policies for many people. In addition, there are many domestic issues of interest to only small segments of the population, and thus they might not have much impact on election outcomes. Many domestic policies, however, resonate strongly with many voters *most* of the time. Presidents can easily find domestic issues with which they can play congressional blame games, and results in this chapter indicate that they do.

The results in Table 5.6 also reveal other similarities in presidential decision making across the four policy domains. One, interest rates affect decisions for three of the four domains. Other environmental factors, such as other economic indicators and war, influence either one or none of the policy areas. Somewhat remarkably, war never affects presidential attention to any of the four policy domains.

The size of government (outlays) affects three of four policy domains, suggesting that administrative responsibilities structure much presidential legislative agenda decision making, as Jones (1984) first proposed. Deficits affect attention to the two largest components of the legislative agenda, international affairs and domestic policy, implying that resources constrain the president in submitting proposals from these two policy domains.

Partisan differences arise for two policy areas, government operations and domestic policy. This is the second instance in which government operations and domestic policy seem to differ from national sovereignty and international affairs, the other being the equilibrium rate. I argued previously that national sovereignty might resemble international affairs substantively because of the inclusion of Native American policies in this domain.

CONCLUSION

Three main points emerge from the analysis in this chapter. First, it can be important to disaggregate by policy type. Descriptively we find different time paths for presidential attention across the four policy domains. Perhaps most importantly, almost all of the rise in presidential proposing in the post-World War Two era derives from social welfare policy. To a degree, modern presidents are social welfare policy presidents. The rise of the social welfare state in the United States can be partly explained by the increased attention of modern presidents to that policy cluster.

Second, unlike much of the rest of the literature on agenda building, decisions to promote one policy type are not independent of decisions about other policy types. Two processes could link agenda-building decisions across policy types – policy competition and logrolling. Policy competition suggests that agendas are finite resources. As attention to one type of policy increases, attention to other policy types will fall. Policy logrolling in agenda building suggests that the different types of policies can be packaged together and/or that some policies can ride the success coattails of other policies. More research into policy competition and logrolling is needed to better specify which policy types compete with each other and which are logrolled together, as well as the conditions that promote these two types of policy linkages.

Finally, this chapter found additional support for the congressional anticipations theory. Anticipations of success versus failure in Congress affect presidential proposals decisions for three of the four policy domains examined here, the only exception being national sovereignty issues. Blame game politics, however, seems to affect presidential proposing of domestic policy issues. Disaggregating by policy type furthered our understanding of presidential agenda building and the conditions under which anticipations of congressional action will affect the president's agenda.

TABLE 5.A. *Congressional, Administrative, Representational, and Partisan Impacts on the Number of Presidential Legislative Proposals by Policy Domain, 1789–2002 (OLS, Single-equation Error Correction Estimation)*

	Policy Domain			
Variable	Sovereignty[a]	Government Operations[a]	International Affairs[a]	Domestic Policy[a]
Dependent Variable-lag	−0.63 (0.10)***	−0.49 (0.08)***	−0.49 (0.09)***	−0.28 (0.06)***
Minority Pres.-lag			4.87 (2.57)#	
Minority Pres.-change				−14.22 (6.67)*
Govt. Outlays % GDP-lag	0.30 (0.16)*	0.63 (0.16)***	1.32 (0.31)***	4.94 (1.14)***
Interest Rates-lag	−1.80 (0.52)***	−1.11 (0.40)**		−6.28 (2.10)**
Deficit % GDP-lag	0.87 (0.39)*	0.72 (0.32)*	1.39 (0.64)*	5.60 (2.04)**
Deficit % GDP-change	0.67 (0.30)*		1.27 (0.42)**	
Recession-lag	−8.00 (2.57)**	−4.62 (1.64)**		
Recession-change	−5.83 (1.96)**			
Republican-lag	4.47 (2.11)*	5.31 (1.68)**		
Republican-change				−40.96 (9.76)***
Constant	18.58 (3.50)***	6.78 (2.26)***	6.12 (2.19)**	21.68 (10.29)*
R^2 / Adj. R^2	0.40 / 0.35	0.34 / 0.30	0.37 / 0.33	0.39 / 0.32
Breusch-Godfrey LM-lag 1[b]	0.14 (.70)	1.22 (0.27)	0.98 (0.32)	0.39 (0.54)
Breusch-Godfrey LM-lag 2[b]	0.77 (0.68)	1.59 (0.45)	1.24 (0.54)	1.78 (0.41)
Breusch-Godfrey LM-lag 3[b]	0.78 (0.86)	4.66 (0.20)	1.37 (0.71)	1.81 (0.61)
Breusch-Godfrey LM-lag 4[b]	0.88 (0.93)	4.78 (0.31)	3.18 (0.53)	4.99 (0.29)
n	101	101	104	101

[a] Cell entries are b (SE).
[b] Cell entries for Breusch-Godfrey LM test are chi-square and p-value.
*** $p < 0.001$.
** $p < 0.01$.
* $p < 0.05$.
# $p < 0.10$.

Source: Presidential Legislative Request Database.

CHAPTER 6

Divided Government and Presidential Policy Moderation

The November 2010 midterms handed congressional Democrats and President Barack Obama a sound electoral defeat. House Republicans gained 63 seats, enough to assume control of the next Congress, whereas the Democratic majority in the Senate fell from 57 to 53. Somewhat surprisingly, the lame duck interregnum from the election to the convening of the new Congress in January 2011 produced a flurry of major legislation, much of it promoted and supported by the president.

Why was the 111th Congress so legislatively productive after the election results came in, especially with a new partisan majority that would assume control of the House in the next Congress? One possibility is that the outgoing Democrats in Congress viewed November and December 2010 as their last chance to forge legislation to their liking before the 112th Congress took session. Republicans in the 111th Senate had enough votes to stymie legislative progress to the end of the session by filibustering, however, and presidential veto threats could not force recalcitrant Republicans to produce legislation given the short time span until the new Congress convened.

One resolution of this puzzle of unexpected congressional productivity is that Barack Obama moved to the center, which allowed Republicans to get essentially the same policy outputs that they would have received had they waited for the 112th Congress to begin. In addition, both parties may have seen advantages to quick legislative action, especially on the tax cut bill passed and signed in mid-December, 2010.

The 2010 tax cuts provide a good case for illustrating these themes. Passing tax legislation was pressing because the Bush tax cuts, originally enacted in 2001, were set to expire in 2010. If these cuts were allowed to expire, all taxpayers would see federal income tax increases for 2011. Two advantages would accrue to both parties if Congress passed a tax bill before the year's end. First, the economy, already mired in a deep recession, appeared to be softening. Allowing the Bush tax cuts to expire could harm the economy. Second, if tax cuts were delayed, either party could potentially be blamed for playing politics instead of being concerned with the economy. Republicans were more exposed on this front than Democrats, because the GOP seemingly had an incentive to wait until the next Congress, when its legislative position would be strengthened.

Also important was Barack Obama's move to the center on the tax bill in the wake of the election results. The president characterized the midterm losses his party suffered as a "shellacking" the day after the results and vowed to cooperate with Republicans in fashioning tax cut legislation (Baker and Hulse, November 3, 2010). Throughout Obama's presidency, tax policy differences between the president and Democrats with the Republicans were wide and deep, especially over the tax rate for high earners.

As enacted in 2001, the Bush tax package cut the income tax rate for high earners more sharply than it did for middle- and low-income earners. Critics charged that too much benefit went to the rich and that such tax policy added to the growth in long-term economic inequality. Economic inequality did widen during the Bush years in office, leading Obama and the Democrats to run in 2008 on a plank to repeal the high-earner tax cuts, to make the rich pay more, their "fair share." With the Bush taxes about to expire in 2010, Obama and the Democrats saw an opportunity to implement their tax program merely by letting the Bush tax rates expire, reverting to the tax rates of the Clinton years. Between the November election results and mid-December, however, Obama and the Democrats caved in to the Republican demand to extend all the Bush tax rates for two more years (Herszenhorn, December 17, 2010). Majorities in both parties supported the extension in both chambers. In the House,

138 Republicans and 139 Democrats voted for the extension; only 36 Republicans and 112 Democrats opposed it. In the Senate, thirteen Democrats, one Independent, and five Republicans opposed the bill, with forty-four Democrats, one Independent, and thirty-six Republicans supporting it.

From the vantage point of this research, the tax bill of 2010 illustrates the impact of divided government on presidential policy making. In this case, the prospect of divided government might have forced the president's hand even before the opposition party had come to congressional power. As the theory of congressional anticipations hypothesizes, presidents can moderate their policy positions in the face of divided government, the policy moderation hypothesis. Obama moderated his policy stance on tax policy in late 2010 by moving toward the Republican position on taxes. In fact, we can argue that he essentially allowed the critical Republican position on taxes to stand, the extension of tax cuts to all earners, and he did so before divided government would take effect.

Still, the 2010 tax bill provides us with merely an illustration of divided government-policy moderation dynamics. This chapter tests this hypothesis more systematically. Do presidents moderate when confronted with divided government, or is the 2010 tax bill an exceptional case, perhaps a function of stakes involved and the depth of the recession? In this chapter, I also test the policy moderation hypothesis against a strong theoretical rival, which looks at the impact of the party nomination reforms of the 1970s on the presidential policy making. Some argue that the nomination reforms of the 1970s contributed to the growth of party polarization witnessed over the last third of the twentieth century. That perspective suggests that just as the reforms polarized party and congressional politics, they should have also polarized the presidency, such that Democratic presidents will take decidedly liberal policy positions and Republicans will take decidedly conservative ones.

This chapter differs from the previous chapters with regard to data used to measure presidential policy extremism versus moderation. No methodology yet exists for locating a presidential proposal, like the data used in the previous chapters, in a policy space. Existing methodologies rely on roll call vote distributions, such as for Congress or the Supreme Court, where voting patterns of individuals across votes and across sessions can be compared. With each presidential proposal for legislation being essentially one vote, the president's, we have no way to compare how liberal versus conservative two proposals are, much less comparing the liberalness of proposals across presidents.[1]

We can, however, take advantage of voting alignments on proposals that receive congressional roll calls, as a large literature using a variety of techniques has done. By knowing the policy leanings of members of Congress who vote for or against the president, we have some knowledge of the liberal/conservative support for presidential proposals. Even this is a laborious process for scaling all presidential proposals for which we have votes.

Hence the analysis in this chapter relies on readily available indicators of presidential roll call liberalism. These series, such as the American for Democratic Action (ADA) liberal support score, exist only since the end of the Second World War, which further limits the temporal scope of the analysis in this chapter. Plus, these indicators do not distinguish between presidential positions on roll calls that come from the president's agenda (proposals) and those not from the president's agenda, but from members of Congress, on-agenda versus off-agenda roll calls (Covington, Wrighton, and Kinney, 1995). The divided government-policy moderation hypothesis should not be specific to on-agenda rolls. Based on that hypothesis, presidents facing divided government should also be inclined to take moderate positions on off-agenda roll calls, just as they will moderate their on-agenda proposals.

The next section of this chapter lays out the party reform thesis, following by the logic of the divided government-policy moderation hypothesis. Then I present the data and the results of the analysis. Foreshadowing the results, we find support for the divided government-policy moderation hypothesis, adding to the support already detected for the theory of congressional anticipations.

---

[1] Wood (2009a) develops a methodology to assess presidential liberalism from their policy rhetoric, but policy rhetoric and policy proposing are not the same, however related they may be.

PARTY ACTIVISTS AND PRESIDENTIAL POLICY EXTREMISM

Many studies contend that party activists were important catalysts of the heightened party polarization of the last third of the twentieth century and first decade of the twenty-first (Aldrich, 1995; Aldrich and Rohde, 2001; Fiorina et al., 2005; Jacobson, 2000; Layman, Carsey, and Horowitz, 2006; Layman et al., 2010; King, 1997, 2003; Saunders and Abramowitz, 2004; Shafer, 2003). Here it is useful to conceptualize party activists broadly to include those who work in candidate campaigns, financially contribute to candidates and the parties, and attend the national conventions, as well as interest groups that seek to influence the nomination and election of candidates for office.

Party activists could stimulate polarization for several reasons. One, they hold relatively extreme policy views compared to voters and rank-and-file members of parties. Two, they play a critical role in selecting the parties' candidates for office, especially in the post-reform era since the early to mid-1970s. Three, they provide considerable resources for candidates' primary and general election contests. Thus, in the era of party activist influence, candidates for office and office holders will either resemble the policy extremism of activists or be policy responsive to their views, repaying activists for their vital electoral support and/or trying to secure their support in the upcoming election.

The reforms of the early to mid-1970s heightened the influence of activists on their respective parties, which had several consequences. One consequence of the reforms was to replace party caucuses and other devices with primaries for nominating candidates. As a result, party activists supplanted traditional party leaders in selecting the parties' nominees. Owing to their critical role in the primary and nomination process (Cohen et al., 2008), activists became critical gatekeepers, ensuring that the party's nominees would reflect the activist strata's policy preferences. This in turn pushed the parties' nominees and office holders toward the policy extremes.[2] As the influence of activists within the parties grew, the Democratic Party moved to the left and the Republican Party to the right.

[2] Several studies document the influence of party activists on the policy stances of candidates since the reforms of the mid-1970s. See Masket (2007) and Miller and Schofield (2003).

The reforms of the presidential selection process in the 1970s exposed the presidency to the newfound influence of party activists. By this account, presidents and presidential aspirants accommodated to the growing influence of party activists within their parties through selection and/or conversion-adaptation effects. Selection effects mean that as party activists became increasingly important in the nomination process, politically extreme candidates would be more likely to win the nomination than moderates. Conversion-adaptation effects mean that aspirants for the nomination would move to the political extremes to gain the support of the party activists. Mitt Romney's move to the right in the 2008 Republican presidential nomination contest illustrates this conversion-adaptation process.

The motivation for office, including renomination, links the nomination and election processes to governing, thus affecting the policy positions that presidents take. Presidents' policy positions in office affect their ability to be renominated. Taking positions at variance with the preferences of the party activists might undermine their chances for renomination. No president seeking renomination has been denied it since the reforms of the mid-1970s, perhaps an indication that presidents cater to their party activists. The lukewarm (if not cold) reception that John McCain received in 2008 among conservative Republican Party activists also illustrates the linkage between governing and nomination-election politics.[3] Second-term presidents also have an incentive to accommodate these party activists, even though they cannot run for the presidency again. By maintaining their "extreme" policy credentials, they ensure some ability to influence whom the party selects as their successor, which could be important for the president's legacy.

This party activist perspective leads to the hypothesis that presidents of the party reform era should be more policy extreme than presidents prior to those reforms. Furthermore, presidents and presidential candidates should become increasingly extreme as party activist polarization has grown from the mid-1970s to the present. Layman et al.

---

[3] In 1980 many Democrats thought that Jimmy Carter was too moderate, and liberal stalwart Senator Edward Kennedy challenged him for the nomination that year, a suggestion of the implication of a president who bucks the activists in the post-reform era.

(2010) find that party activists have increasingly polarized on ideological and policy grounds over the past thirty years. Based on this perspective, we should see presidents becoming more extreme since the party reforms of the 1970s.

One relevant issue is the speed with which the reforms led to activist influence in their parties. In the analysis that follows, I initially assume relatively immediate effects of the reforms on activist influence. Because the major reforms were implemented before the 1976 election, I first use this as a marker to distinguish the pre-reform from the post-reform era. Data on polarization, for instance, the Poole-Rosenthal DW-Nominate scores for Congress, suggest that the uptick in polarization did not begin in earnest until the late 1970s, however, and it is not until the mid-1980s that appreciable levels of polarization become evident. The data collected by Layman et al. (2010) on party activists suggest a steadier increase in polarization across the 1970s, but it is not until the mid-1980s that their data suggest much polarization between the parties. Thus, the analysis also uses other cut-points (1980/1981 and 1984/1985) to distinguish the pre- from the post-reform era. Using these later cutpoints, however, also attenuates the connection between the implementation of the party reforms and presidential behavior.

CONGRESSIONAL ANTICIPATIONS, DIVIDED GOVERNMENT, AND PRESIDENTIAL POLICY MODERATION

Chapters 4 and 5 tested and found support for two hypotheses of the theory of congressional anticipations, the divided government-size of the agenda and the presidential blame game hypotheses. The theory of congressional anticipations argues that expectations about eventual success with Congress will affect whether the president submits a proposal to Congress for legislative consideration. When prospects for enactment appear slim, the president will refrain from submitting the proposal. Presidents can also modify their proposal, however, making it more appealing to Congress. By modifying a proposal, a president can improve the likelihood that Congress will enact it. Because support for the president is lower under divided than united government, presidents will find a greater need to modify their proposals during divided than united government. This leads to the hypothesis that presidents will be more moderate during divided than united government.

Polarization between the parties could condition how much minority presidents will moderate their policy stance. To understand the possible implications of polarization on presidential moderation during divided government, assume that we can locate a president's and a pivotal congressional member's preferred policy in a unidimensional liberal-conservative policy space. Let us also define the pivot as the member of Congress whose support the president needs for a policy proposal to pass.[4]

Define the president's utility, U, for a policy as a function of two distances, 1) the distance from the president's preferred policy and pivotal member of Congress, either the median from the president's party or the opposition party, whichever party is in the majority; and 2) the policy distance between the medians of both parties. Also assume that utility declines as distances from preferred positions increase. The president faces an optimization problem, constrained by the preferences of the pivotal member of Congress as well as his party's median member.

Why should the president care about his party median when all it takes is a compromise with the congressional pivot to pass a policy? Disregard instances when a president needs voters from his party for his policy to be enacted. Even when the president does not need his party's support for passage, he still will take into account the preferences of his party. Members of the president's party might rebel if the president cohabits too often with the opposition. Disgruntled members of his party might even try to deny him renomination for a second term. The president could also harm his party's reputation with the public if it cannot share in the credit for policy enactment. Harming the party's image with voters might undermine the election chances of candidates for office of the party. By working with the opposition and

---

[4] Considerable controversy in the literature on congressional policy making surrounds the identification of this pivot, whether the pivot is the median member of the chamber (Krehbiel, 1998) or the party majority median, or some other member (Smith, 2007). We need not enter this debate. Whether the pivot is the chamber or party median generates the same basic hypotheses.

Panel A: President's Party is in the Majority.

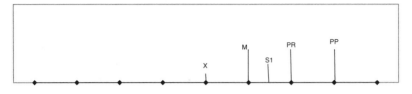

Panel B: President's Party is in the Minority.

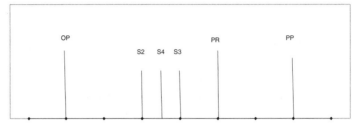

Figure 6.1. Presidential Policy Choice under Majority versus Minority Status and Different Degrees of Party Polarization.

not his own party in building policy, the president also could allow the opposition party to gain a reputation for governance, responsibility, and bipartisanship, which could further undermine the president's party in upcoming elections. Thus, presidents will take into account their own party's preferences in making policy, even when they do not need their votes for passage.

Figure 6.1 presents several schematics that help to illustrate policy behavior under four conditions, when the president's party is in the majority or minority and polarization is either high or low: 1) Majority-Low Polarization, 2) Majority-High Polarization, 3) Minority-Low Polarization, and 4) Minority-High Polarization. As we shall see, the policy dynamics for situations 1 and 2 wind up being the same – when the president's party controls Congress, polarization does not factor into policy making.

Figure 6.1, Panel A presents the case when the president's party is in the majority. On that figure, M represents the pivotal member of Congress, PR is the president's preferred policy position, PP is the president's party policy position, and X the opposition party median. When the president's party is in the majority, by definition, the congressional pivot will be in the president's party. In this case, the president will negotiate with the pivotal member, M, settling on a policy, S1, the midpoint between their positions. If the congressional pivot happens also to be the presidential party median, that is M = PP, then the midpoint between PR and PP (not shown) is the policy result. Notice that X, the minority party median, does not enter into policy production under majority government in this model, but also notice that by definition X is farther from the president's position than M, a point that becomes more important later on when considering policy production under minority government.

In this example, M stands to the left of the president. The president moderates slightly to S1, but if M were to the right of the president, then the president would become more extreme, moving to the right and away from the center. With majority rule, whether the president moderates or becomes more extreme depends on his position relative to that of his party. The more important point, however, is that presidents need move only a slight distance under majority rule compared with minority rule. For instance, assume the opposition party controls Congress and the congressional pivot becomes X instead of M. The midpoint between PR and X will be further to the left of S1; presidents will moderate more under divided than united government, all else being equal.

All else, however, is not equal, and the model suggests that presidents take into account the preferences of their party when making policy. Figure 6.1, Panel B illustrates these dynamics, but now OP stands for the opposition party median. First, consider the case when there is no polarization between the parties, but the opposition party controls Congress. Although unrealistic, this baseline helps to illustrate the dynamics involved, especially the interaction between polarization and minority status on policy production. On Figure 6.1 Panel B, this would mean that OP = PP, that is, that both parties have the same policy preferences. The policy midpoint between the president, PR, and the opposition party median, OP, becomes S2.

Now assume a high degree of party polarization, with the median for the president's party located at PP. The policy midpoint between the president's party and the opposition majority party is S3, to the right of S2, the solution with no polarization. When polarization between the parties exists under minority rule, presidents must take into account the policy preferences of both the majority opposition and the minority presidential party; that is, the president must find some compromise between S2 and S3. On the figure, S4 represents that new policy solution. Notably that solution is to the right of S2; that is, presidents move a shorter distance to S4 than S2. Under minority government, polarization constrains the distance that presidents will move toward the opposition. Presidents will moderate less under minority government in the presence of high versus low levels of party polarization. Party polarization is not relevant when the president's party controls Congress, because the president has to negotiate with only his own party; polarization between the parties does not affect that negotiation. This model leads to two hypotheses:

> *H1*: Presidents will be more moderate during divided than united government.
>
> *H2*: Presidential will moderate less during divided government as polarization between the parties increases.

DATA

Testing the party activist and congressional context theories of presidential policy choice requires measuring the degree of moderation versus extremism in presidential policy positions. We also would like data spanning the more polarized present era, as well as times characterized with lower levels of polarization, such as the 1950s to the early 1970s. There are three relevant data series available for us to use: ADA scores, Poole and Rosenthal's DW-Nominate scores, and ideal point estimates. Because each has its own recommendations and pitfalls, the analysis that follows uses several measures.[5]

---

[5] There are two other major attempts at coding presidential policy stances, but both rely on rhetoric, not roll calls. Cohen (1997) coded each sentence in presidential State of the Union Addresses (SUA) from 1953 through 1989 for liberal-conservative direction. For present purposes there are several limitations to Cohen's measure. One, it ends in 1989, and thus misses the extreme polarization of the post-1989 years. Two, the SUA misses all presidential positions taken throughout the year but not mentioned in the SUA. Second, building upon Cohen, Wood (2009a) content analyzes all presidential rhetoric from 1945 to 2005. Wood's series, however, although positively correlated with the three roll call measures, is only significantly associated with one, the adjusted ADA scores. Presidential rhetoric and roll call stances may differ for several reasons. Presidents can take many more rhetorical

Kenny and Lotfina (2005), updating Zupan (1992), calculate presidential liberalism by using presidential positions on ADA votes with a series that extends from 1947, the first year that ADA selected key votes, through 2000. There are well-known issues with using ADA roll calls for creating a comparable time series, primarily agenda composition effects, in which the votes/issue across years are not comparable. Because of this problem, Groseclose, Levitt, and Snyder (1999) have developed a method to adjust the ADA scores across time to provide temporal comparability. The analysis below uses these ADA scores, adjusted as Groseclose et al. (1999) recommend, following the Kenny-Lotfina (2005) procedure by averaging the ADA presidential scores for the House and Senate. Anderson and Habel (2009) bring the conversion scores up to date.[6]

Second, Poole and Rosenthal have calculated DW-Nominate scores for presidents. The DW-Nominate scores are well known and well studied, especially for Congress. DW-Nominate scores for presidents are calculated based on all positions that the president took while in office and thus cannot vary over time for an individual person. At most therefore we would be able to compare only presidents, and not whether an individual president's policy position shifts during his time in office. Third, Bailey (2007) has calculated ideal point estimates for presidents, as well as the House, Senate, and the Supreme Court for 1951 to 2002.[7] Bailey's ideal point estimates are calculated for each year, allowing us an intra-administration dynamic perspective that the DW-Nominate scores do not allow.

---

positions and have greater freedom in selecting what to speak about than is the case for roll call measures. But as our concern is with presidential positions vis-à-vis Congress, the impact of the congressional context on presidential policy positions, the roll call-based measures are more appropriate for our needs than the rhetorical ones.

[6] Still, caution is in order in using the ADA data. Ragsdale (1998, pp. 410–411) presents her own ADA series for 1960 through 1996, which is in several instances quite discrepant compared to the Zupan-Kenny-Lotfina (ZKL) scores. For example, in 1970 Ragsdale gives Nixon an ADA score of 50 compared to 16 for ZKL. Again in 1967, Ragsdale gives LBJ a 90 to 56 by ZKL, and in 1966, Ragsdale gives LBJ a 90 to 75 by ZKL. Of the years of overlap between the two series, 34, only 13 years have identical scores, usually when the president scored either a 100 or a 0. Although it is unclear as to the source of these discrepancies, it may be that ZKL do not count presidential absences in their calculations, but Ragsdale does.

[7] Accessed from: http://www9.georgetown.edu/faculty/baileyma/.

The analysis below uses all three of these measures, the adjusted ADA scores, the DW-Nominate scores, and the ideal point estimates, to ensure that the findings are not a result of different measurement strategies. I folded each series at their "midpoints" to create the three presidential extremism variables. This entails taking the absolute value of each case from either the natural midpoint or a calculated mean for the entire series. The natural midpoint for the Bailey ideal point estimates and DW-Nominate scores is 0. For the adjusted ADA scores, I use the actual mean of the series as the midpoint (45.6).[8] Despite differences in underlying assumptions and calculation methodologies, all three measures of presidential extremism are significantly correlated with each other, with correlations ranging from 0.45 to 0.72.[9]

Figure 6.2 plots the three series. Because each series employs a different metric, the plot uses their z-scores. Small z-scores (negative values) indicate moderate presidents, whereas large z-scores (positive values) indicate extreme presidents. A z-score of 0 indicates average presidential extremism in the series. The first notable point is that in general the series travel together, although on occasion we can also see some notable divergences. For instance, the ADA score gives LBJ a moderate score in 1967, but the ideal point estimate suggests strong extremism.

Although it is hard to discern visually any distinct temporal trends in these data, each series hints at greater extremism for post-reform than pre-reform presidents. Table 6.1 presents some descriptive statistics for the three series comparing pre-reform and post-reform presidents using these years to define the two eras: pre-reform (1951–1976) and post-reform (1977–2002). In each case, post-reform presidents exhibit on average greater extremism than pre-reform presidents, but each series also indicates within-era variance. Relatively moderate and extreme presidents served in each era.

---

[8] For unadjusted ADA scores the "natural midpoint" would be 50, indicating that a president votes with the ADA 50%; the variable can range from 0% to 100%. Using 50 for the adjusted scores makes little sense because a value in one year is not comparable to the same value in another year. Thus, I use the actual mean to locate the midpoint for creating the folded variable.

[9] The correlation between the ADA score and the DW-Nominate is 0.72 ($p < 0.001$) and 0.45 ($p < 0.001$), and 0.56 ($p < 0.001$) between the DW-Nominate and ideal point estimates.

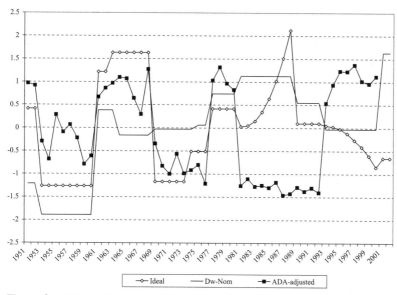

Figure 6.2. Three Measures of Presidential Policy Extremism 1951–2002: z-scores.

TABLE 6.1. *Descriptive Statistics for Three Measures of Presidential Extremism, 1951–2002*

Years	Variable	n	Mean	sd	Min.	Max.
All	Ideal Points	52	0.77	0.41	0.25	1.64
	DW-Nom.	52	0.53	0.19	0.17	0.83
	ADA	50	32.30	12.66	2.42	51.02
1951–1976	Ideal Points	26	0.70	0.51	0.25	1.44
	DW-Nom.	26	0.40	0.17	0.17	0.60
	ADA	26	25.30	11.51	2.42	44.57
1977–2002	Ideal Points	26	0.84	0.27	0.42	1.64
	DW-Nom.	26	0.65	0.10	0.52	0.83
	ADA	24	41.06	7.62	18.77	51.02

For ideal point estimates, see Michael A. Bailey's Web page:
    http://www9.georgetown.edu/faculty/baileyma.
For presidential DW-Nominate scores see Keith Poole's nominate Web page:
    http://voteview.com/dwnl.htm.
For the ADA scores see Kenny-Lotfina (2005), corrected using Anderson and Habel (2009).
Source: See text for details.

TABLE 6.2. *Dickey-Fuller Unit Root Tests for Variables Included in the Analysis*

Variable	Levels	Changes
President Ideal Points	−2.51*	−7.08
President DW-Nominate	−1.41*	−7.04
President ADA	−3.81	−11.81
Divided Government	−3.10*	−6.95
Party Polarization	1.49*	−8.45
Interaction of Divided Government and Party Polarization	−2.64*	−6.97
Pre-Post Reform Dummy	−0.98*	−7.07
Reform Era Counter	8.17*	−1.00*
Public Mood-folded	−4.04	−8.94
Critical Value at 0.01	−3.58	−3.58

* Indicates nonstationary at .01 level.
Source: See text for details.

ANALYSIS ISSUES

Before we proceed to the estimation, diagnostics revealed nonstationarity in the presidential extremism series' (Table 6.2).[10] First differencing produces stationary series. Also, as some of the independent variables also display nonstationarity, I again use a single-equation error correction model (ECM).

To test the party activist hypotheses, I use a pre-post reform dummy, coded 0 for 1951–1976 = 0 and 1 for 1977–2002, and a counter, coded 1951–1976 = 0 and 1977 to 2002 is a counter with 1977 = 1 up to 2002 = 26. The dummy tests whether post-reform presidents are more extreme than pre-reform presidents, and the counter tests whether extremism among presidents has grown during the post-reform era. The estimation uses only the lagged form of these variables. Differencing them leads to variables equal to 1 when there is the shift from pre- to post-reform, with 0 for all other cases. The party activist theory leads to the expectation of positive and statistically significant coefficients for the period dummy and counter.

To test divided government-moderation hypotheses, I use a dummy for divided government, coded 1 if the opposition party controls at least one house and 0 for united government. I measure the degree of

---

[10] The augmented Dickey-Fuller statistic for the ADA series, with one-lag, a trend, and constant is also nonstationary (statistic = −3.35, with a critical value of −4.15).

polarization with the absolute value of the difference in DW-Nominate scores for the median member of the two parties in each chamber, using the average distance for the two chambers. The interaction of divided government and polarization multiplies these two variables. Under united government, the interaction equals 0 but takes the party polarization value with divided government. The model developed earlier suggests a negative effect for divided government; that is, presidents will moderate under divided government. Polarization will be positively associated with extremism, and the interaction term will have a positive sign. Finally, the estimation includes a control for Stimson's public mood variable. As the mood variable ranges from conservative to liberal, I also fold it, using the numerical mean of the series as the midpoint (58.2).[11]

One disadvantage of single-equation ECM models is that they can eat up degrees of freedom quite quickly. This might be a problem for the full ECM estimations here, where we have fifty or fifty-two cases and eleven variables. Secondly, there is a hint of multicollinearity between the differenced and levels form of the congressional variables, especially the divided government and interaction variables. Thus, I ran several different estimations, one set using all variables, another set using only the differenced form of the congressional variables, and a third set employing only the lagged form of those variables. I did the same for the public mood variable. In all cases, the differenced form of the congressional and mood variables was a stronger predictor than the lagged form of those variables. In fact, the lagged forms never get close to being statistically significant, even in estimations without the differenced variables. Hence I show only the results for the differenced variables, excluding the lagged variables.

RESULTS

Table 6.3 presents results of the estimations for each presidential extremism measure. Analysis of residuals finds that all are white noise. Despite the modest number of variables included, each estimation

---

[11] There is one issue in using the folded mood variable. It is possible for the public to be extreme in the opposite direction from the president. Thus, I also ran the analysis using the unfolded mood variable. The unfolded mood variable never reaches statistical significance, but the folded one does, as reported later.

TABLE 6.3. *Impact of Party Activists, Congressional Context, and Public Mood on Presidential Policy Extremism, 1951–2002*

	Presidential Policy Measure					
	Ideal Points		DW-Nominate		Adjusted ADA	
	b (SE)	t	b (SE)	t	b (SE)	t
Dep. Var.-Lag	−0.17* (0.08)	−1.96	0.91*** (0.09)	10.68	−0.54*** (0.14)	−3.76
Divided-change	−1.46* (0.64)	−2.28	−0.34[+] (0.22)	−1.54	−55.27* (26.43)	−2.09
Polarization-change	1.26 (2.16)	0.58	0.55 (0.75)	0.74	30.86 (90.47)	0.34
Interaction-change	1.91* (1.05)	1.82	0.52[+] (0.37)	1.43	99.26* (43.62)	2.28
Mood-lag	0.03* (0.02)	1.74	0.01* (0.006)	2.05	2.01* (0.82)	2.45
Pre-Post Reform Dummy-lag	0.12 (0.11)	1.10	−0.001 (0.05)	−0.02	9.72* (5.10)	1.90
Pre-Post Reform Counter-lag	−0.01 (0.01)	−1.61	0.0002 (0.002)	0.07	−0.20 (0.29)	−0.67
Constant	0.12 (0.07)	1.59	0.05 (0.04)	1.35	13.63 (3.92)	3.48
R^2/Adj. R^2	0.48	0.40	0.85	0.83	0.54	0.46
n	50		50		48	
Breusch-Godfrey LM-lags 4/Prob. χ^2	2.10	0.72	3.58	0.53	1.02	0.91

*** $p < 0.001$, ** $p < 0.01$, * $p < 0.05$, [+] $p < 0.10$.

accounts for a considerable amount of the variance in presidential policy extremism, 40% for the ideal point measure, nearly one-half for the adjusted ADA scores, and more than 80% in the case of the DW-Nominate measure. The lagged dependent variable is the major factor accounting for the DW-Nominate variance. The large coefficient for the lagged DW-Nominate variable also indicates its predictive strength. As a consequence of the lagged dependent variable, the other independent variables do not emerge as strong as they do for the ideal point and ADA measures, but the DW-Nominate measure might be the weakest one for these purposes, because it does not vary across congresses, only across presidents.

Overall, these results provide little support for the party activist theory. In only one case, ADA scores, is the pre-post reform dummy significant. That coefficient indicates a nearly 10% increase in presidential extremism in the post-reform compared with the pre-reform era. For two of three cases, the post-reform counter actually has the wrong sign, although they do not attain statistical significance.

In contrast, analysis provides more support for the divided government-party polarization hypothesis. The divided government variable is properly signed for all three measures and is statistically significant at the 0.05 level for the ideal point and ADA measures. For the DW-Nominate indicator, the divided government dummy only reaches a significance level of 0.10, not quite significant using the conventional 0.05, but perhaps close enough to warrant some attention. Turning to substantive implications, using the ADA measure, shifting from united to divided government results in presidents being 55% less extreme, about the difference between the least and most extreme presidents. Divided government has similar effects using the ideal point measure, reducing presidential extremism by 1.46, which again is about the difference between the least and most extreme presidents. Even for the DW-Nominate measure, divided government reduces extremism by 0.34 units, or about 40% of the range between the least and most extreme presidents.

Polarization by itself has no significant effect on presidential extreme once the interaction between divided government and polarization is controlled for, as predicted. The interaction term is significant for the ADA and ideal point measures, however, whereas for the DW-Nominate scores, it just misses, at $p < 0.10$. For the ADA score, a one-standard deviation shift in polarization, about 0.10, is associated with approximately a 10-point rise in extremism. A more useful comparison is between very low (0.47) and very high polarization (0.87), capturing the full effects of the rise of polarization the past several decades. Using this comparison, presidents will be 40% more extreme during periods of highest versus lowest polarization, offsetting most of the effect of divided government. A president during both high polarization and divided government will moderate only about 15%. Substantively the results are similar when inspecting the ideal point measure, and although not as potent using the

DW-nominate measure, the interaction between divided government and high polarization undercuts most of the moderating influence of divided government alone. These results point to strong support for the congressional context theory.

The public mood always affects presidential extremism. Presidents become more extreme as the public does. This finding varies with Wood (2009a), who found that presidential rhetorical liberalism does not respond to public liberalism. The difference here might be in the measures of presidential policy, with Wood using a rhetorically based measure and the measures here relying on congressional roll calls. Despite the statistically significant impact of public mood on presidential extremism, however, the substantive effects appear marginal, swamped by the congressional effects. If we use the ADA scores, a maximum shift in the public mood of about 6% leads to approximately a 12% shift in presidential extremism. Rarely does the public mood swing so much from year to year. Only in 4 of the 50 years here does it move more than 3 points. A one-standard deviation shift in public mood, about 2 points, results in a 4% shift in presidential extreme, a substantively modest impact.

Finally, there is the issue of the timing of the reform effects. The pre-post variables with 1976/1977 as the cutpoints suggest a nearly immediate or speedy effect of the reforms on the influence of party activists, to which presidents also respond quickly. There might be a lag between the implementation of the electoral reforms of the 1970s and party activist realization of increased influence. To test for this possibility, I experimented with two alternatives for the pre-post reform dummy and counters by using 1980/1981 and 1984/1985 as the cutpoints. Substituting 1980/1981 cutpoints finds that these new variables perform nearly identically to the original variables, except for minor differences in the size of coefficients and standard errors. For the ideal point and DW-Nominate measures, again the 1984/1985 cutpoint variables work similarly to the original ones. For the adjusted ADA scores, however, the size and significance of the coefficient grow somewhat ($b = 0.76$, SE $= 0.21$, $t = 3.60$, $p = 0.001$). The counter variable now attains statistical significance but points in the wrong direction ($b = -1.22$, SE $= 0.45$, $t = -2.69$, $p = 0.010$).

Most important for this analysis is that the divided government and polarization variables maintain their impact on presidential extremism in the face of controls for the public mood. In contrast, the party activist perspective receives much less, and only scattered support. The congressional context, as the theory of congressional anticipations argues, looms large in presidential policy choice.

CONCLUSION

This chapter adds support for the theory of congressional anticipations. That theory argues that presidents care whether they win or lose before Congress. Consequently they will adjust their legislative agendas to maximize legislative success. Presidents allow themselves to be defeated only when they can use those defeats for other ends, such as reelection for divided government presidents. Presidents can avoid congressional defeat in essentially two ways, by withholding proposals that appear destined for defeat or by modifying proposals to align more closely to congressional policy preferences. Chapters 4 and 5 focus on the first of these behaviors. Consistent with the divided government hypothesis, those chapters found smaller presidential agendas during divided than united government, except during reelection years, the latter consistent with the presidential blame game hypothesis.

This chapter turned to the second behavior, modifying presidential proposals. The logic of the theory of congressional anticipations suggests that presidents are more likely to moderate their agenda and policy positions under divided than united government. Analysis in this chapter provides support for this hypothesis but also finds that polarization affects the degree to which presidents modify their policy positioning. Minority government presidents moderate less when polarization between the parties is wide rather than narrow.

Chapters 4 to 6 round out the empirical tests of the theory of congressional anticipations on presidential agenda building and position taking. That theory has implications for the sources of presidential success in Congress as well, the topic of the next chapter.

CHAPTER 7

From the White House to Capitol Hill

The Congressional Fate of the President's Legislative Proposals

The president's greatest influence over policy comes from the agenda he pursues and the way it is packaged.

  Jon R. Bond and Richard Fleisher, *The President in the Legislative Arena*, 1990, p. 230

To interpret Bond and Fleisher's famous quote, we ask what in particular is it about the president's agenda and the way that it is packaged that provides presidents with policy influence. This book is an attempt to better specify the factors that affect presidential agenda building and how that decision process affects presidential success with Congress. Recognizing that the presidential agenda-building process is complex and multifaceted, I have focused deeply on how the congressional environment influences presidential agenda building. I start with a simple proposition, that presidents want to win in Congress and avoid defeat. The congressional environment, especially whether their party controls Congress, provides presidents with useful information about how receptive Congress is to their legislative proposals. In general, Congress is more receptive and open to the president's proposals when his party is in control than when the opposition's party is in control.

  Expectations for success, partly a function of party control in Congress, therefore condition the president's agenda. This theory of congressional anticipations leads to several hypotheses regarding the shape of the president's agenda. The previous chapters presented and tested these hypotheses, finding support for them. First, when expectations for success decline, the president's agenda shrinks as presidents withhold proposals destined for defeat. Second, presidents are more likely to modify their proposals, making them more acceptable to more members of Congress when expectations of success are low as opposed to high. Because expectations for success are lower during divided compared with united government, the president's agenda will be smaller and more moderate when confronting an opposition-controlled Congress than when the president's party controls the legislature.

Plus, presidents also might seek resources to enhance their bargaining situation with Congress, especially when they are under some political and public pressure to submit legislation to Congress. Modern presidents in particular find themselves facing heightened expectations to be active in the legislative policy-making process compared with traditional presidents. Results of the analysis in Chapter 4 found that the great surge in presidential activism took off only once those resources were in place, a decade after Franklin Roosevelt assumed office, after the end of the Second World War, and only with the establishment of the central legislative clearance processes. Thus, the congressional anticipations theory, which argues that presidents try to minimize or lessen the likelihood of being defeated in Congress, was shown to explain much of presidential agenda building.

This chapter considers the effects of these agenda-building decisions and presidential behaviors on success in Congress, testing the Bond and Fleisher perspective, but with specific hypotheses. The theory of congressional anticipations hypothesizes that there should be a positive relationship between the size of the president's agenda and success. Moreover, once we control for agenda size, the direct effect of divided government on success, which existing research finds to be so important, should diminish in power. Similarly, we should find that a positive association between presidential policy moderation and success, but only during periods of divided government. The congressional anticipations theory also has implications for the success of modern versus traditional presidents. First, because modern presidents possess resources that they can deploy in bargaining with Congress that traditional presidents do not have, modern presidents should be more successful with Congress than traditional presidents. Plus, there should be a positive interaction effect between the size of the president's agenda and being a modern president. Presidential success with Congress should rise as the agenda grows, but only for modern presidents.

This chapter offers several tests of these hypotheses concerning presidential success in Congress. The next two sections present two tests of the agenda size and divided government hypotheses. One set of tests uses a measure of success at the individual proposal level, whereas the other uses a measure of success aggregated to the congress level. Although the individual level measure allows us to control for characteristics of the proposal, such as its specific timing and policy area, the individual level test also raises some thorny estimation issues. The aggregate level test helps with those estimation issues, although it raises another set of statistical issues. Testing the hypotheses at both levels allows us to compare results. Given the statistical and estimation issues that each test raises, our confidence will be bolstered if both tests produce similar results. The succeeding section presents tests of the modern presidency hypotheses. Finally, the fourth section turns to the moderation-success hypothesis.

AGENDA SIZE AND PRESIDENTIAL SUCCESS IN CONGRESS AT THE INDIVIDUAL PROPOSAL LEVEL: TEST 1

The theory of congressional anticipations, as developed in Chapter 3, suggests several hypotheses regarding the effects of agenda size and divided government on presidential success with Congress. Recall that the theory of congressional anticipations argues that presidents calculate a proposal's estimated chance for success. They will be less likely to forward a proposal to Congress with a weak chance for success. On average, proposals have better enactment chances when the president's party controls Congress than when the opposition party is in control. Consistent with these points, we found that the presidential agenda is smaller under divided than united government. Extending this logic to success, we should find a positive relationship between agenda size and success: Presidents submit more proposals when the prospects for success are high compared with low, the size-success hypothesis.[1]

The agenda size hypothesis also has implications for the effect of divided government on success. Divided government routinely is found to be a major factor conditioning presidential success with Congress. The theory of congressional anticipations argues that divided government's effect is felt indirectly on success through its impact on the size of the presidential agenda. Thus, we should find that divided government's direct effect on success will decline once we control for the size of the presidential agenda.

The next section discusses construction of a presidential success measure from the proposal data. I then discuss other independent variables used in the analysis. These other variables serve two purposes. First, they act as controls on our primary independent variables of interest, size of the agenda and divided government, ensuring that any effects of these two variables of interest are not spurious. Second, the controls provide tests of other hypotheses on the sources of presidential success in Congress.

DEPENDENT VARIABLE: PRESIDENTIAL PROPOSAL SUCCESS

How should we measure presidential success with Congress? The literature on presidential success offers several indicators, from presidential support to concurrence (roll call success).[2] In this study I

---

[1]   The agenda size-success hypothesis is not a direct test of the theory of congressional anticipations but only a test of an implication of the theory. A direct test of the theory would involve a two-stage process. The first stage would model the presidential decision to submit a proposal to Congress, with the second stage modeling the success of those submitted proposals, such as through a Heckman selection model. We cannot do such a test because proposals that the president did not submit are unobserved. As explained in Chapter 1, we only have information on proposals submitted by the president to Congress. Consequently, we can test only implications of the theory, as done in this chapter.

[2]   There has been considerable debate in the literature over which type of measure to use. Edwards (1985) argues that support of the president by members of Congress is the preferable measure because it allows one to determine which factors lead individual members to vote with or against the president. Individual support is also the building block of all aggregated measures. Edwards (p. 669) does admit, however,

depart from most of the extant literature, which focuses on roll call votes, by asking whether Congress enacts a presidential proposal. As Beckmann (2010, p. 65) argues, "[t]he president's ultimate objective: outcomes, not necessarily roll call votes... [t]he White House wants to change the nation's laws, so the paramount metric of presidential success is the substantive result... tests of presidential influence should... highlight outcomes."

Here I define success as whether Congress enacted a presidential proposal. Despite the simplicity and intuitive appeal of such a measure, constructing such a measure from the proposal data used in this study is neither easy nor straightforward. First, the presidential proposal data set does not contain enactment information, but the Rollreq tables data set from the larger Database of Historical Congressional Statistics (DHCS) provides us with information that we can use to construct an enactment measure.

The Rollreq data set consists of all roll calls on a presidential request for legislation. Excluded are roll calls in which the president took a position but that did not come from the president's agenda, in other words, roll calls derived from the agenda of members of Congress (the off-agenda). To create our measure of congressional action on presidential proposals requires matching the proposal from the proposal data set to the roll call from the Rollreq data set, not a straightforward or easy thing to do.

First, the roll calls from the Rollreq data set span only the first 100 congresses (1789–1988), where the proposal data used in the earlier chapters continues through 2002. Being limited to the 1789-to-1988 period, 200 years, still provides us with information on final congressional action for 12,076 (85%) of the total number of presidential requests from 1789 to 2002.

that aggregate measures, like presidential box scores, can be useful in making comparisons across congresses, although it loses information at the individual level. Bond and Fleisher (1990), in contrast, argue that one should focus only on nonconsensual roll calls, that is, those with at least 20% of members voting against the president. Rivers and Rose (1985), like Beckmann, contend that passage of presidential legislative initiatives is the preferable measure. As I discuss in the conclusion of this book in more detail, each of these measures provides information on different aspects of presidential-congressional relations. All will be necessary for developing a complete theory of presidential-congressional relations.

Configuration 1: One-to-One Correspondence: Each Proposal Results in One Roll Call.

Configuration 2: Splits: One Proposal Is Split into Multiple Roll Calls.

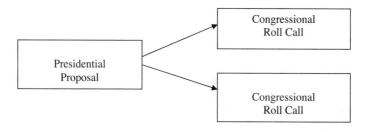

Configuration 3: Fusions: Multiple Proposals Are Combined into One Roll Call.

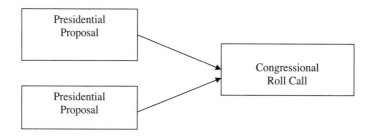

Configuration 4: No Roll Call Is Associated with a Proposal.

Figure 7.1. Creating a Roll Call Data Set from a Presidential Proposal Data Set.

Second, and more important, there is no one-to-one correspondence between presidential legislative proposals and roll calls. Figure 7.1 illustrates the various relationships between a presidential proposal and congressional roll calls. Easiest to comprehend is when each proposal corresponds to one roll call in the House and/or

Senate, here termed *one-to-one correspondence*. (Assuming passage in the first voting chamber, a second roll call will be held in the other chamber.) A presidential proposal can be "split" into two or more roll calls in either chamber, however, diagrammed in the second panel on Figure 7.1. Third, two or more presidential proposals can be bundled into one roll call vote, termed *fusions*, the third panel on Figure 7.1. Finally, there might not be a corresponding roll call to a presidential proposal, as suggested by the fourth panel in the figure. I matched each presidential proposal to the corresponding roll call, noting the various configurations from Figure 7.1, for the House and Senate separately; then the matches between the proposal and House roll calls were combined with the matches between the proposals and Senate roll calls, creating a master data set for analysis. Based on this procedure, the original 12,076 proposals from 1789 to 1988 produced 14,073 proposal-roll call *matches*, the new unit of analysis.

A third limitation is that we have no information on other types of congressional action on presidential requests, like committee hearings. This restricts the analysis to the input (presidential request) and final output (congressional roll call vote), but we are able to compare roll call action in the House with roll call action in the Senate.

Fourth, we are not able to link presidential requests and congressional action on those proposals to actual public laws. As Clinton and Lapinski (2008) show, the possibility exists that a presidential request became a public law without Congress holding a recorded roll call vote. Recorded roll call votes are critical in determining congressional action on the president's proposal. Clinton and Lapinski also find that recorded roll calls are more likely on important as opposed to less-important legislation. We have no way to measure the importance of a presidential request. All the existing methods of measuring importance look at the public and historical record, such as contemporary news reports and histories (e.g., Clinton and Lapinski, 2006; Grant and Kelly, 2008; Mayhew, 2005). Rarely do presidential requests make it into this public record, and historically, presidential requests are even less likely to appear in public records like news reports than in the more modern era, when there is more extensive reporting on the president and his legislative program.

The possibility of enactment without a recorded roll call is real and could undermine this analysis, however. To partly account for this possibility, I include in the analysis only presidential requests from one of the four major policy domains (i.e., sovereignty, government organization, foreign policy, and domestic policy), excluding all others, assuming that the excluded requests are less important than the requests in the four policy domains. There are 413 matches that did not come from one of the four policy domains. Only 19.9% of these "less important" matches have a roll call in at least one chamber, compared with 36.9% of matches in one of the four policy domains. This is consistent with the idea that nonpolicy domain requests are less important than policy domain requests.

Thus, this analysis assumes a minimal level of importance for presidential requests from one of the four policy domains. Owing to the prestige and constitutional position of the presidency, when a president submits a policy request from one of the four major policy domains, I am assuming that that request is more important than requests on other issues and topics, and that requests from one of the four policy domains will rarely be enacted without a recorded roll call vote. Such might be even more the case in the traditional period (pre-1946) than the modern era, because traditional era presidents felt constrained in their legislative activism and in lobbying Congress for their preferred policies. The possibility still exists, however, that some presidential requests will result in a public law without a recorded roll call vote in both chambers.

Lacking information on public laws, a presidential success in these data exists when both houses of Congress pass the presidential request. This assumes that the president will sign into law all of his proposals that passed both legislative chambers, a reasonable assumption. (Because treaties require only senatorial action, however, Senate passage of the treaty also constitutes a presidential success.) Thus I define a presidential success as when both houses pass the presidential request, and for treaties, when the Senate passes the treaty request. Defeats occur when at least one house fails to vote on the president's request (except for treaties) and/or when at least one house defeats the president's request on a roll call. Narrowly defined, therefore, the dependent variable measures the outcome on congressional roll calls pertaining to a presidential proposal, noting the possibility that some proposals might be enacted without a recorded roll call vote. This produces a binary dependent variable, 1 = success, 0 = defeat.

Based on these definitions and data, most presidential defeats occur before the roll call stage. Fully 63.1% (8,630) of matches never reach either chamber's floor.[3] Presidential odds of success improve once a match reaches a floor vote: Of the matches that make it to the floor of at least one chamber (5,037), the president wins 53.6% of the time. Possessing a majority seems to result in a higher percentage of matches getting to the floor of at least one chamber, as well as higher success rates for matches receiving floor attention. During majority congresses, 42% (3,529 of 8,398 matches) receive at least one floor vote, compared with 28.6% (3,763 of 5,271) during minority congresses, and during majority congresses, presidents win on 58% of matches with at least one floor vote (2,054 of 3,529), compared with 42.9% (647 of 1,508) during minority congresses.

Modern (1946–present) presidents seem only slightly more successful with Congress than traditional presidents, somewhat contrary to conventional wisdom about the impact of modernity on presidential success with Congress, but in line with Cohen's (1982a, 1982b) analysis, which showed that premodern presidents, especially during periods of majority control, could be highly successful with Congress. Where modern presidents get to at least one floor 38.2% of the time (3,030 of 7,941 matches), traditional presidents do so 35% of the time (2,007 of 5,728). Moreover, once their proposals get to the floor stage, both traditional and modern presidents seem to win with nearly equal frequency, 53.6% for modern presidents compared with 51.9% for traditional presidents. This initial analysis suggests that unified control might confer some advantage to the president over divided government, but modern presidents appear no more successful with Congress than premodern incumbents.

INDEPENDENT VARIABLES: DIVIDED GOVERNMENT AND SIZE OF THE AGENDA

The key independent variables are a dummy variable for divided government, measured 1 if the opposition party controls at least one

---

[3] Again, except for those that receive nonrecorded roll calls and are enacted into public law.

legislative chamber and o otherwise, and the size of the legislative agenda, measured as the number of legislative proposals submitted in the same congress as the presidential proposal-roll call *match*. We expect a negative sign for divided government on success, but a positive sign for the effect of agenda size on each match. Large agendas indicate presidential expectations for success. Proposals submitted in congresses with large agendas will have higher prospects for enactment than proposals submitted in congresses with small agendas.

CONTROL VARIABLES

Congressional Polarization

Under some conditions, the degree of polarization between the congressional parties might affect presidential success in the legislative arena. Party polarization denotes not only the policy distance between the parties but also the internal cohesion, or loyalty, of members to their party. During periods of high polarization, there is a large distance in policy between the two parties, and members will exhibit strong loyalty to their respective parties. Presidents also might have a hard time securing the support of opposition party members for their legislative initiatives when polarization is high. In contrast, when polarization is low, presidents might be able to pick up opposition support. For instance, Republican President Dwight Eisenhower and Lyndon Johnson, the Democratic Senate majority leader, had a good working relationship during a period of relatively low party polarization. In general, from the 1940s to the 1960s, Republican presidents found it quite easy to work with Southern Democrats in Congress on several issues, like civil rights and economic regulation, the well-known "conservative coalition."

High levels of polarization might not affect presidential success when the president's party is in the majority. Majority presidents might be successful merely by relying on support from their own party. Support from opposition party members might not be necessary as long as the majority party remains cohesive. Minority presidents, in contrast, require some opposition party support for enactment of their proposals. Gaining such support, even from a relatively small number of opposition party members, becomes increasingly more difficult when polarization is high than when it is low. Hence party polarization and party control of Congress interact in affecting presidential success with Congress. Polarization dampens success only when the president's party is in the minority, the *divided government-polarization interaction hypothesis.*

I use the DW-Nominate distance between the median members of the two (largest) parties, averaged across both chambers, to measure polarization, expecting a negative sign. For the interaction effect, I multiply the minority status (1 = presidential party minority, 0 = majority) and polarization variables. The interaction variable is 0 when the president's party controls both chambers but takes on a polarization value if the president's party is in the minority in one or both chambers.

The Economic and Budgetary Context

The state of the economy may affect presidential success in Congress. Presidents tend to be blamed or rewarded for the state of the economy. A vast literature has found that presidential approval declines when the economy falters. Although presidential approval polls date to only the mid-1930s and thus we cannot say much about the linkage between the economy and presidential approval prior to then, other research detects a strong effect of the economy on the electoral success of the president and his party. Even before the age of the modern president, there are indications that the public held the president and his party responsible for the economy at the ballot box. For instance, the economic panic of 1837 was a major factor in Martin Van Buren's defeat for reelection in 1840, as well as widespread defeats of Democratic candidates for office that year (Formisano, 1993). Lynch's (1999, 2002) studies of presidential elections from 1872 to 1996 find economic effects across the entire period. Curry and Morris (2010) find the same in their study of presidential elections dating from 1828 to 2008. If the public blames the president (and his party) for bad economic times, either at the ballot box or through approval ratings, then members of Congress have an incentive to distance themselves from the president. One way to demonstrate that distance, even among members of the president's party, is to vote against presidential policy proposals on economic and perhaps noneconomic matters. By this account, presidential success in Congress should fall as the economy weakens.

There are also many examples of presidents getting the economic policies that they wanted from Congress during periods of economic distress. For example, Congress swiftly acted on several major economic proposals that Franklin Roosevelt put before them in the early days on his assuming office in March 1933. Barack Obama also received fast support for his economic stimulus package in 2009. How can we square these and other major presidential policy accomplishments during periods of economic distress with the blame-reward theory?

Consistent with the blame-reward theory, presidents *in office during the period of economic decline* are likely to be blamed for that decline, and the processes associated with the traditional perspective should set in. If severe enough, bad economic times should lead to the ouster of the sitting president and possibly his party from office in the upcoming election. New presidents coming to office when the economy is ailing, in contrast, should enjoy some agenda success, but only for a short time. The success of newly elected presidents in bad economic times comes from the signal that the election sends to policy makers. Often, the previous administration loses the White House and seats in Congress. Policy makers can read such election results as voter rejection of the policies of the previous administration. The new administration, however, enters office with a store of public support to implement policies to address the down economy. For a time, a new president can blame the weak economy on his predecessor. As time goes on, however, if the economy does not improve, the president's standing with the public should begin to erode and Congress might be less willing to support the "weakened" president's proposals. Economic distress provides these new presidents with only a short period of opportunity to prove themselves and their policies. The window of opportunity might last perhaps no longer than from their election until the first midterm. In other words, presidents can take advantage of a weak economy to further their policy agenda only if they are not associated with the bad economy. The longer a new president serves in office, the more likely it is that the public will come to blame him for the state of the economy. There are time limits for how long a new president can blame his predecessor for what ails the economy. Once the public begins to blame or hold the president responsible for the weak economy, presidential success with Congress should decline as members of Congress try to distance themselves from the besieged president.

I use two measures of the economy, a dummy variable for whether the nation was in recession during the Congress of the proposal and interest rates. To measure the "presidential window of opportunity" associated with economic downturns, I multiply these economic measures by a dummy variable for the first congress (first two years) of a new president. I suppress the interest rate interaction variable to 0 when interest rates range from 0% to 7%, however. Again, the assumption is that the interest rate-new president interaction has an impact on success only for high interest rates, defined as 7% or greater.[4] I expect a positive sign between economic distress and success during the "window" period, but negative signs between economic distress and success during other periods.

Two aspects of the federal budget, the size of the deficit and the size of government relative to the economy, also can affect presidential success. High deficits and large government limit the ability to finance programs. When deficits are high, policy makers look for ways to curtail government spending, to bring it in line with government revenues. When government is large relative to the economy, opponents of large government also seek to reduce the size of government by eliminating and/or reducing the size of programs. When deficits and government spending are high, legislative energy is aimed at managing the fiscal side of government, providing less opportunity, willingness, and/or time to consider aspects of the president's agenda on nonfiscal matters. Presidential success with Congress should fall during periods of large deficits and big government. I use deficits as a percentage of GDP and federal outlays as a percentage of GDP, averaged across the two years of the Congress of the match, expecting a negative sign between both and success.

---

4   In this series, interest rates averaged 5.7%. Experimentation found that the interaction term became statistically significant only when interest rates neared or topped 7%.

The International Context

The international context, in particular war, also can affect presidential success with Congress. Prospects for success with Congress should rise early during wartime. As the war goes on, however, those prospects should fade, even turning against the president, which is partly a function of mounting war casualties and war fatigue. Furthermore, the longer the war drags on, the more people may question the president's war policy and his leadership.[5] Such questions erode support for the president in Congress.

Typically the public rallies behind the president, and the opposition party tends to mute its criticism of the president with the outbreak of war. The early period of a war is when the nation coalesces and unites, and domestic controversies and divisions are suppressed, at least for a time. This political harmony improves the likelihood that Congress will enact the president's legislative proposals. Some of those proposals, of course, concern the war itself, and the president's constitutional role as commander-in-chief leads Congress to support whatever the president deems necessary for the war effort. Presidents can also link nonwar proposals to the war, arguing that they are necessary for the nation's defense. To keep from appearing unpatriotic and disloyal, Congress will give the president much of what he asks for in the early stages of war. The outbreak of war should lead to higher presidential success with Congress, the *war rally hypothesis*.

As the war continues, however, war wariness may set in, especially if the war and the president's leadership and war strategy appear unsuccessful. Opposition leaders can begin to criticize the president and his war leadership, and an unsuccessful or costly war can even sow dissent within the president's party. These processes can reduce the likelihood that presidential proposals will receive congressional approval. Opposition party members might think it necessary and politically advantageous to block the president's proposals, whereas members of the president's party also might distance themselves from an administration because of its failing war policies and the erosion of support that accompanies failed or costly war policies.

---

[5] On public opinion during war, see Berinsky (2009), Gelpi, Feaver, and Reifler (2009), and Baum and Groeling (2010). On presidential-congressional relations during wartime, see Howell and Pevehouse (2007).

Conversely, even when the nation is confident of victory, presidential success with Congress can fade as the war continues. Confidence of eventual victory reduces the perceived threat of the war to the nation, and public attention returns to the issues and concerns that the war pushed off of the agenda. As those issues rise on the agenda, political divisions will re-emerge on the nation's political agenda, and opposition party leaders might start criticizing the president and his policies. Thus, whether the war appears a success or a failure, as it goes on, prospects for legislative success should begin to fall from the high levels of the early war period, the *war continuation hypothesis.*

Two variables are used to capture these related dynamics, a dummy variable for whether the United States is at war at the time of the proposal and a counter for the number of months that the United States has been at war at the time of the proposal. These hypotheses predict a positive sign for the war dummy, but a negative sign for the monthly counter.

Proposal-specific Characteristics

One advantage of an individual proposal level model as is laid out here is that we can control for characteristics of the proposal. Some types of proposal have an easier (or harder) time with Congress.[6] The two presidencies literature, for example, argues that presidents have some advantages with foreign policy legislation lacking for other types of proposals.[7] Thus, I control for policy domain with two dummy variables, one for whether the proposal is from the international relations domain, and a second for domestic policy proposals (as defined in Chapter 5), hypothesizing a positive sign for international relations proposals but having no expectations about domestic policy proposals. Using similar logic, we expect treaties to have higher odds of

---

[6]   Ideally we would like a measure of the distance of the president's proposal from the congressional median (or pivot), but as discussed earlier, this is not possible with these proposal data.

[7]   The literature on the two presidencies thesis is quite large, dating to Wildavsky's (1966) seminal article. Steven Shull (1991) collected most of the relevant studies. Also see the recent study by Canes-Wrone, Howell, and Lewis (2008).

acceptance than other types of proposals, using a dummy variable, $1 =$ treaty proposal, $0 =$ non-treaty proposal.[8]

Other Characteristics

Finally, I include dummy variables for lame-duck status, second-term status, and the postfilibuster era. Lame duck is a dummy variable for whether a president submits a proposal in the period from the presidential election to the end of his term in office (e.g., November of an even-numbered year to January or March of the next calendar year). We expect a negative sign for lame-duck status. Modern lame-duck presidents rarely submit legislation to Congress.[9]

There are two primary motivations for lame-duck presidents to submit proposals to Congress. First, some issues come up that need attention, such as the Trouble Asset Relief Program (TARP) that George W. Bush requested to handle the economic meltdown of late fall-winter 2008. We can think of these as policy emergencies or crises that call for government action. Second, until 1934, presidents issued their State of the Union Addresses (SUAs), which contain many of their legislative proposals, in December for congressional action the next calendar year. Furthermore, new presidents were not inaugurated until March of the following year, a gap of nearly five months from the election to the inauguration. In 1934, at FDR's behest, Congress changed the date for inauguration to early-to-mid-January, and FDR changed the timing for the SUA to late January-early February. FDR sought to reduce the time between the election and the inauguration, allowing the new president to take action on pressing policy issues more quickly than in the past.

I also control for whether the proposal were submitted in the second two years of the presidential term (years 3 and 4), expecting a negative sign here. Several factors associated with the second half of a term can affect presidential success, such as the loss of seats that usually comes with midterm elections, declining public support compared

---

[8] Treaties also might have an easier time gaining acceptance because they require only the Senate and not both chambers for passage.

[9] There are only nine cases for the post-1934 period. Congress failed to enact any of these proposals.

with the level when the president came to office, and the run-up to the next presidential election, a period in which Congress focuses more on reelection than legislative matters and when Congress might be waiting for the presidential election results to decide how to handle some issues. The opposition party in Congress, in particular, has strong incentives to stymie the president's proposals, hoping that defeating him will weaken him and his party in the upcoming election. Congress is usually less legislatively productive in years 3 and 4 of a presidential term than the first two years (Lapinski, 2008).

Finally, I control for the institution of the filibuster rule, coded 0 for the period prior to the filibuster (1789–1918) and 1 for the filibuster era (1919–present).[10] The Senate enacted the cloture vote, Rule 22, to end debate in 1917, and implemented it in 1919, in part at the urging of Woodrow Wilson. Prior to that, any Senator could delay a floor vote simply by speaking on any topic; no formal process existed for terminating a filibuster and moving to a floor vote. The cloture vote rule created a process to end a filibuster and also set the number of senators needed to overcome a filibuster, two-thirds, until 1975, when the threshold became three-fifths. Rule 22, cloture, despite creating a formal supermajority needed to overcome a filibuster, advantaged presidents over those in office during the pre-cloture era. With cloture, presidents would know how many members it would take to end a filibuster and thus could either tailor their legislative proposals to avoid such opposition or work with Senate leaders to end a (threatened) filibuster. Rule 22 provided the president with better information about potential opposition to his legislative proposals and put limits on the ability of a filibuster or its threat to stop legislation. We therefore expect presidential success to improve with the institution of the filibuster rule.

ANALYSIS ISSUES

Because the unit of analysis is the individual proposal, with the dependent variable scored 1 for a success and 0 for a failure, I use probit. There is a possibility that victory or defeat of one presidential

---

[10] On the filibuster see Wawro and Schickler (2006) and Koger (2010).

proposal might spill over into other proposals, affecting their chances for victory. For example, when a president wins on a proposal, his reputation as a legislative leader could rise and his support with the public could increase (Brace and Hinckley, 1992; Rivers and Rose, 1985). This addition to the president's resources and political capital (Light, 1982) could improve the odds that other proposals will also be enacted (Beckmann, 2010). Thus, the success of one proposal is not necessarily independent of the success of other proposals submitted within the same congress. To control for this nonindependence, I cluster the analysis by congress.

FINDINGS

Table 7.1 presents the results of two probit analyses. The first estimation includes all variables except for agenda size. This estimation resembles much research on presidential success in Congress, with the expectation that divided government will have a significant and substantively meaningful impact on success. The second estimation adds the agenda size variable. Based on the previous discussion, we should find a positive effect of agenda size on success, and divided government should have less impact than in the first estimation. The results on Table 7.1 exclude the minority president-polarization interaction. That interaction, which never reaches statistical significance, obscures the effects of divided government on success.

Results on Table 7.1 provide support for the two key hypotheses concerning agenda size and divided government effects on success. Consider first the model without the agenda size term, labeled *divided government* in Table 7.1. Divided government demonstrates a strong and significant dampening effect on success, as found in most of the literature on presidential success in Congress. As probit coefficients are not intuitively interpretable, I convert them to probabilities, presented in the Impact columns on the table. Presidents can expect a 0.08 lower probability that Congress will enact a proposal during divided as opposed to united government. Averaged across all proposals, this equates with 8% fewer proposals being enacted with minority as opposed to majority control of Congress.

TABLE 7.1. *Impact of Agenda Size and Divided Government on Individual Proposal Success, 1st to 100th Congresses, Multivariate Probit (Clustered on Congress)*

Variable	Divided Government Model				Agenda Size Model			
	b	SE	p	Impact	b	SE	p	Impact
Constant	0.14	0.33	0.41		0.50	0.31	0.10	
Proposals					0.002	0.0005	0.0	0.0004
Divided Govt.	−0.32	0.10	0.001	−0.08	−0.20	0.11	0.03	−0.05
War Dummy	0.58	0.24	0.01	0.17	0.32	0.20	0.06	0.09
War Counter	−0.15	0.05	0.001	−0.004	−0.01	.005	0.003	−0.003
New Party Dummy	−0.50	0.18	0.005	−0.11	−0.46	0.19	0.01	−0.10
Recession Dummy	−0.53	0.12	0.0	−0.14	−0.43	0.11	0.0	−0.11
New Party × Recession	0.75	0.18	0.0	0.23	0.69	0.20	0.0	0.21
Interest Rates	0.02	0.02	0.43	0.004	0.04	0.02	0.04	0.09
New Party × Int. Rates	0.04	0.01	0.003	0.01	0.06	0.01	0.0	0.01
Polarization	−1.30	0.46	0.002	−0.33	−2.07	0.44	0.0	−0.52
Treaty Dummy	0.93	0.14	0.0	0.30	0.90	0.13	0.0	0.29
International Relations	0.09	0.08	0.12	0.02	0.14	0.08	0.04	0.04
Domestic Policy	0.11	0.10	0.24[a]	0.03	0.10	0.10	0.30[a]	0.03
Deficit % GDP	−0.03	0.02	0.05	−0.008	−0.10	0.03	0.0	−0.02
Fed Outlays % GDP	−0.04	0.01	0.0	−0.01	−0.09	0.02	0.0	−0.02
Lame-duck Dummy	−0.27	0.15	0.04	−0.06	−0.31	0.16	0.02	−0.07
Second Congress	−0.21	0.14	0.06	−0.05	−0.19	0.10	0.03	−0.05
Filibuster Era	0.62	0.20	0.001	0.14	0.57	0.18	0.001	0.13
n	13,538				13,538			
Wald Chi-sq/p	288.4	0.000			274.5	0.000		
Log Likelihood	−5,912.7				−5,834.2			
Pseudo-R^2	0.12				0.13			

[a] Two-tailed tests; all others are one-tailed tests.

Impact: Probability shift of a one-unit change in the independent variable. For dummy variables, a 0–1 shift.

Adding agenda size into the estimation support lowers effect of divided government and shows the positive association between size and success on success. With agenda size entered into the estimation, divided government's effect falls from 0.08 to 0.05. This reduction in the direct effect of divided government on proposal success is similar in proportion to that found in Marshall and Prins's (2007) study of presidential position taking on roll call success. The effect of divided government controlling for agenda size is still statistically significant, but only at the 0.05 level, compared with 0.002 in the estimation without agenda size.

Agenda size, as hypothesized, is also positively associated with success. Presidents are more successful when their agendas are large as opposed to small, consistent with the idea that presidents submit larger agendas when they think they will have an easier time gaining congressional support. The impact suggests a 0.004 increase in success for each additional proposal. Although this appears to be a small amount, aggregated over proposals, the effect is substantively meaningful. Recall that the number of proposals varies greatly from congress to congress, from 5 to 665, averaging 129, with a standard deviation of 135. Each additional 10 proposals are equal to an increase success probability of 0.04; for 100 additional proposals, this becomes 0.40. Admittedly these probability effects are quite high per proposal, but recall that there are many other factors in the multivariate model that dampen success.

Summary statistics also indicate that the model containing the agenda size variable has a superior fit. For instance, the log likelihood ratio changes from −5,912.7 without agenda size to −5,834.2, indicating a better fit. Furthermore, the AIC and BIC statistics are also smaller for the agenda size than the divided government estimations.[11] This is significant given the increase in parameters with the agenda size estimation.

Although the results thus far provide support for the agenda size hypothesis, the estimations do not necessarily model the underlying theoretical process properly. The theory of anticipated reactions

---

[11] The AIC and BIC for the divided government model are 11861.3 and 11996.6, but 11706.4 and 11849.2 for the agenda size estimations.

suggests that agenda size is a function of expectations for success, such as whether a president is a majority or minority president. Rather than controlling agenda size for divided government, we should endogenize agenda size for divided government. We can do with a two-stage, instrumental variable model, where agenda size is a function of divided government in the first stage, and the second-stage equation for success now has the instrumented agenda size variable as its predictor.

To estimate a two-stage model requires that at least one variable statistically predict to the instrumental variable (total requests) but not have an impact on the dependent variable (enactment). Divided government alone, although we argue that it is exogenous to total requests, still retained some direct statistical effect on enactment. Experimentation reveals three other variables in the two-stage estimation that predict to requests but not enactment, the war dummy, the international relations dummy, and the domestic policy dummy.[12] The Wald test is statistically significant (test statistic $= 6.54$, $p = 0.000$), supporting the exogeneity assumptions here.

Results of the two-stage estimation are presented on Table 7.2. Again, I cluster on Congress for the reasons detailed previously. The column labeled "Endogeneous Variable: Enactment" presents the probit results on enactment success, whereas the column labeled "Endogenous Variable: Number of Proposals" is the regression estimation for the number of proposals. Notably, divided government, as previously found, depresses the number of proposals. Based on these results, presidents submit sixty-two fewer proposals during divided than united government. In this estimation, the size of the agenda has a positive and statistically significant impact on success.

I also ran a second estimation, this time allowing divided government to have both direct effects on enactment and number of proposals. All of the other variables are treated as they are in Table 7.2. For this new estimation, although divided government lowers the total number of proposals ($b = -61.4$, $p = 0.002$), divided government fails to have a statistically significant effect on enactment (Impact Probability $= -0.09$, $p = 0.52$). Total requests, however, is still significant

---

[12] Recall that the other two policy domains are for national sovereignty and government operations, which together act as the criterion category.

TABLE 7.2. *Impact of Agenda Size and Divided Government on Individual Proposal Success, 1st to 100th Congresses, Two-stage Probit (Clustered on Congress)*

Variable	Endogenous Variable: Enactment			Endogenous Variable: Number of Proposals		
	Impact	SE	p	b	SE	p
Constant	1.02	0.380	0.004	−222.38	80.38	0.006
Proposals	0.004	0.001	0.000			
Divided Govt.				−61.84	20.83	0.002
War Dummy				158.78	68.67	0.01
War Counter	−0.01	0.004	0.003	−1.67	1.22	0.08
New Party Dummy	−0.38	0.21	0.03	−11.34	36.83	0.76
Recession Dummy	−0.31	0.12	0.005	−50.15	20.10	0.01
New Party × Recession	0.62	0.23	0.003	19.31	41.01	0.64
Interest Rates	0.06	0.02	0.01	−11.46	4.39	0.005
New Party × Int. Rates	0.07	0.02	0.001	−7.58	4.89	0.06
Polarization	−2.99	0.59	0.000	447.74	106.12	0.000
Treaty Dummy	0.89	0.11	0.000	10.85	8.70	0.11
International Relations				−18.82	6.85	0.003
Domestic Policy				8.53	3.61	0.01
Deficit % GDP	−0.18	0.03	0.000	37.65	3.99	0.000
Fed Outlays % GDP	−0.15	0.02	0.000	26.33	2.77	0.000
Lame Duck Dummy	−0.38	0.16	0.01	24.51	22.72	0.28
Second Congress	0.18	0.10	0.04	−3.62	34.06	0.92
Filibuster Era	0.52	0.18	0.002	29.23	37.47	0.44
n	13,538					
Wald Chi-sq/p	247.3	0.000				
Log Likelihood	−86,043					
/athrho	−0.20	0.08	0.01			
/lnsigma	4.50	0.14	0.000			
Rho	−0.20	0.08				
Sigma	90.46	12.36				

Wald test of exogeneity = 6.54, $p = 0.01$.

The enactment equation uses probit; the proposal equation uses regression.

Impact: Probability shift of a one-unit change in the independent variable. For dummy variables, a 0–1 shift.

(Impact Probability per proposal = 0.003, $p < 0.001$). These results provide further support for treating divided government as a predictor of total requests but without a direct impact on enactment success.

Turning to the results on Table 7.2, the proposal estimation indicates that divided government has a strong dampening effect on the number of proposals. By these estimates, presidents submit sixty-one fewer proposals during divided than united government ($t = 2.90$, $p < 0.004$). The instrumented agenda size variable is significant and positive, and the probability impact analysis[13] suggests that each additional request carries a 0.004 increase likelihood of enactment, an effect the same as that found for the estimations on Table 7.1.

No matter the statistical procedure used thus far, we find support for the agenda size hypothesis: Divided government does not have as much direct affect on success as reported in the literature. With controls for agenda size (Table 7.1), divided government's effect on success declines steeply. Moreover, depending on the estimation, all of divided government's effect on success is mediated through the effect of divided government on the size of the presidential agenda (e.g., the two-stage results on Table 7.2).

Impact of Control Variables

Results of the analysis presented on Table 7.2 also indicate that several of the control variables affect presidential success with Congress. For instance, congressional party polarization affects success. Contrary to the minority status-polarization hypothesis developed earlier, polarization undercuts success for minority and majority presidents alike. The impact effect on Table 7.2 suggests that each one-unit increase in polarization lowers success by 3%. A one-standard deviation shift in polarization (0.13) corresponds to a 3.9% shift in the probability of enactment ($0.13 \times 3.0 = 0.39$). In these data, the highest party polarization score is 0.96, with the mean at 0.61 and the minimum at 0.18. A president facing the most polarized congress will see a 11% reduction in the probability that a proposal will be enacted compared with a president facing average congressional polarization. Presidents facing the least polarized congress see the best chances for the enactment of their proposals, 13% better compared with average polarization levels and 23.4% better than a president facing the most polarized congress. Clearly, polarization has significant effects on legislative success both in statistical and substantive terms.

War has complex impacts on proposal success. First, the two-stage results indicate that war and the war counter both affect the size of

---

[13] I used the ivprobit command in STATA 11.0, but I report only the probability impact effects on Table 7.2 because the STATA output does not report the probit coefficients.

the president's agenda, with war increasing the agenda but the war counter decreasing it. That war would lead to an increase in agenda size might appear counterintuitive, because one might expect war to divert attention away from domestic and non–war-related issues and policies. War can, however, require new policies and programs for the prosecution of the war effort, to regulate and manage the economy in service of war needs, and to generate and maintain public support for the war. Plus, seeing his support in Congress rise because of rally effects associated with war, at least during the initial stages, a president might view war as an opportunity to move stalled policies through the legislative process, especially if he can frame them as elements of the larger war policy. The results here also indicate that with each passing month that the war continues, it leads to reductions in the size of the president's agenda. Thus, part of the impact of war on success is mediated through the effect of war on agenda size. War itself has no direct impact on success once the effect of war on agenda size is taken into account; however, the probability of success drops by 0.01, 1% per proposal, for each additional month that the war continues. At the end of one year, war will reduce the prospects of success by 12%, a hefty amount.

The analysis used two sets of economic variables, one set for recession and another for interest rates. Recession influences success both through the effect of recession on agenda size and directly. Indirectly, recession affects success by leading to smaller agendas. In addition, recession decreases the prospects for success directly by a hefty 38%. Recession, however, offers newly elected presidents legislative opportunities. Whereas recession dampens the size of the agenda for sitting presidents, recession is associated with comparatively larger agendas for newly elected presidents in their first year in office. For instance, whereas recession will result in fifty fewer proposals for sitting presidents, the net effect of recession on newly elected presidents is a reduction of forty-two proposals.[14] In other words, newly elected presidents submit eight more proposals than sitting presidents during recessionary periods.

---

[14] To arrive at this figure, we need to aggregate the three variables necessary for the interaction term, the new president dummy (−11), recession dummy (−50), and the interaction of new presidents and recession (19). Adding the effects of the three variables equals 42.

Recession also follows the "window of opportunity" model, in which new presidents come to office with greater prospects for success than presidents in office during recessions. The results indicate that sitting presidents will suffer a 31% decline in the probability of success owing to recession. In contrast, recessions provide new presidents with improved, albeit not great, prospects for success in their first year in office, a net effect of −0.07, or only a 7% decline in the probability of success.[15] This is about a 24% improvement in success compared with presidents who have recessions continuing after their first year in office.

Interest rates also follow a window-of-opportunity dynamic. Higher interest rates always lead to decreases in agenda size. Each 1% increase in interest rates reduces the number of proposals by 11.5 for sitting presidents and nearly 31 for new presidents. At very high interest rates, for example 10%, these effects can aggregate into a large impact on the size of the agenda, but such high interest rates are rare.

Increases in interest rates, however, boost presidential success. A 1% increase in interest rates is associated with a 0.06 increase in the probability of success. At the average interest rate of nearly 6%, this translates into a 36% probability effect. For newly elected presidents, however, the net effect of a 1% increase in interest rates is −0.18, but at an average interest rate of 6%, new presidents receive a net effect of +0.40, that is, a 40% probability improvement in their success rates.[16] Both recession and interest rates improve the opportunities for success for new presidents compared with sitting presidents.

Government finances and size also affect success in Congress, as hypothesized. Each seems to be associated with larger presidential agendas. It might be that in the face of rising deficits and large government, presidents' agendas enlarge as presidents offer proposals designed to handle these problems. Large government, as Charles Jones (1994) argues, also forces the president to concern himself with a larger number of policies and programs. Without a detailed look at the proposal itself, we cannot be sure of the reason for larger agendas when deficits are high and government is large.

---

[15] Again, to calculate this effect we need to add the impact of the three terms, −0.38 (new president) − 0.31 (recession dummy) + 0.62 (interaction) = −0.07.

[16] −0.38 (New President) + 0.06 × 6 (Interest Rates) + 0.07 × 6 (Interaction) = 0.40.

Both deficits and large government depress presidential success with Congress, however. Each 1% increase in the deficit and size of government outlays relative to GDP leads to a −0.18 and −0.15 decrease in the probability of success. These are substantively massive effects, especially when deficits and government size begin to grow, but some of these dampening effects are counterbalanced by the effects of deficits and government size on the size of the president's agenda. A 5% deficit, taking into account direct and mediated effects of the deficit on agenda size, leads to a probability effect of −0.15.[17] The comparable effect at government that is 15% of GDP is −0.67, extraordinarily high.[18]

The individual level proposal estimation allows us to test whether characteristics of proposals affect success. Drawing on the two presidencies thesis, the analysis looked at the effects of international relations, domestic policy, and treaty proposals on success. Results in Table 7.2 suggest that neither international relations nor domestic policy have direct effects on success compared with the criterion category of combined national sovereignty and government organization proposals. Both international relations and domestic policy indirectly affect success through agenda size, however. Here the topic of international relations seems to dampen the size of the agenda, whereas domestic policy leads to larger agendas. The dampening effect of international relations on agenda size, which leads to lower success, seems contrary to existing research.

The estimation here controls also for treaty effects, however. All treaties are in international relations domain by definition. These results suggest that presidents gain strong congressional support for their treaties, as expected. First, treaties show a modest impact on the size of the agenda, which aggregates into a small positive impact on treaty success;[19] however, treaties are 89% more likely to be approved by Congress than nontreaty proposals. Presidents rarely lose on treaty votes. The high rate of treaty success, and separating treaties from

---

[17] (5% × −0.18 Direct deficit) + (37.7 × 5% × 0.004 Indirect through agenda size) = −0.15.

[18] (15% × −0.15 Direct government size) + (15% × 26.3 × 0.004 Indirect through agenda size) = −0.67.

[19] (10.85 × 0.004) = 0.04.

international relations proposals, accounts for the insignificant effect of international relations proposals on success. Future research on the two presidencies should consider distinguishing treaties from other types of international relations proposals.

Finally, lame-duck status, the second half of a presidential term, and the filibuster rule all directly affect presidential success. None, however, affects agenda size. Thus we find that lame duck presidents see a large decline in success, 38%, compared with non–lame-duck presidents. It makes sense that Congress generally would be unwilling to support a legislative proposal from a lame-duck president; however, presidents seem somewhat more successful in years 3 and 4 of their term than in years 1 and 2. We might expect otherwise, given the possibility of honeymoon effects and that the presidential party usually suffers seat losses after the midterm elections. Light's (1991, 1999a) cycle of increasing effectiveness would predict that presidents, being more experienced, would have a better sense of what can pass in Congress, would be better at crafting legislation, and would probably be better at negotiating with Congress, however. Under the pressure of reelection, presidents might also be more selective in what they submit to Congress during years 3 and 4, selecting those items with strong public backing. Such proposals might be harder for Congress to resist than less popular ones.

Finally, these results indicate that presidents are better off during the filibuster than the pre-filibuster era. During the pre-filibuster era, a lone senator could stymie legislation at will. The cloture rule, which allowed the floor of the Senate to end a filibuster effort, required those supporting a filibuster to organize their efforts if they wanted to ensure that their filibuster could withstand cloture. More important, perhaps, cloture allowed Senate majorities, admittedly supermajorities, to overcome a filibuster. In the pre-filibuster age, a tiny minority, even one senator, could kill legislation. Ironically, by formalizing filibusters, the president and other opponents of a filibuster, are in a stronger position to overcome opposition to legislative efforts. The results here indicate the effect is large, too, 0.52. One topic for future research is to look more closely at how rules changes in Congress, like the filibuster, affect presidential success in Congress, a rarely studied question.

Agenda Size and Presidential Success At the Aggregate Level: Test 2

The previous analyses, using individual level proposals, presented support for the hypothesized impacts of divided government and agenda size on presidential success in Congress. That analysis found, consistent with the theory of congressional anticipations, that once controlling for the size of the president's agenda, divided government's effect on success fades, and in some instances exhibits no direct effect on success. Rather, divided government affects presidential success indirectly, through its impact on the size of the president's agenda. As the theory of congressional anticipations hypothesizes, because presidents expect less support in Congress with divided than united government, they will scale back their legislative agendas during divided party control of Congress. Also consistent with hypotheses from the theory of congressional anticipations, agenda size was positively associated with success. The positive association between agenda size and success is a function of presidential anticipations of congressional action on their proposals. When presidents expect more support from Congress, they submit larger agendas. When they expect a harder time gaining congressional support, the agenda shrinks, because presidents refrain from submitting proposals with low chances for enactment.

The underlying assumption of the theory of congressional anticipations is that presidential proposals to Congress are endogenous to the president's expectations for success. Presidential expectations for success are built on information that the president gleans from the environment. In this book thus far, I focus on divided government, which provides presidents with information on how Congress will likely treat their legislative proposals, but presidents can use other types of information as well.

Divided government provides presidents with static information. By this I mean that the expected effect of divided government on success will be constant across the two years of a congress; however, the prospects for success could rise and fall within a natural two-year congress too, as conditions that affect success change. Presidents can update their expectations for success/failure based on changes in conditions that affect success, modifying their legislative agendas based on that updated information. For instance, assume that presidential approval affects prospects for success with Congress. As approval rises, so can presidential success with Congress, and presidents can decide to take advantage of these newly enhanced opportunities by submitting legislative proposals that they have been sitting on. To a degree, the previous analysis took this possibility into account by clustering proposals by congress. Recall that I argued that success or failure on one proposal might spill over to affect the prospects for success on subsequent proposals. Proposals should not be treated as independent events. Success on one proposal could be contingent on the success of previous proposals.

These updated expectations can affect proposals that presidents submit during the legislative session, after the initial flurry of proposals that comes with the SUA and the transmission of the presidential program to Congress early in the congressional session. Presidents might take into account previous success/failure with Congress in deciding whether to submit these "later" proposals. Thus, the size of the presidential agenda might be not only endogenous to divided government but also to past success/failure during the current congressional session. Presidents might be emboldened to submit additional proposals if Congress has acted positively on previous proposals. In contrast, if presidents have been having a difficult time with Congress during the session, they might refrain from submitting additional proposals to the legislature.

The two-stage estimation of the last section is consistent with this view of strategic presidential behavior. This section offers an additional test of this dynamic by aggregating presidential success to the natural congress. The dependent variable for this aggregate analysis is the presidential success rate per congress, defined as the percentage of successful "matches" per congress. Recall that the unit of analysis in the previous analysis was the match between a presidential proposal and congressional action on that proposal. As Congress can split or merge proposals when casting roll calls on them, there is not always a direct one-to-one correspondence between proposals and roll calls. If this aggregated analysis produces results similar to that of the individual proposal analysis presented earlier, we will have additional support for theory advanced in this study.

Figure 7.2 plots aggregate presidential success. By this measure, presidents appear less successful than other indicators, like roll call

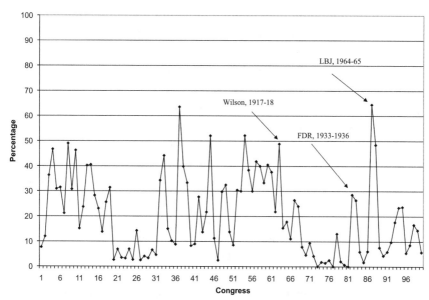

Figure 7.2. Aggregate Presidential Success, by Congress, 1st to 100th Congress.

support, suggest. For instance, here aggregate success varies from a low of 0.0 to a high of 64.5% for FDR in the 74th Congress (1935–1936), with a mean of 20% and a standard deviation of 16.4%. These figures also report a 52.1% success rate for LBJ during the 89th Congress (1965–1966). Ragsdale reports concurrence rates of 93.1% and 78.9% combined House and Senate concurrence for 1965 and 1966, considerably higher, but recall the important differences between the construction of concurrence rates and success as measured here. Concurrence is based on the president being on the winning side on congressional roll calls. Any presidential position on legislation that does not receive a roll call is not used to construct concurrence. As those positions that fail to get to the congressional floor would likely be defeated on the floor if a roll call were held, the concurrence rate will have higher scores for presidents than the aggregate success rate as measured here. Both the concurrence scores and aggregate success point to the same presidents as being successful or not with Congress. Figure 7.2 also identifies other peaks in presidential success that conform with common historical understandings, such as Johnson, FDR (1933–1936), and Wilson (1917–1918). There is much more information in this figure than can be easily digested through visual inspection.

I use two-stage least squares to account for the endogeneity between success and the size of the president's agenda. Here I define agenda size as the number of proposals from the four policy domains that the president submits to Congress, which I term *important proposals*. This definition of the president's agenda differs from that used in the analyses in Chapters 4 and 5, which used all proposals. The two measures of agenda size, important versus all proposals, however, correlate at 0.99 ($p < 0.000$), and so there might be little practical implication. Moreover, variables that affect agenda size, defined as all proposals, similarly affect the number of important proposals, with only minor differences in the size of the coefficients. Like all proposals, important proposals are not stationary. First, differencing produces a stationary variable.[20] Given the nonstationarity of important proposals, I will use the differenced form and also use the first difference for aggregate success, to match the two equations in the two-stage least squares estimation.[21] For first-differenced aggregate success, the key descriptive statistics are average (−0.25), minimum (−28.4), maximum (57.5), and standard deviation (13.6).

Table 7.3 provides the results of the two-stage least squares estimation. To arrive at these final results, I began with separate estimations for each of the two endogenous variables (important proposals and aggregate success). Those preliminary estimations found several variables that predicted to important proposals, but not aggregate size, a necessary condition for us to employ the two-stage estimation approach. As Table 7.3 reports, the lag of federal deficits, the lag of federal outlays, and change to/from a Republican president affect size but not success. Furthermore, the table also shows that divided government in lag and changes affects size but not success. Finally,

---

[20] The Dickey-Fuller test reports a value of −2.40, against a test statistic of −3.527 at the 0.01 level, −2.900 at 0.05 and −2.59 at 0.10, with a Dickey-Fuller value of −9.42 for the first-differenced variable.

[21] Aggregate success is stationary in levels, with a Dickey-Fuller value of −4.36 and test statistic of −3.52 at the 0.01 level. For the first differenced form the Dickey-Fuller value is −12.17.

TABLE 7.3. *Impact of Agenda Proposal Success, 7th to 100th Congresses, Congressional Level, Aggregate Analysis, Two-stage Least Squares*

Variable	Endogenous Variable: Number of Proposals Per Congress (changes)			Endogenous Variable: Enactment Rate Per Congress (changes)		
	b	SE	p	b	SE	p
Constant	20.40	15.06	.05	18.24	4.56	0.000
Enactment Rate-lag				−0.66	0.10	0.000
Size-changes				0.04	0.02	0.023
Size-lag	−0.31	0.08	0.000			
Years 3 and 4	−14.39	12.93	0.27[a]	−1.66	3.22	0.31
Divided Govt-lag	−36.26	26.16	0.08	3.52	6.62	0.60[a]
Divided Govt-changes	−45.68	16.99	0.004	4.95	4.55	0.28[a]
Interaction: DG *YR3 and 4, Lag	75.62	40.11	0.03	−18.08	10.40	0.04
Interaction: DG * YR3 and 4, Changes	45.56	23.52	0.03	−10.96	6.13	0.04
Interest Rates-lag	−4.73	2.56	0.035	1.18	0.64	0.035
Deficit %-Lag	7.14	2.86	0.007			
Outlays %-Lag	7.07	1.71	0.000			
Republican Pres.-lag				−15.12	3.44	0.000[a]
Republican Pres-changes	−51.99	13.79	0.000			
Democratic Pres-changes				−6.72	4.07	0.10[a]
War-lag				−5.76	2.88	0.024
89th Congress-lag	431.20	96.90	0.000			
89th Congress-changes	378.49	50.98	0.000			
91st Congress-lag	−3.22	0.87	0.000			
91st Congress-changes	−2.35	0.60	0.000			
R^2	0.76			0.44		
F	16.47			5.32		
p	0.000			0.000		

[a] Two-tailed test; all other p values are one-tailed tests.

I added dummy variables for changes and lags associated with the 89th and 91st Congresses because they revealed the largest congress-to-congress shifts in size of the important agenda. Inclusion of these dummies does not affect the other variables that predict to size of the agenda, although it increases the R^2. Inclusion of the dummies does not affect the second-stage estimation for success, although it lowers the coefficient for agenda size (changes) on success from 0.07 to 0.04. Because inclusion of these dummies does not affect overall findings but reports some more conservative estimates for the effects of agenda size on success, Table 7.3 reports results using these congress dummies.

If we turn to the results for aggregate success, the lag in the success rate (e.g., presidential success) is negatively associated with changes in presidential success, suggesting an equilibrium to success. The strong coefficient here suggests that presidential success reverts to its equilibrium level relatively quickly. This makes sense theoretically. If, as the theory argues, presidents adjust the expectations based on previous successes, then as conditions that affect success change, presidents should speedily adjust to the changing conditions.

On the key issue of the relationship between agenda size and success, the results repeat the positive association between size of the president's agenda and success. From Table 7.3, each additional proposal is associated with a 0.04% increase in aggregate success. Although the increment appears trivial, a one-standard deviation increase in the size of the agenda (about 80 important proposals) cumulates to a 3% increase in success, a modest but statistically significant effect in the hypothesized direction. This finding, coupled with similar findings reported in this chapter, all point to the positive association between agenda size and success as the theory of congressional anticipations hypothesizes.

The theory of congressional anticipations and the previous analyses in this chapter also suggested that once controlling for the effect of agenda size, divided government should not have as large an effect on success as reported in the extant literature. Results on Table 7.3 support that hypothesis. Neither divided government lagged nor in changes has a direct effect on aggregate success, but both have strong effects on agenda size.

The interaction between minority status and reelection congresses (year 3 and 4 of a presidential term), the presidential blame game, shows a negative effect for both the lag and changes of this interaction term. The lag effect is −18% and the change effect is −11%. These results are consistent with the idea that presidents are submitting proposals to Congress that they know will be defeated, perhaps for reelection campaign purposes, as discussed previously. Notably, these effects on success are independent of the impact of divided government-reelection on the size of the agenda. Both the lag and change forms of the interaction have strong positive and substantively meaningful effects on agenda size.

Several other variables also affect presidential success in these estimations. First, the lag of interest rates boosts presidential success. Each 1% increase in interest rates is associated with a 1% increase in presidential success. Here Congress and the president might be jointly responding to the effects of rising interest rates on the economy, and the potential negative political consequences for both. The lag of a Republican in office and changes to a Democrat depress success. Finally, the lag of war leads to lower presidential success of nearly 6%. This finding is consistent with the previously reported finding, which is that as war continues, presidential success falls.

Putting all of the findings of this chapter thus far into perspective, we find strong support for the basic contentions of the theory of congressional anticipations. As that theory predicts, there will be a positive association between the size of the presidential agenda and success, which is what we have found in all the analyses presented. We should not read this as agenda size is related to presidential *influence* but rather that presidents adjust their agendas to expectations for success based on their reading of the congressional environment. As Bond and Fleisher (1990; also Beckmann, 2010) argue, there is a difference between success and influence. With the data at hand we can observe success but not influence. Second, and also consistent with the theory of congressional anticipations, results in this chapter show that divided government has much less direct impact on presidential success than reported in the extant literature. Most of divided government's effects are mediated through the size of the agenda. Divided government is among the most important factors conditioning the president's agenda, because presidents can expect their success with Congress to fall when facing an opposition as opposed to same-party control.

MODERN PRESIDENTS AND PRESIDENTIAL PROPOSAL SUCCESS

As detailed in Chapter 4, modern presidents, defined as those serving since the establishment of the central clearance process, submit on average five times as many legislative proposals to Congress as pre-modern presidents, 300 compared with about 60. Heightened expectations for presidential leadership are usually cited to account for this rise in legislative activism (e.g., Greenstein, 1978, 1988); however, the literature on presidential success with Congress suggests that modern presidents have a difficult time with Congress (e.g., Krutz, Fleisher, and Bond, 1998). Thus the modern presidency puzzle: Why the steep increase in presidential proposals to Congress if presidents can expect rough times gaining congressional support for their proposals?

The theory of congressional anticipations argues that presidents mold their legislative agendas partly based on expectations of how Congress will treat their legislative proposals. Presidents can withhold proposals with little prospect for enactment, but they might also try to amass resources that enhance their bargaining situation with Congress. The central clearance process, argued in Chapter 3, centralizes bureaucratic expertise in the president's hands. Through that process, presidents regulate congressional access to bureaucratic expertise, insofar as Congress wants or needs that expertise to inform how it crafts legislation. Thus, the central clearance process provides modern presidents with a resource that enhances their bargaining situation with Congress, something that premodern presidents did not possess.

This discussion suggests two hypotheses. First, if this is the case, then we should see modern presidents being more successful in their dealings with Congress than premodern presidents were. Thus, to the analysis presented in Table 7.1, we can add a dummy variable for modern presidents, 1946 to the present (modern $=1$, premodern $=0$), using the rise of central clearance to differentiate modern from premodern presidents, rather than the traditional definition, which cites FDR as the first modern president. The timing of modernity might vary, depending on the characteristic of the presidency we are regarding. This modern president dummy variable should be positive and statistically significant.

An important complication, however, is that we have already demonstrated that the size of the agenda is positively associated with presidential success, but the modern presidency dummy variable is collinear

TABLE 7.4. *Impact of the Modern Presidency on Individual Proposal Success, 1st to 100th Congresses, Multivariate Probit (Clustered on Congress)*

Variable	Modern Presidency Model[a]				Interaction Model[a]			
	b	SE	p	Impact	b	SE	p	Impact
Constant	0.69	0.32	0.03		0.86	0.29	0.003	
Modern Presidency	0.20	0.33	0.27	0.05	−1.03	0.002	0.000	−0.27
Proposals	0.002	0.0005	0.000	0.0004	−0.009	0.002	0.000	−0.002
Modern Pres. × Proposals					0.01	0.002	0.000	0.003
n	13,538				13,538			
Wald Chi-sq/p	255.3	0.000			310.8	0.000		
Log Likelihood	−5,862.9				−5,779.9			
Pseudo-R^2	0.13				0.14			

[a] The estimation also includes the following variables from Table 7.1: Divided government, War Counter, New Party Dummy, Recession Dummy, New Party × Recession, Interest Rates, New Party × Interest Rates, Polarization, Treaty Dummy, Deficit % of GDP, Federal Outlays % of GDP, Lame-duck Dummy, Second Congress (Years 3 and 4 of a presidential term), and Filibuster Era Dummy.

Impact: Probability shift of a one-unit change in the independent variable. For dummy variables, a 0–1 shift.

with the size of the agenda.[22] Thus we have the second hypothesis, which argues that there should be an interaction effect between presidential modernity and success. Everything else being equal, each proposal of a modern president should have a higher prospect of success than a proposal from a premodern president. We can capture this effect with an interaction term (*modern president × size of the agenda*), which we expect to be statistically significant with a positive sign.

Table 7.4 presents the analysis on individual level proposal success. That analysis uses the model estimated in Table 7.1, the agenda size model.[23] To conserve space, the table only presents the results for the

---

[22] The correlation between modern presidents and the size of the agenda is 0.84 ($p <$ 0.000).

[23] Three variables, the war dummy and the dummies for international relations and domestic policy, are not used because they are not statistically significant. I also attempted to implement the two-stage probit model, but the estimation would not converge with the inclusion of the additional variables, the modern president dummy and the interaction term.

TABLE 7.5. *Impact of the Size of the President's Legislative Policy Agenda on the Probability of Individual Proposal Success in Congress for Premodern and Modern Presidents*

Size of Agenda	Premodern Presidents (1789–1945)		Modern Presidents (1946–1988)	
	Agenda Size	Probability of Enactment[a]	Agenda Size	Probability of Enactment[a]
Minimal	5	−0.01	145	−0.13
Average	61	−0.12	320	+0.05
Maximum	145	−0.29	665	+0.39

[a] Probability of enactment for each proposal, based on the results from Table 7.4, the interaction model.

key variables for this analysis. The other variables behave as they did in Table 7.1. The left-side estimation, labeled *modern dummy*, adds the modern presidency dummy. As expected, the modern dummy by itself is statistically insignificant ($b = 0.20$, $p = 0.27$), but the interaction term for modernity and size of the agenda is positive and strongly statistically significant ($b = 0.01$, $p < 0.000$). Above and beyond the effects of all the other variables in the model, each additional proposal by a modern president has a 0.003 probability (or 0.3%) increase of enactment.

Although this increment appears tiny, recall the large size of the agenda of modern presidents. To fully appreciate the impact of the interaction between modernity and agenda size, we need to take into account all three terms that comprise the interaction – the modernity dummy, the size of the agenda, and the interaction between them. Table 7.5 presents the probabilities of enactment for agendas at varying sizes that roughly correspond to small, average, and large agendas for premodern and modern presidents.[24]

For premodern presidents, as the agenda grows, controlling for all the other variables, the probability of enactment declines. Increasing the size of a premodern presidential agenda from its smallest (5) to average size (61) reduces the prospects of enactment from each proposal from −0.01 to −0.12. At the largest agenda of premodern

[24] To make these calculations, I use these probabilities: modernity = −0.27, agenda size = −0.002, modernity × agenda size = +0.0026.

presidents, 145, the prospects of enactment fall further, to −0.29 per proposal. Legislatively ambitious premodern presidents do not possess the resources to influence Congress to support their initiatives, especially as their legislative ambitions grew. Something other than prospects for success must motivate the large agendas of legislatively ambitious premodern presidents.

Modern presidents, in contrast, see the prospects of success rise as their agendas grow in size and ambition. As Table 7.5 indicates, the probability of enactment per proposal is −0.13 for the smallest agendas (145) of modern presidents. Matters improve as the size of the agenda grows. At average-sized agendas (320), presidents can expect a +0.05 probability for each proposal; however, it is the largest agendas (665) of modern presidents that see the highest enactment rates at +0.39. These findings are consistent with the modern presidency hypothesis of the congressional anticipations theory.

Table 7.6 presents results using the aggregate measure of success from Table 7.3 as a further test of the modern presidency-success hypothesis. To estimate the effects of modernity on aggregate success, I add to the second stage (enactment success estimation) a dummy variable for modern presidents (80th Congresses and after = 1; 0 otherwise) and an interaction term between modernity and the size of the agenda (restricted to important proposals) to the variables previously included. With these variables included, the war lag and interest rates variables fall to statistical insignificance. The modern presidency-agenda size interaction improves in performance when these war lag and interest rates variables are dropped.[25] Table 7.6 presents the results of this estimation without the war and interest rates variables.

Results of the aggregate analysis parallel those of the individual proposal analysis already reported. The interaction term is positive and statistically significant. Each additional proposal for modern presidents is associated with a 0.22% increase in success. Again, to calculate the full impact of the interaction requires combining the effects

[25] With war-lagged and interest rates-lagged, the modernity-agenda size interaction has a $b = 0.17$ and a p value = 0.11. Without the war-lagged and interest rates-lagged variable the modernity-agenda size interaction rises to $b = 0.22$ and a p value = 0.04, which is now clearly statistically significant, but the R^2 falls from 0.44 to 0.27.

TABLE 7.6. *Impact of the Modern Presidency on Agenda Proposal Success, 7th to 100th Congresses, Congressional Level, Aggregate Analysis, Two-stage Least Squares*

Variable	Endogenous Variable: Number of Proposals Per Congress (changes)			Endogenous Variable: Enactment Rate Per Congress (changes)		
	b	SE	p	b	SE	p
Constant	29.40	15.06	0.05	25.06	5.02	0.000
Enactment Rate-lag				−0.65	0.11	0.000
Modern Pres. Dummy-changes				−44.92	21.10	0.02
Modern Pres-Size-changes				0.22	0.13	0.04
Size-changes				−0.18	0.13	0.08
Size-lag	−0.31	0.08	0.000			
Years 3 and 4	−14.39	12.93	0.27^a	−5.66	4.11	0.17^a
Divided Govt-lag	−36.26	26.16	0.08	8.59	7.57	0.13
Divided Govt-changes	−45.68	16.99	0.004	4.30	4.98	0.20
Interaction: DG × Yr. 3 and 4, Lag	75.62	40.11	0.03	−24.55	12.42	0.09
Interaction: DG × Yr. 3 and 4, Changes	45.56	23.52	0.03	−13.47	7.09	0.03
Interest Rates-lag	−4.73	2.56	0.035			
Deficit %-Lag	7.14	2.86	0.007			
Outlays %-Lag	7.07	1.71	0.000			
Republican Pres.-lag				−15.16	3.93	0.000
Republican Pres-changes	−51.99	13.79	0.000			
Democratic Pres-changes				−8.20	4.53	0.04
89th Congress-lag	431.20	96.90	0.000			
89th Congress-changes	378.49	50.98	0.000			
91st Congress-lag	−3.22	0.87	0.000			
91st Congress-changes	−2.35	0.60	0.000			
R^2	0.76			0.27		
F	16.47			4.07		
p	0.000			0.000		

[a] Two-tailed test; all other p values are one-tailed tests.

of the three terms comprising the interaction model – the modernity dummy, size of the agenda, and their interaction. Based on the coefficients reported on Table 7.6, a modern president of an average-sized agenda (300) will have a success rate 6 percentage points higher than a modern president with the smallest agenda (150). An agenda of above-average size (450) will increase aggregate success another 6 percentage points over the average-size agenda, or 12 percentage points higher than for the smallest agenda. At the largest-sized agenda, 650 or so, modern presidents record aggregate success 20 percentage points higher than for presidents of the smallest agenda.[26] In contrast, for premodern presidents, as the agenda grows, the aggregate success rate falls, similar to what we reported for the individual proposal analysis. A one-standard deviation increase in the size of premodern presidential agendas is associated with a 5.8 percentage point *decline* in the aggregate success rate.[27]

These findings suggest that the boost in success associated with the institutions and resources of the modern presidency, like the central clearance process, are indeed potent and considerable. At least in regard to legislative relations, the modern presidency differs from the premodern one. Not only is the modern president more legislatively active than premodern presidents, a not-too-surprising finding, but modern presidents are more successful with Congress than premodern presidents merely by being modern. The modern office possesses institutional resources that can be converted into legislative success.

This leads us to a different understanding of the modern presidency compared with the existing literature. The existing literature emphasizes the presidential response to demands for presidential leadership. Clearly those demands partly explain the great rise in legislative activism of modern presidents. Those demands might also have

---

[26] The results of the estimation that includes the war-lagged and interest rate-lagged variables show essentially the same effects. With b for modernity = −35.5, the b for agenda size = −0.125, and the b for the interaction = 0.17, an average agenda (300) improves success over a small agenda (150) by 6.8%. For above-average (450) and largest (650) the improvement over the small agenda is 13.5 and 22.5 percentage points, nearly the same as that for the estimation with the war and interest rate variables.

[27] The decline in aggregate success is 4%, using the results of the estimation that includes the war-lagged and interest rate-lagged variables.

impelled presidents to seek out new resources, such as central clearance, that can be used in the legislative arena. Finding that those newfound institutional resources improve the president's bargaining situation with Congress, and thus bring success, modern presidents might have stoked public expectations for their policy and legislative leadership. The story of the modern presidency and its consequences is therefore more complex than what is found in the existing research.

CONGRESSIONAL ANTICIPATIONS, POLICY MODERATION, AND PRESIDENTIAL SUCCESS

The theory of congressional anticipations hypothesizes that presidents can react in several ways when faced with unfavorable conditions in Congress: 1) they can withhold legislative proposals with slim prospects for enactment; 2) they can acquire resources to enhance their bargaining position with Congress; and/or 3) they can modify their proposals to make them more acceptable to Congress. The previous sections of this chapter tested the first two approaches and found support for them. This section turns to the third approach, strategic modification.

The strategic modification hypothesis argues that presidents will moderate their policy positions when faced with divided government to increase their success levels. The analysis presented in Chapter 6 showed support for the idea that presidents moderate their policy positions during divided but not united government, conditional on the degree of party polarization. Presidents are less inclined to moderate their position taking when polarization is high than when it is low. Does policy moderation in the face of divided government lead to higher success levels, as the strategic modification hypothesis argues? This section tests the success implications of the strategic modification hypothesis.

As in Chapter 6, we cannot test the divided government-moderation hypothesis with the presidential proposal data. For the reasons outlined in Chapter 6, we do not yet possess the capability of locating presidential proposals in an ideological or policy space. Hence, I again turn to the presidential ADA support scores to measure presidential policy stances, noting that the ADA scores are based on presidential positions on roll calls. Roll calls measures differ from the presidential proposal data in two regards. First, roll call measures do not include presidential proposals that do not receive a roll call. Second, roll call measures include presidential positions on items not from the president's agenda, such as bills that members of Congress introduced. With these roll call data we cannot test whether presidents moderate their legislative agendas, but presidents should moderate the positions they take on roll calls. The logic of the strategic modification hypothesis applies to both position taking and presidential agenda building.

The dependent variable for this analysis is total annual House and Senate concurrence with the president from 1952 to 2000 (Ragsdale, 2009, pp. 500–502).[28] Concurrence is the number of roll calls supporting the president divided by the total number of roll calls on which the president took a position. I use the concurrence scores of the two chambers combined because the strategic modification hypothesis argues that presidents moderate when the opposition party holds at least one chamber.

The strategic moderation-success hypothesis argues that moderation leads to success only during periods of divided government. Moderation implies that a president moves closer to the policy preferences of the opposition party and away from his own party. By moving closer to the opposition party's policy preferences during divided government, the president should increase the likelihood of forging a legislative compromise with the opposition, increasing presidential success.[29] Presidents need some opposition support to win during divided government. Conversely, if during divided government presidents do not moderate but take positions close to their own party, the likelihood of success should fall. Presidential extremism in the face of divided government reduces the likelihood of picking up support from opposition legislators, which is necessary for success on roll calls. In contrast, presidents do not have to moderate when their party controls

---

[28] Total concurrence is a weighted average of House and Senate concurrence rates, the number of roll calls in each chamber being the weighting factor.

[29] This case is a good illustration of the difference between presidential success and influence. Here presidents can increase their success by accommodating to Congress, that is, when they are least influential.

both legislative chambers but should locate near their party's center. As long as their party stays cohesive, presidents do not need opposition support to prevail on roll calls during untied government.[30] To measure this interaction model, I use the following equation:

$$\textit{Presidential Success} = \textit{Constant} + b_1 \,(\textit{Divided Government})$$
$$+ \, b_2 \,(\textit{Presidential Policy Extremism}) + b_3 \,(\textit{Divided Government}$$
$$\times \textit{Presidential Policy Extremism}) + b_n(\textit{Other Factors}) + e$$

As in Chapter 6, divided government is a dummy variable, coded 1, if the opposition party controls at least one legislative chamber and presidential policy extremism is the annual corrected folded ADA presidential support score. High ADA scores indicate presidential extremism, whereas low scores indicate presidential moderation. The strategic moderation hypothesis predicts a statistically significant and negative sign to the interaction term, b_3 (Divided Government × Presidential Policy Extremism).

For b_n (Other Factors), I include dummy variables for presidents, a dummy variable for years 3 and 4, and presidential approval. The president dummies pick up unmeasured factors associated with individual presidents that can affect success, such as presidential skill with Congress. Experimentation found two presidential dummies with significant effects on success, Nixon and Reagan. To preserve degrees of freedom, the other president dummies are deleted from the analysis. Presidential success tends to be lower during years 3 and 4 of the term.[31] Finally, time series analysis of presidential success, like this

---

[30] This assumes that the president's party is large and united enough to overcome filibusters in the Senate or that the opposition is unlikely to threaten the president with a filibuster.

[31] Past research has generally found that presidential success rises during the first or honeymoon year and falls during the lame-duck or last year in office for a president. Bond and Fleisher (1990); Edwards (1989); Frendreis et al. (2001); Grossback et al. (2006); Lockerbie et al. (1998); Peterson (1990); and Peterson et al. (2003) report honeymoon effects, defining the honeymoon as the first year in office of a new president. Beckmann and Godfrey (2007) offer a formal model to account for higher presidential success during the honeymoon period. There is much less work on lame-duck effects, but Eshbaugh-Soha (2005) and Barrett and Eshbaugh-Soha (2007) find lower success for presidents during lame-duck periods. Based on these findings, I experimented with several variables to pick up these cyclical effects on success and the simple dummy distinguishing the first two years (1 and 2) of a term

TABLE 7.7. *Presidential Policy Extremism, Divided Government, and Presidential Success in Congress, 1952–2000*

Variable	b	SE	t	p
Divided Government	−7.11	6.68	−1.06	0.29
Policy Extremism	−0.07	0.17	−0.41	0.69
Divided Government × Policy Extremism	−0.48	0.20	−2.39	0.01[a]
Years 3 and 4	−8.80	2.57	−3.42	0.001[a]
Nixon	8.95	3.60	2.49	0.02
Reagan	14.24	3.32	4.29	0.00
Approval	0.20	0.10	1.96	0.03[a]
Constant	81.88	8.57	9.55	0.00

[a] One-tailed test; all others are two-tailed tests.
See text for variable definitions.

analysis, finds that approval affects success (Bond, Fleisher, and Wood, 2003, 2008; Rivers and Rose, 1985).

Table 7.7 presents the results. I use OLS because diagnostics revealed that the dependent variable was stationary and had no serial correlation in the residuals.[32] First, the overall model fits the data well, with an adjusted R^2 of 0.77. Second, as expected, presidential approval has a statistically significant and positive, albeit marginal, effect on success. Each one-percentage point gain in approval improves success by 0.2 percentage points. A one-standard deviation rise in approval (13%) leads to a 2.6% increase in success. Results also find that presidents fair better in their first two than their second two years in office. During the first half of their term, presidents can expected nearly 9% higher concurrence from Congress than during the second half of their term. Also, the president dummies indicate that Nixon and Reagan were 9.5% and 14% more successful than the other presidents.

from the second two years (3 and 4) worked best and preserved degrees of freedom. The primary purpose of this variable is as a control. Deleting this variable does not affect the interaction term, our variable of key interest, although the interaction term is slightly stronger and produces a larger R^2 with the dummy variable for years 3 and 4 included. Foreshadowing presentation of the results, without the year 3 and 4 variable, the interaction term has a $b = -0.45$, SE = 0.22, t =−1.99, $p < 0.03$, and adjusted $R^2 = 0.75$, compared to $b = -0.48$, SE = 0.20, t = −2.39, $p < 0.01$, and adjusted $R^2 = 0.77$.

[32] The Dickey-Fuller test statistic for success is −3.621 against critical values of −3.600 at the 0.01 level and −2.938 at the 0.05 level.

The variable of key interest is the interaction between divided government and policy extremism. Results on Table 7.7 indicate a statistically significant and negative effect of presidential extremism on success, as hypothesized. To calculate the effect of policy moderation/ extremism in the face of divided government requires taking into account the three variables necessary for estimating the interaction effect: the divided government dummy, presidential extremism, and their interaction. During divided government, presidential extremism ranges from 2.4 to 50, with an average of 34.2 and a standard deviation of 14.2. An average extreme president during divided government will be 17.5% less successful than the least extreme president, whereas the most extreme president will be 8.7% less successful than an average extreme president during divided government. The most extreme president will be about 26% less successful than the least extreme president during divided government.[33] Moderation versus extremism appears to have substantively potent effects on presidential success during divided government, consistent with the strategic moderation hypothesis.

These findings not only bear on our strategic moderation hypothesis but also inform us of the consequences of party polarization in Congress on presidential success. Recall from Chapter 6 that polarization offsets the tendency of presidents to moderate when confronted with divided government. This means that presidents moderate less when polarization is higher during divided government, which translates into lower success. Presidents can be quite successful during periods of divided government, but only if they can moderate, that is, shift their policy stances closer to the opposition and away from the

---

[33] I also ran separate regressions for divided and united government congresses. These regressions repeat the previous finding, that policy extremism is associated with lower success during divided government but has no impact for united government. The results of policy extremism for divide government on success are $b = 0.53$, SE $= 0.14$, $t = -3.84$, and $p < 0.001$; but for united government $b = -0.06$, SE $= 0.12$, $t = -0.55$, $p < 0.30$. We should be cautious in making direct comparisons of the two b coefficients here because the variances of the policy extremism and presidential success variables differ for divided as opposed to united government. The variances for policy extremism for divided and united government are 205.6 and 102.2, whereas for presidential success the variances are 180.9 (divided) and 32.8 (united). See Wright (1976) for more on this point and why interaction models are preferable to splitting data into subsets.

center of their own party. Polarization between the parties creates barriers and disincentives for such presidential movement during divided government.

CONCLUSION

In their groundbreaking study of presidential success in Congress, Bond and Fleisher (1990) argue that the way presidents package their agendas has implications for their success within the legislature. The theory of congressional anticipations developed earlier links presidential agenda-building decisions to success in Congress and suggests three testable hypotheses: the divided government, modern presidency, and strategic modification hypotheses. This congressional anticipations theory also helps to resolve the two puzzles that motivated this study, 1) the divided government puzzle, why presidents lose at such higher rates during divided than united government, when they can expect such high loss rates; and 2) the modern presidency puzzle, why modern presidents persist in submitting such large agendas to Congress, knowing full well the difficulties that they will face in persuading Congress to support these policy proposals.

This chapter tests the three major hypotheses derived from the theory of congressional anticipations as related to presidential success in Congress and found support for all three. The divided government hypothesis maintains that presidents will not submit to Congress legislative recommendations that they expect to be defeated. Defeat in Congress imposes costs on presidents that they would like to avoid. One way to avoid those costs is to refrain from submitting legislative proposals with low prospects for enactment. Earlier chapters find, consistent with the divided government hypothesis, that presidential agendas are smaller when facing opposition than majority congresses. A second implication is that once we have controlled for the size of the president's agenda, divided government should not have as large a direct impact on presidential success as is found in the literature. With the presidential proposal data at the individual proposal level and aggregated by Congress being used, this is what the analyses in this chapter find. In some estimations, divided government has no direct statistical effect on presidential success. This is not to suggest that divided government is unimportant to presidential success, but that rather than affecting the roll call votes of members directly, divided government affects the agenda that presidents submit to Congress.

The modern presidency hypothesis grows out of another puzzle: Why do modern presidents submit such large legislative agendas when the literature on presidential-congressional relations suggests that presidents often encounter difficulty in persuading Congress to enact their legislative proposals? Part of the answer to the modern presidency puzzle, of course, is the standard one found in the literature – the transformation of the political system in the mid-twentieth century that led to increased expectations for presidential policy leadership. The large agendas of modern as opposed to premodern presidents are partly a response to these heightened expectations, but this conventional answer is incomplete. It does not take into account the costs of legislative defeat to the policy leadership of modern presidents.

The modern presidency hypothesis argues that modern presidents acquired institutional and other resources that would enhance their bargaining situation with Congress, thereby improving the odds that Congress will enact their legislative proposals. For instance, the establishment of central clearance procedures in the early post-World War Two years, I argue, centralized bureaucratic expertise in the hands of the president. The president, through central clearance, could regulate congressional access to that expertise. Inasmuch as bureaucratic expertise is important to Congress when forging legislation, the president's bargaining role with Congress is enhanced through the executive's control over that expertise. It might not be entirely coincidental that the president's agenda rapidly ballooned in size with the codevelopment of central clearance.

This understanding of the modern presidency has implications for presidential success in Congress. Everything else being equal, modern presidents should be more successful than premodern ones, and if size of the agenda tells us about presidential expectations for legislative success, then we should find an interaction effect between presidential modernity and size of the agenda. This is what the analysis finds, using both the individual level and aggregated proposal data. For modern presidents, as size of the agenda grew, so also did success with Congress. In contrast, as size of the agenda grew for premodern presidents, success rates fell. Compared with modern presidents, premodern executives do not possess the resources to move ambitious agendas through Congress. This finding itself presents a new puzzle to explore – why some premodern presidents have ambitious legislative agendas and how they sought to gain congressional support for them.

Finally, the theory of congressional anticipations argues that presidents can avoid defeat by modifying their legislative proposals. Such strategic modification is most evident when the president faces an opposition-controlled Congress. When the opposition controls Congress, by definition, presidents need support from some member of the opposition for enactment of his legislative initiatives and positions. Analysis in Chapter 6 finds that presidents facing divided government do moderate their policy positions, subject to the amount of polarization between the congressional parties. This chapter looks at the implications of presidential moderation on success. As the hypothesis predicts, presidential moderation is associated with higher success levels when the opposition party controls at least one house of Congress.

The analysis in the chapter then finds support for each of the major hypotheses pertaining to success in Congress that were derived from the theory of congressional anticipations, just as earlier chapters find support for the impact of congressional anticipations on presidential agenda building. As Bond and Fleisher maintained, agenda-building decisions affect presidential success in Congress. The theory of congressional anticipations adds to that insight in two ways. First, conditions in Congress that might affect presidential success affect presidential agenda building. Second, the theory of congressional anticipations leads to several testable hypotheses regarding the impact of Congress on presidential agenda building and the impact of attributes of the presidential agenda on success with Congress. The theory of congressional anticipations integrates two bodies of literature, that on agenda building with that on presidential success in Congress.[34]

---

[34] Light (1991) suggests that the congressional environment affects presidential agenda building but he does not investigate what Congress does with presidential proposals, or whether presidential agenda-building decisions affect presidential success in Congress.

CHAPTER 8

Conclusion

This book opened with two puzzles, the divided government puzzle and the modern president puzzle. The divided government puzzle asks, Why do presidents allow themselves to be defeated so often when faced with an opposition-controlled Congress when there are things that they can do to avoid or lessen the high rate of defeat, such as refraining from submitting legislative proposals that are destined for defeat? The modern government puzzle asks, Why do modern presidents submit such large legislative agendas to Congress when the research on their relations with Congress suggests that they will have difficulty obtaining support from Congress for their proposals?

Although seemingly different, these two puzzles ask essentially the same question, but in different contexts: Why do presidents allow themselves to be defeated so often? To resolve these puzzles, I offered the theory of congressional anticipations. That theory argues first that presidents read the congressional environment for clues concerning the likely action that Congress will take on their legislative proposals. The theory then argues that presidents want to avoid congressional defeat of their proposals because of the costs of such defeats. Presidents have several options if they expect a proposal to be defeated. They can withhold the proposal, that is, not submit it for legislative consideration, they can modify the proposal to make it more acceptable to Congress, or they can accumulate additional resources to enhance their bargaining situation with Congress.

The empirical sections of this book provided support for each of these strategic adaptations to the congressional environment. In particular, we found that

- The president's legislative agenda is smaller during divided than united government, because presidents strip proposals destined for congressional defeat from their agenda, as the divided government hypothesis predicts.
- Once the size of the president's agenda is taken into account, divided government no longer has such a pronounced direct effect on success in Congress as found in the extant literature. Most of the effect of divided government on success is mediated through the size of the president's agenda, again as predicted by the divided government hypothesis.
- Presidents will moderate their policy positions during divided as opposed to united government. Such policy moderation improves the odds for presidential success during divided but not united government, which the policy moderation hypothesis predicts.
- Moderation leads to higher presidential success during periods of divided government, another prediction of the policy moderation hypothesis.
- Beginning with the full implementation of the legislative clearance process in 1949, the size of the president's agenda grew remarkably. The legislative clearance process gave modern presidents a newfound institutional resource that increased their prospects for success in Congress. Consequently, the legislative agendas for modern presidents are larger than those of traditional, pre-1949 presidents.
- Modern presidents are more successful with Congress than traditional presidents, and there is a positive relationship between the size of the agenda and success for modern presidents. There is a negative relationship between agenda size and success for traditional presidents, however. Modern presidents have larger agendas than traditional ones partly because they foresee greater success with Congress than their traditional counterparts, as the modern presidency hypothesis predicts.

An important contribution of this study is to link the presidential agenda-building process with the later legislative process. Although most research acknowledges a linkage between presidential agenda building and congressional action on the president's agenda (as the quote from Jon R. Bond and Richard Fleisher, which opens Chapter 7, illustrates), the bulk of the empirical work tends to treat the two as distinct processes. Thus, we have work on presidential agenda building and other work on presidential success in Congress. Rarely do we have work that explicitly joins the two, except as passing comments and references.

There are still limitations to this research, including unanswered questions, and this research speaks to other questions and issues related to the presidency that are not directly addressed in these pages. The remainder of this concluding chapter highlights some of the major limitations of this study, lists some questions left unanswered, and relates the findings presented earlier to other research topics and controversies associated with the presidency and presidential development.

LIMITATIONS

One of the major limitations of this study concerns the empirical design and strategy. The study of presidential agenda-building decisions shows that legislative proposals that are not submitted to Congress are unobserved, and there might be little that we can do systematically to identify those potential but unsent proposals. Unsent proposals tend not to leave a record or paper trail in either official government documents or newspapers.

We confront a situation that is somewhat similar to critiques of David Mayhew's seminal study of lawmaking, *Divided We Govern* (1991). Mayhew asked whether the president and Congress could overcome divided government and produce major legislation. His methodology basically compared the number of major pieces of legislation that government passed during divided and united government. Contrary to the conventional wisdom, which argued that divided government erects a high hurdle to legislative productivity, Mayhew found divided government was on average equally productive as united government. Mayhew's study spawned a large literature critiquing his work. Among the most relevant critiques for my study was Binder's (1999, 2003), which argued that a better measure of productivity was not the total number of major pieces of legislation enacted but rather the percentage of major issues that resulted in enactment. She found that during divided government, Congress enacted a smaller proportion of active items than during united government.

We can draw a parallel between the Mayhew-Binder studies and this one. Our data on presidential proposals is like Mayhew's list of major legislation. Binder in contrast identified the entire legislative agenda, distinguishing those agenda items that resulted in enactment from those that did not. This is similar to the potential presidential agenda discussed in Chapter 2, where I distinguished between proposals that were submitted to Congress and those not submitted. Ideally, we would like to replicate Binder and identify those proposals that the president did not send to Congress for legislative consideration. We could then directly compare those two sets of proposals and test the underlying assumption of the theory of congressional anticipations, that presidents are more likely to submit proposals with a stronger chance for enactment than those with a weaker chance for enactment.

Unsent proposals do not leave a paper trail in either newspapers (which Binder used for identifying failed legislative efforts) or government documents. Newspaper coverage of presidential agenda decisions is especially poor and weakens the further back in history one goes. For example, Cohen (2008) demonstrates the paltry level of newspaper coverage of the presidency prior to the mid-twentieth century. He also finds that until the advent of the modern presidency in the mid-twentieth century, the president tended to be an actor in a congressional news story. News coverage of the presidency tends to revolve around official actions of the president, like announcements and the submission of major reports (e.g., the State of the Union Address [SUA] or the budget). Only on a scattershot basis are there news stories about the internal workings of the presidency. For these reasons, newspapers do not provide a complete enough picture for us to identify unsent proposals, even for modern presidents.[1]

Nor does the government documentary record provide us with an alternative source for identifying unsent proposals. Proposals might be discussed between the president and his advisers/staff, but there might not be a written record of these discussions. An alternative could be to look more closely at the legislative clearance process and compare legislative proposals from the bureaucracy that the administration rejects from those that the president forwards to Congress (e.g., Rudalevige, 2002; Wayne, 1978, p. 76). The limitation of this approach is that we still lack information on presidential decisions before the central clearance process, and we do not know what happens to proposals that come to the president from other sources, like White House staffers and allies in Congress.

In statistical terms, we confront a problem of selection effects, in which we lack information on the parameters of our population of interest. To conduct a study with the historical scope as done here, I had to compromise and employ essentially a Mayhew-style research design. Like Mayhew, who compared legislative production for divided and united government, here I compare characteristics of the presidential agenda, like its size, from congress to congress. This allowed me to statistically model the dynamics of the president's agenda but not to test directly the core assumptions of the theory of congressional anticipations. Instead I had to settle for "what if" hypotheses, the secondary implications for agenda building if the president took into account the congressional environment in building his legislative agenda.

---

[1] In a related vein, I tried to recover news coverage about the proposals that the president did submit to Congress by using key word searches particular to each proposal from various newspaper databases. My aim was to try to develop a measure of proposal importance, somewhat similar to Mayhew (1991) and Clinton and Lipinski (2006). Although such a data collection effort would probably have been impossible for all 14,000 proposals, I found that I could not use this technique even on a sample: It was impossible to find news coverage of presidential proposals the further back in history I went, and even for more modern times, only a small percentage of presidential proposals received coverage near the time of proposing. Lack of data is a major hurdle to doing historical, comparative, and systematic research on the president.

Some of the core assumptions of the theory of congressional anticipations are left untested, however. Barring long-scale historical, systematic, and quantitative work, like that presented in these pages, case
studies of particular presidents and legislative proposals might be a
useful way of assessing whether presidents exclude or modify legislative proposals, as the theory of congressional anticipations suggests.
Light's (1991, 1999) interviews with White House staffers suggest that
they do. Supplementing case studies with interviews that focus on these
hypotheses, as did Light, also could be useful. Case studies that rely on
diaries of presidents and their advisers, and other records, might be
useful for peering into this issue for earlier presidents, perhaps giving
us a new way of looking at premodern presidents. They could prove
to be more strategic in this sense than our standard accounts suggests
(e.g., McCarty, 2009 on the early use of the veto).

UNANSWERED QUESTIONS

Several unanswered and new questions were raised earlier. First,
legislatively ambitious premodern presidents did not fair well with
Congress, which contrasts sharply with modern presidents. We found
a positive association between the size of the legislative agenda and
success for modern presidents, those of the legislative clearance era.
The argument offered was that presidents submit proposals that have
a good chance for enactment but withhold those with a weak chance.
Thus, large agendas indicate presidents who expect comparatively
high levels of support from Congress. To a degree this also holds
for premodern presidents. Their agendas are smaller during divided
than united government, the understanding being that presidents will
receive less cooperation from Congress during divided than united
government. Controlling for this and other factors, however, we found
that as the agendas of premodern presidents grow, their enactment
odds decline. Unlike modern presidents, premodern presidents do
not seem to possess the necessary resources to move ambitious agendas through the legislative process.

This raises the question: Why are some premodern presidents
legislatively ambitious? Is it in response to external, environmental
demands (some of which we already controlled for in the statistical

estimations presented in these pages)? Do they misread the legislative environment? Despite a few examples to the contrary, like John Quincy Adams and James K. Polk, most premodern presidents are characterized as lacking legislative ambitions, or as not being highly active or involved in the legislative process. One possible hypothesis to account for the negative association between legislative ambition and success for premodern presidents is their lack of follow-through or lobbying of Congress on behalf of their agendas, once submitted. Another possibility is that the costs of legislative defeat are not so dear for premodern as opposed to modern presidents, the latter serving in an era of heightened public expectations for presidential leadership. Without being so tethered to such public expectations and/or without feeling that they have to supply policy leadership, premodern presidents with legislative ambitions might be less concerned about the costs of defeat. This perspective runs counter to the finding of their sensitivity to divided government, however. This finding thus remains puzzling but opens up new areas of inquiry in presidential-legislative relations in the premodern era.

Second, findings reported in Chapter 5 suggest interconnections among presidential proposals. This view differs from the unstated assumption of much research on agenda setting, which tends to look at issues and proposals in isolation from other proposals on the agenda. The *issue isolation* perspective is most evident in case studies of agenda setting, which tend to look at one issue at a time, asking why and when a particular issue attains agenda status.[2]

Clearly, other research contends that the agenda status fate of issues might have similar roots. For instance, the larger political, economic, and social context could affect the agenda status of large numbers of issues at the same time (Baumgartner and Jones, 1993). If the public is in an activist mood, issues might have an easier time gaining a foothold on the policy agenda than when the public mood leans in a conservative, antiactivist direction. From another perspective, the ability to apply a "popular" policy solution might enhance the prospects that an issue will make it onto the agenda (Kingdon, 1995; Light, 1991,

---

[2] A useful critique of case study agenda-setting research can be found in Baumgartner and Jones, 1993, ch. 3.

1999). In the late 1970s and early 1980s, deregulation was such a policy solution. From its early application to topics like telecommunications, transportation, and banking (Derthick and Quirk, 1985), the deregulatory solution was applied to noneconomic policy areas like education (Brown, 1995).

The point that I am making is different, that the presidential (or other agenda setters) choice to put one issue on the agenda directly affects the likelihood that another issue will get onto the agenda. In Chapter 5, I offered two ways to link issues: policy competition and logrolling. Policy competition suggests that when presidents decide to go with one issue, another issue is blocked from attaining agenda status. For instance, there may be trade-offs between issues, perhaps because of natural "conflicts" between issues, limited resources (e.g., budgets), and/or limited attention. To a degree the old adage that a nation cannot pursue both "guns and butter" at the same time evokes the policy competitiveness idea between domestic and foreign policies.

Logrolling suggests that two possibly disparate issues might be linked. Unlike the popular policy solution perspective noted earlier, logrolling does not necessarily involve applying the same or similar policy solution or problem definition to the issues. Rather, logrolling is an attempt to widen the base of support for each policy by erecting a "temporary" coalition: Supporters of Issue A will support Issue B if Issue B's supporters also support Issue A. Logrolling is an often-noted technique for narrow-based issues to emerge as a policy in majoritarian institutions like legislatures. The president sometimes engages in issue-based logrolling to further the prospects that Congress will enact several elements of his agenda. In fact, presidents might adopt an issue onto their agenda merely to advance the prospects of another issue of higher priority to the president. Little research to date exists on the impact of policy competition and logrolling in presidential agenda setting, and this topic is ripe for future research.

THE DEVELOPMENT OF THE PRESIDENCY

Several other findings reported in this study not only raise unanswered questions but also have implications for our understanding of the institutional development of the presidency. Clearly, the presidency of the past sixty to seventy years differs fundamentally from the office of earlier times. For convenience, let's call these recent presidents "modern" and their predecessors "traditional." Modern presidents receive more news coverage and occupy a larger place in the popular imagination than did their predecessors (Cohen, 2008). A larger, more expert, and better organized staff apparatus supports modern presidents compared with what their traditional predecessors had to work with (Dickinson and Lebo, 2007). Modern presidents also play a larger role in the legislative policy-making process, providing more leadership on policy issues, lobbying Congress more systematically in favor or in opposition to policy options, and as detailed here, submitting larger policy agendas for Congress to work on. One of the puzzles in understanding these developments is how they occurred without fundamentally altering the constitutional foundations of the presidency.

Greenstein (1988) offered one of the first statements that addressed this question. Events and personalities play a large part in Greenstein's account. The combination of the Great Depression and Franklin Roosevelt's ambitions, according to Greenstein, partly explain the rise of the modern presidency in the middle twentieth century.[3] Students of the presidency often forget, however, that the intellectual roots of modern executive leadership had been in place for thirty to forty years prior to FDR, a legacy of the Progressive movement (Arnold, 1986; Landy and Milkis, 2000). The Progressive movement, which emphasized among other elements strong executive leadership and responsibility, swept across the states in the late 1800s and early 1900s. Many state and local governments had been modern in form for a generation or so before modernity came to the presidency. Progressivism also came to the federal government before FDR, with the creation of the executive-centered budget process in the early 1920s (Seligman and Covington, 1989).

---

[3] To be fair, Greenstein's discussion of the development into the modern presidency transcends those two elements, FDR and the Great Depression, but many treatments of the modern-traditional divide focus heavily on FDR and the Depression to explain the transformation of the presidency.

Greenstein's modern presidency idea came under criticism soon after it appeared. Of the many critics, two stand out, Jeffrey Tulis's (1987) rhetorical presidency notion and Stephen Skowronek's (1993, 2002, 2008) political time thesis. Whereas Greenstein's idea marks the mid-1930s as the fundamental transition period for the presidency, distinguishing presidents from 1789 to 1932 as premodern and those from FDR to the present as modern, Tulis's cites the early 1900s, the presidencies of Theodore Roosevelt and especially Woodrow Wilson, as an earlier (and perhaps more important) transition era.

Greenstein suggests that several factors – the president's role in legislating, White House staffing, the position of the United States in international politics, and the public presidency – had to come together to produce the modern presidency. The modern presidency in Greenstein's view is complex and multifaceted. In contrast, Tulis emphasizes the public presidency, especially the use of rhetoric to mobilize public support behind the president and his policy initiatives. According to Tulis, this transformed the character of the polity from a republic to a democracy, with most democratic attention being placed on the president.

Skowronek takes a completely different tack. Unlike Greenstein and Tulis, who identify important moments that transformed the presidency, Skowronek argues that the presidency is best understood from a cyclical perspective. Skowronek argues that the president's place in political time explains more of the president's behavior, leadership, and impact on the political system than either the rise of the rhetorical or the modern presidency. Thus modern presidents of articulation (Lyndon Johnson) or disjunction (Carter), for example, have much in common with premodern presidents during the articulation (Monroe) or disjunction (Pierce) phases of the political time cycle.

Greenstein's, Tulis's, and Skowronek's work has stimulated numerous elaborations, specifications, refinements, and critiques. One common type of study asks, Who was the first modern-rhetorical president, Theodore Roosevelt or Woodrow Wilson, or someone else? Such studies often present an indicator, based on presidential rhetoric, to demonstrate who was first in using that rhetorical attribute, and then argue that so-and-so is the first rhetorical president.[4] Although historically it would be nice to know who was first or when certain presidential behaviors, rhetorical or otherwise, initially appeared, this type of fine-tuned dating might be beside the point for understanding the institutional development of the presidency.

As argued here (also Woolley, 2005), we need to develop theories about the causes of certain types of presidential behaviors. Rhetorical traits might provide useful dependent variables, but we also need independent variables, derived from theories, and to test whether those independent variables actually affect the behavior under scrutiny. In this study I measure certain aspects of the president's legislative policy agenda as the dependent variables, including its size and policy content. I focused in particular on anticipations of the congressional reaction to presidential proposals to explain these attributes of the president's agenda, while also identifying several other independent variables that might affect temporal variation in the president's agenda. The basic design employed here is rare in studies trying to account for the long historical development of the presidency, although the approach is more common for other types of studies of "modern" presidential behavior, such as speech making, roll call success, and congressional support.

What do we learn substantively from taking this type of analytic approach? First, we learn something about the evolution of the president's agenda from looking at the time trends of certain traits. For example, the size of the presidential agenda grew across the entire history of the office, but a great surge in agenda size occurred shortly after the Second World War concluded. The president's legislative agenda continued to grow in size, peaking in the 1960s. After reaching that peak, the size of the president's legislative agenda receded, settling at levels still higher than pre-1945 presidents. Furthermore, much of the post-1945 surge in the size of the agenda came from increased presidential attention to domestic, especially social, policies. Moreover, this increase in legislative activism also accompanies the institution of the legislative clearance process. All told, this provides a more detailed and nuanced portrait of this aspect of presidential development than

---

[4] See for instance the debate between Teten (2003, 2007, 2008) and Murphy (2008).

is found in much of the literature and leads to several new directions for studying the development of the presidency.

First, this research bears on the utility of the modern presidency concept and the "big bang" (Skowronek, 2002) approach to understanding the emergence of the modern office. At least as it pertains to legislative activism, there is a modern presidency that differs fundamentally from the traditional office. As noted, in the mid-to-late 1940s, there was a rapid and steep surge in the size of the president's legislative policy agenda, and the high level of presidential proposing has persisted to the present. Both the modern and "big bang" approaches (or "line drawing," see Woolley, 2005) are useful for understanding this aspect of presidential behavior.

Saying this for legislative activism does not mean that both the modernity and big bang concepts are also applicable to all other aspects of presidential behavior and institutional development, however. It is quite possible that some aspects of the office developed incrementally and/or far earlier than conventional dating of the modern presidency (mid-twentieth century).

The coincidence of the surge in legislative activism with presidential attention to domestic policy also deserves more scholarly attention. That modern presidents have paid much attention to domestic policy is not a novel finding, but it is somewhat puzzling that they would do so, sometimes at the expense of attending to foreign policy, in the era when the United States emerged as the world's leading superpower and was engaged in a Cold War with the Soviet Union. What are the connections among the rise of the modern presidency, the erection of the legislative clearance process, and the accumulation of larger presidential staffs, to the presidential attention turn to domestic policy? We need more research on these linkages.

Furthermore, the theory of congressional anticipations suggests an under-explored rationale for the creation of the legislative clearance process. Most studies of the history and development of that process emphasize the control over the bureaucracy that presidents gained from the legislative clearance process, as well as the ability to set the congressional agenda (e.g., Berman, 1979; Neustadt, 1954, 1955; Rudalevige, 2002; Wayne, 1978).

Central clearance can be thought of as part of the development of the president's legislative policy program. Through central clearance, the president channels bureaucratic and other proposals for legislation to Congress, usually accompanied with drafts of bills. Neustadt (1955) remarks on the potential value of these drafts of bills to Congress as a starting point for its legislative efforts, while also providing the president with a way to set the legislature's agenda, to enable it to work on items that the president deems important (1955, p. 1015). Cameron and Park (2008) have formalized Neustadt's idea with their burden-sharing model. Larocca (2006) too argues that institutional advantages accrue to the president through these mechanisms and services.

I take a slightly different approach, arguing that through the regulation of bureaucratic expertise to Congress by the central clearance process and the preparation of the president's program, presidents enhanced their bargaining situation with Congress, which results in higher success. This book finds empirical support for this proposition, but did this logic affect presidents when they were building and instituting central clearance and the president's program? Did presidents see the central clearance and presidential program processes as possibly resulting in greater influence with Congress, or was that heightened success merely a by-product of developing those processes, motivated primarily by political and public expectations for presidential leadership and the need to control an increasingly large bureaucracy?

LEGISLATIVE AND EXECUTIVE MODES OF PRESIDENTIAL POLICY MAKING

Besides the legislative route, presidents can make policy through unilateral means, the most important being executive orders. Presidents have been issuing executive orders since the earliest days of the Republic. In his first year in office in 1789, George Washington penned three executive orders, and seven overall in his first term. Except for occasional spurts in using executive orders, as in 1842 when Tyler issued fourteen and in 1847 when Polk signed twelve, issuance of executive orders generally remained light until after the Civil War, when it became common for presidents to issue nearly twenty orders per year. A swell in the volume of executive orders began with Theodore Roosevelt's second term, when he averaged more than 200 per year, a level that persisted through Franklin Roosevelt's tenure. Just as legislative proposing rates surged with Harry Truman, however, executive order rates began to fall, dropping to less than 100 per year for most subsequent presidents (Ragsdale, 2009, pp. 447–454).

What are the connections between these two modes of presidential policy making? How do conditions in Congress affect use of both forms of policy making, the legislative and the unilateral? Studies on executive orders have addressed the second question, but except for Howell (2003), research on the first question is rare.

As to conditions in Congress, two perspectives permeate the literature. First, presidents turn to executive orders when Congress is blocking their legislative initiatives. Second, presidents turn to executive orders when confronting friendly and legislatively productive congresses. Executive orders are used to fill in the details of legislation; when Congress enacts numerous policies, there is a greater need for presidents to issue executive orders. Although numerous studies now exist on this question, considerable debate exists on the impact of congressional conditions on presidential issuance of executive orders.[5] Most of that research, too, is limited to the post-World War Two era. The brief historical review earlier on the volume of executive orders suggests that the relationship between executive order use and legislative proposing varies across time periods.

Krause and Cohen (2000), two of the few researchers to study executive orders quantitatively before the advent of the modern presidency, suggest three epochs in their use by presidents, a *preinstitutionalized* presidency period (1990–1930), an *institutionalizing* period (1930–1970), and an *institutionalized* presidency period (1970–present). Such a temporal conceptualization might help to link presidential use

---

[5] Leading recent studies of executive orders include Deering and Maltzman (1999); Howell (2003, 2005); Howell and Mayer (2005); Krause and D. Cohen (1997); Krause and J. Cohen (2000); Lewis (2005); Marshall and Pacelle (2005); Mayer (1999, 2001); Mayer and Price (2002); and Moe and Howell (1999). Useful overviews of the literature on executive orders, and unilateral action more generally, can be found in Mayer (2009), Pious (2009), and Waterman (2009).

of executive orders with legislative proposing. Connections between the two could vary across differing historical periods.

Howell (2003) links legislative productivity in Congress directly to issuance of executive orders. He argues that when Congress has a harder time producing legislation, presidents turn to executive orders for making policy. Using seemingly unrelated regression, Howell finds that his measures of congressional policy-making difficulty have different impacts on the production of legislation versus executive orders – as difficulty increases, legislative production drops, whereas executive order issuance increases.[6] Controlling for this congressional barrier to producing legislation, Howell finds that divided government results in both fewer legislative enactments and executive orders. Howell's analysis has only twenty-seven time points (congresses), however, which limits the number of controls that can be applied. Because Howell's analysis is for the post-World War Two period, it cannot shed light on the development of these two policy-making modes.

Future research should avoid exclusive analysis of either the legislative or unilateral policy-making modes to designs that address both. When making policy, presidents ask themselves which approach is best for attaining their policy aims. Both legislation and unilateral devices are hard to overturn. Howell (2003) shows that Congress or the Courts rarely reverse an executive order, but a new president may easily reverse an existing executive order by issuing a new one. Furthermore, sometimes presidents require legislation because the authority to take certain actions simply does not exist. These points argue for the superiority of legislation over unilateral devices for policy making; however, executive orders are much easier to accomplish than legislation.

This highlights one of the limitations of this study, as well as others that look at executive orders or legislation isolated from other forms of presidential policy making. When presidents are considering submitting legislative proposals to Congress, they not only ask themselves about legislative prospects but also if the unilateral route might

---

[6] Howell uses two indirect measures of congressional difficulty in producing legislation, the size of the majority party and an index of legislative productivity potential, which combines the size of the majority and minority parties and the internal cohesiveness of the two parties.

accomplish their policy ends. These points suggest several recommendations for future research on presidential policy making that links legislative and unilateral approaches. First, such research should extend as far back historically as possible, especially before the modern presidency began. As demonstrated here, much is to be gained by comparing policy making of premodern and modern presidents. If staffing resources and processes associated with the modern presidency have implications for legislative success, we might find that premodern presidents opt for unilateral devices when they have policy ambitions but limited resources for influencing Congress. This could account for the rapid rise and high level of executive order issuance from the late 1800s through the mid-twentieth century.

Second, whereas Howell (2003) compares legislation with executive orders, we can learn much about presidential policy making by also looking at presidential proposals for legislation rather than the final output of the legislative process. As detailed here, most presidential proposals do not make it to a floor vote, much less get enacted into law. What do presidents do when Congress kills a proposal or fails to consider it? Do presidents shift gears and proceed down the unilateral policy-making path, or not? Can presidents employ "unilateral policy-making threats," somewhat analogous to "veto threats" (Cameron, 2000) to motivate Congress to take action on their proposals? As these questions suggest, many new issues come up when we begin to think of the connections between unilateral and legislative routes to policy making.

Third, Howell (2003) looks at major legislation and executive orders. He quite imaginatively builds on Mayhew (1991, 2005) for identifying major executive orders, but Cameron and Park's (2008) burden-sharing model suggests that presidential influence from bill drafting is greater for less important legislation because Congress has strong incentives to invest resources and energy into important legislation. Although it is natural to be attracted to the study of important policy, the vast bulk of policy making is not on matters of such high importance. These lesser matters are not trivial either. Pairing Howell and Cameron-Park suggests the possibility that the connection between unilateral and legislative policy making could vary with the importance of the policy.

To address this possibility, however, requires that we measure the importance of presidential proposals. I tried to do so by looking at news coverage of presidential proposals, for example, but found that record to be too sketchy, even in the modern era when the president is the major topic of political reporting (Cohen, 2008). Another alternative is to use the databases on public presidential papers, for instance the American Presidency Project (http://www.presidency.ucsb.edu/), housed at the University of California at Santa Barbara, under the direction of John Woolley and Gerhard Peters. Based on the language that presidents use when transmitting their proposals to Congress, one can identify key words for searching within that database to see how often presidents refer to the proposal, assuming that presidents spend more time on proposals that are important to them than for less important proposals. This approach to measurement still must contend with the reticence of premodern presidents to lobby Congress and the public actively and publicly. Other than the document used to submit the proposal, we might not find any other references to the policy proposal until the modern era. Although this might undermine such a strategy for measuring importance, it might be quite informative about the development of the presidency, providing a way to study linkages across the rhetorical policy agenda, the public presidency, legislative proposing, and interactions with Congress.

Past research on presidential agenda building also has focused almost exclusively on domestic policy. I argue in these pages that we must incorporate foreign policy into the study of presidential agenda building and policy making more generally and to go beyond the crude distinction between domestic and foreign policy by looking at more refined policy categories. Doing so has paid off in greater understanding of presidential policy making and the development of the office.

Different factors affect presidential attention to foreign and domestic policy in their legislative agendas. The topic of foreign affairs is always a major presence on the president's legislative policy agenda, much as Durant and Diehl (1989) argue. Presidential attention to domestic policy increased incrementally over the long course of U. S. history but took off in the post-World War Two era, becoming the major preoccupation of the legislative agenda. Moreover, unlike foreign affairs, representational concerns seem to motivate presidential attention to domestic policy. In fact, the statistical models had a relatively difficult time accounting for presidential attention to foreign policy, presumably because of the actions of other nations, which stimulate or force a presidential response. Using a more refined policy typology than the domestic versus foreign policy dichotomy also could have dividends. The postwar surge in presidential attention to domestic policy related primarily to social policies. In terms of legislative policy attention, the modern presidency is to some degree a social policy presidency.

If we return to the issue of unilateral versus legislative policy-making modes, what is the relative policy mix for unilateral devices? It is quite likely that there are important distinctions in policy emphasis across the two policy-making approaches. Recall from Ragsdale's executive order data, mentioned previously, presidential use of executive orders fell in the postwar era just as legislative proposing began to take off. This difference in trends suggests possible differences in the policy composition of the two agendas, the administrative-unilateral and the legislative.

This analysis did not fully mine the policy data collected, however. Although I made some comparisons across the four major policy domains of the Katznelson-Lapinski policy categorization scheme, except for the disaggregation of domestic policy to try to understand more deeply the basis for the growth in the legislative agenda in the postwar years, the analysis rarely made much use of the more refined policy categories, yet another task for future research.

Bibliography

Aberbach, Joel D. and Bert A. Rockman. 2000. *In the Web of Politics: Three Decades of the US Federal Executive.* Washington, DC: Brookings Institution Press.

Ackerman, Bruce A. 2005. *Failure of the Founding Fathers: Jefferson, Marshall and the Rise of Presidential Democracy.* Cambridge, MA: Belknap Press of Harvard University Press.

Adler, E. Scott and John Wilkerson. 2005. "The Scope and Urgency of Legislation: Reconsidering Bill Success in the House of Representatives." Presented at the American Political Science Association annual meeting, Washington, DC, 2005.

Aldrich, John H. 1995. *Why Parties? The Origin and Transformation of Political Parties in America.* Chicago: University of Chicago Press.

Aldrich, John H. and David W. Rohde. 2001. "The Logic of Conditional Party Government: Revisiting the Electoral Connection." In *Congress Reconsidered,* eds. Lawrence C. Dodd and Bruce I. Oppenheimer. Washington, DC: CQ Press. 7th ed, pp. 269–292.

Alesina, Alberto and Howard Rosenthal. 1995. *Partisan Politics, Divided Government, and the Economy.* New York: Cambridge University Press.

Anderson, James E. 2003. *Public Policy-Making: An Introduction,* 5th ed. Boston: Houghton Mifflin.

Anderson, Sarah and Philip Habel. 2009. "Revisiting Adjusted ADA Scores for the U.S. Congress, 1947–2007." *Political Analysis* 17 (No. 1): 83–88.

Andrade, Lydia and Garry Young. 1996. "Presidential Agenda Setting: Influences on the Emphasis of Foreign Policy." *Political Research Quarterly* 49 (No. 3): 591–605.

Andres, Gary. 2005. "The Contemporary Presidency: Polarization and White House/Legislative Relations: Causes and Consequences of Elite-Level Conflict." *Presidential Studies Quarterly* 35 (December): 761–770.

Arnold, Peri E. 1986. *Making the Managerial Presidency: Comprehensive Reorganization Planning, 1905–1980.* Princeton, NJ: Princeton University Press.

Arnold, Peri E. 1995. "Determinism and Contingency in Skowronek's Political Time." *Polity* 27 (Spring): 497–508.

Arnold, R. Douglas. 1990. *The Logic of Congressional Action.* New Haven, CT: Yale University Press.

Bachrach, Peter and Morton S. Baratz. 1962. "Two Faces of Power." *American Political Science Review* 56 (December): 947–952.

Bachrach, Peter and Morton S. Baratz. 1963. "Decisions and Nondecisions: An Analytical Framework." *American Political Science Review* 57 (September): 632–642.

Bailey, Jeremy D. 2007. *Thomas Jefferson and Executive Power.* New York: Cambridge University Press.

Bailey, Michael A. 2007. "Comparable Preference Estimates across Time and Institutions for the Court, Congress and Presidency." *American Journal of Political Science* 51 (July): 433–448.

Baker, Baker and Carl Hulse. 2010. "Deep Rifts Divide Obama and Republicans." *New York Times*, November 3, 2010, accessed online on March 17, 2011 at http://www.nytimes.com/2010/11/04/us/politics/04elect.html?scp=1&sq=obama%20shellacking&st=cse.

Barabas, Jason. 2008. "Presidential Policy Initiatives: How the Public Learns about State of the Union Proposals from the Mass Media." *Presidential Studies Quarterly* 38 (June): 195–222.

Barrett, Andrew W. and Matthew Eshbaugh-Soha. 2007. "Presidential Success on the Substance of Legislation." *Political Research Quarterly* 60 (March): 100–112.

Bartels, Larry M. 2000. "Partisanship and Voting Behavior, 1952–1996." *American Journal of Political Science* 44 (January): 35–50.

Baum, Matthew A. 2004. "Going Private: Public Opinion, Presidential Rhetoric, and the Domestic Politics of Audience Costs in U.S. Foreign Policy Crises." *Journal of Conflict Resolution* 48 (October): 603–631.

Baum, Matthew A. and Tim J. Groeling. 2010. *War Stories: The Causes and Consequences of Public Views of War.* Princeton, NJ: Princeton University Press.

Baumgartner, Frank R. and Bryan D. Jones. 1993. *Agendas and Instability in American Politics.* Chicago: University of Chicago Press.

Baumgartner, Frank R. and Bryan D. Jones. 2009. *Agendas and Instability in American Politics.* 2nd ed. Chicago: University of Chicago Press.

Baumgartner, Frank R., Jeffrey M. Berry, Marie Hojnacki, David C. Kimball, and Beth L. Leech. 2009. *Lobbying and Policy Change: Who Wins, Who Loses, and Why.* Chicago: University of Chicago Press.

Beckmann, Matthew N. 2010. *Pulling the Levers of Power: Presidential Leadership in U.S. Lawmaking, 1953–2004.* New York: Cambridge University Press.

Beckmann, Matthew N. and Joseph Godfrey. 2007. "The Policy Opportunities in Presidential Honeymoons." *Political Research Quarterly* 60 (June): 250–262.

Beckmann, Matthew N. and Vimal Kumar. 2010. "Opportunism in Polarization: Presidential Success in the U.S. Senate, 1953–2008." Paper presented at the American Political Science Association meeting, Washington, DC, September 2–5, 2010.

Beckmann, Matthew N. and Anthony McGann. 2008. "Navigating the Legislative Divide: Polarization, Presidents, and Policymaking in the US." *Journal of Theoretical Politics* 20 (April): 201–220.

Beer, Samuel. 1978. "In Search of a New Public Philosophy." In Anthony King, ed. *The New American Political System.* Washington, DC: American Enterprise Institute, pp. 5–44.

Bergeron, Paul H. 1987. *The Presidency of James K. Polk.* Lawrence: University Press of Kansas.

Berinsky, Adam J. 2009. *In Time of War: Understanding American Public Opinion From World War II to Iraq.* Chicago: University of Chicago Press.

Berman, Larry. 1979. *The Office of Management and Budget and the Presidency, 1921–1979.* Princeton, NJ: Princeton University Press.

Bernstein, Irving. 1996. *Guns or Butter: The Presidency of Lyndon Johnson.* New York: Oxford University Press.

Binder, Sarah A. 1999. "The Dynamics of Legislative Gridlock, 1947–96." *American Political Science Review* 93 (September): 519–533.

Binder, Sarah A. 2003. *Stalemate: Causes and Consequences of Legislative Gridlock.* Washington, DC: Brookings Institution Press.

Binkley, Wilfred E. 1947. *President and Congress.* New York: Knopf.

Bond, Jon R. and Richard Fleisher. 1990. *The President in the Legislative Arena.* Chicago: University of Chicago Press.

Bond, Jon R. and Richard Fleisher. 2001. "The Polls: Partisanship and Presidential Performance Evaluations." *Presidential Studies Quarterly* 31 (September): 529–540.

Bond, Jon R., Richard Fleisher, and B. Dan Wood. 2003. "The Marginal and Time-Varying Effect of Public Approval on Presidential Success in Congress." *Journal of Politics* 65 (February): 92–110.

Bond, Jon R., Richard Fleisher, and B. Dan Wood. 2008. "Which Presidents Are Uncommonly Successful in Congress?" In Bert A. Rockman and Richard W. Waterman (eds.), *Presidential Leadership: The Vortex of Power.* New York: Oxford University Press, pp. 191–213.

Brace, Paul and Barbara Hinckley. 1992. *Follow the Leader: Opinion Polls and the Modern Presidents.* New York: Basic Books.

Brady, David and Joseph Stewart, Jr. 1982. "Congressional Party Realignment and Transformations of Public Policy in Three Realignment Eras." *American Journal of Political Science* 26 (May): 333–360.

Brambor, Thomas, William Roberts Clark, and Matt Golder. 2006. "Understanding Interaction Models: Improving Empirical Analyses." *Political Analysis* 14 (No. 1): 63–82.

Brown, Frank. 1995. "Privatization of Public Education: Theories and Concepts." *Education and Urban Society* 27 (February): 114–126.

Burke, John P. 1992. *The Institutional Presidency.* Baltimore: Johns Hopkins University Press.

Burns, James MacGregor. 1966. *Presidential Government.* Boston: Houghton-Mifflin.

Burstein, Paul. 2003. "The Impact of Public Opinion on Public Policy: A Review and an Agenda." *Political Research Quarterly* 56 (March): 29–40.

Burstein, Paul. 2005/2006. "Why Estimates of the Impact of Public Opinion on Public Policy Are Too High: Empirical and Theoretical Implications." *Social Forces* 84 (June): 2273–2291.

Calabresi, Steven G. and Christopher S. Yoo. 2008. *The Unitary Executive: Presidential Power from Washington to Bush.* New Haven, CT: Yale University Press.

Cameron, Charles M. 2000. *Veto Bargaining: The Politics of Negative Power.* New York: Cambridge University Press.

Cameron, Charles M. 2002. "Studying the Polarized Presidency." *Presidential Studies Quarterly* 32 (December): 647–663.

Cameron, Charles M. and Nolan McCarty. 2004. "Models of Vetoes and Veto Bargaining." *Annual Review of Political Science* 7: 409–436.

Cameron, Charles M. and Jee-Kwang Park. 2008. "A Primer on the President's Legislative Program." In Bert A. Rockman and Richard W. Waterman, eds. *Presidential Leadership: The Vortex of Power.* New York: Oxford University Press, pp. 45–80.

Canes-Wrone, Brandice. 2001. "A Theory of Presidents' Public Agenda Setting." *Journal of Theoretical Politics* 13 (April): 183–208.

Canes-Wrone, Brandice. 2006. *Who Leads Whom? Presidents, Policy, and the Public.* Chicago: University of Chicago Press.

Canes-Wrone, Brandice and Scott de Marchi. 2002. "Presidential Approval and Legislative Success." *Journal of Politics* 64 (May): 491–509.

Canes-Wrone, Brandice, William G. Howell, and David E. Lewis. 2008. "Toward a Broader Understanding of Presidential Power: A Reevaluation of the Two Presidencies Thesis." *Journal of Politics* 70 (January): 1–16.

Carey, George W. 1978. "Separation of Powers and the Madisonian Model: A Reply to the Critics." *American Political Science Review* 72 (March): 151–164.

Casper, Gerhard. 1995. "Executive-Congressional Separation of Power during the Presidency of Thomas Jefferson." *Stanford Law Review* 47 (February): 473–497.

Chamberlain, Lawrence. 1946. *The President, Congress, and Legislation.* New York: Columbia University Press.

Chernow, Ron. 2010. *Washington: A Life.* New York: Penguin Books.

Clausen, Aage R. 1973. *How Congressmen Decide: A Policy Focus.* New York: St. Martin's.

Clausen, Aage R. and Carl E. Van Horn. 1977. "The Congressional Response to a Decade of Change: 1963–1972." *Journal of Politics* 39 (August): 624–666.

Clausen, Aage R. and Clyde Wilcox. 1991. "The Dimensionality of Roll-Call Voting Reconsidered." *Legislative Studies Quarterly* 16 (August): 393–406.

Clinton, Joshua D. and John S. Lapinski. 2006. "Measuring Legislative Accomplishment, 1877–1994." *American Journal of Political Science* 50 (January): 232–249.

Clinton, Joshua D. and John S. Lapinski. 2008. "Laws and Roll Calls in the U.S. Congress, 1891–1994." *Legislative Studies Quarterly* 33 (November): 511–541.

Cobb, Roger W. and Charles D. Elder. 1972. *Participation in American Politics: The Dynamics of Agenda-Building.* Baltimore: Johns Hopkins University Press.

Cobb, Roger, Jennie-Keith Ross, and Marc Howard Ross. 1976. "Agenda Building as a Comparative Political Process." *American Political Science Review* 70 (March): 126–138.

Cohen, Jeffrey E. 1980. "Presidential Personality and Political Behavior: Theoretical Issues and an Empirical Test." *Presidential Studies Quarterly* 10 (No. 4): 588–600.

Cohen, Jeffrey E. 1982a. "The Impact of the Modern Presidency on Presidential Success in the U.S. Congress, 1861–1972." *Legislative Studies Quarterly* 1982 (7): 515–532.

Cohen, Jeffrey E. 1982b. "A Historical Reassessment of Wildavsky's 'Two Presidencies' Thesis." *Social Science Quarterly* 1982 (63): 549–555.

Cohen, Jeffrey E. 1995. "Presidential Rhetoric and the Public Agenda." *American Journal of Political Science* 39 (February): 87–107.

Cohen, Jeffrey E. 1997. *Presidential Responsiveness and Public Policy-Making: The Public and the Policies that Presidents Choose.* Ann Arbor: University of Michigan Press.

Cohen, Jeffrey E. 2008. *The Presidency in the Era of 24-Hour News.* Princeton, NJ: Princeton University Press.

Cohen, Jeffrey E. 2010. *Going Local: Presidential Leadership in the Post-Broadcast Age.* New York: Cambridge University Press.

Cohen, Jeffrey E. and Matthew Eshbaugh-Soha. 2012. "Durability and Change in the President's Legislative Policy Agenda, 1799–2002," in Jeffrey A. Jenkins and Eric M. Patashnik, eds. *Living Legislation: Political Development and Contemporary American Politics.* Chicago: University of Chicago Press, pp. 48–70.

Cohen, Marty, David Karol, Hans Noel, and John Zaller. 2008. *The Party Decides: Presidential Nominations before and after Reform.* Chicago: University of Chicago Press.

Conley, Patricia Heidotting. 2001. *Presidential Mandates: How Elections Shape the National Agenda.* Chicago: University of Chicago Press.

Cooper, Phillip. 2002. *By Order of the President: The Use and Abuse of Executive Direct Action.* Lawrence: University Press of Kansas.

Copeland, Gary W. 1983. "When Congress and the President Collide: Why Presidents Veto Legislation." *Journal of Politics* 45 (August): 696–710.

Cornwell, Elmer E., Jr. 1966. *Presidential Leadership of Public Opinion.* Bloomington: Indiana University Press.

Covington, Cary R. 1987. "'Staying Private': Gaining Congressional Support for Unpublicized Presidential Preferences on Roll Call Votes." *Journal of Politics* 49 (August): 737–755.

Covington, Cary R., J. Mark Wrighton, and Rhonda Kinney. 1995. "A Presidency-Augmented Model of Presidential Success on Roll Call Votes." *American Journal of Political Science* 39 (November): 1001–1024.

Cox, Gary and Mathew D. McCubbins. 2006. *Setting the Agenda: Responsible Party Government in the U.S. House of Representatives.* New York: Cambridge University Press.

Crenson, Matthew. 1971. *The Unpolitics of Air Pollution: A Study of Non-decision-making in the Cities.* Baltimore: Johns Hopkins University Press.

Cronin, Thomas E. 1975. *The State of the Presidency.* Boston: Little Brown.

Cronin, Thomas E. and Michael A. Genovese. 1998. *The Paradoxes of the American Presidency.* New York: Oxford University Press.

Cummins, Jeff. 2008. "State of the Union Addresses and Presidential Position Taking: Do Presidents Back their Rhetoric in the Legislative Arena?" *Social Science Journal* 45 (September): 365–381.

Curry, Jill and Irwin L. Morris. 2010. "The Effect of the U.S. Economy on Presidential Elections, 1828–2008." Paper presented at the 2010 American Political Science Association, Washington, DC, September 2–5, 2010.

De Boef, Suzanna and Luke Keele. 2008. "Taking Time Seriously." *American Journal of Political Science* 52 (January): 184–200.

Deering, Christopher J. and Forrest Maltzman. 1999. "The Politics of Executive Orders: Legislative Constraints on Presidential Power." *Political Research Quarterly* 52 (December): 767–783.

Derthick, Martha and Paul J. Quirk. 1985. *The Politics of Deregulation.* Washington, DC: Brookings Institution.

Dickinson, Matthew J. 1997. *Bitter Harvest: FDR, Presidential Power and the Growth of the Presidential Branch.* New York: Cambridge University Press.

————. 2004. "Agendas, Agencies, and Unilateral Action: New Insights on Presidential Power?" *Congress & the Presidency* 31 (No. 1): 99–109.

————. 2008. "The Politics of Persuasion." In Bert A. Rockman and Richard W. Waterman, eds. *Presidential Leadership: The Vortex of Power.* New York: Oxford University Press, pp. 277–310.

Dickinson, Matthew J. and Matthew J. Lebo. 2007. "Reexamining the Growth of the Institutional Presidency, 1940–2000." *Journal of Politics* 69 (February): 206–219.

Di Salvo, Daniel R. 2007. *Intraparty Factions in American Political Development.* Ph.D. Dissertation, University of Virginia.

Dolan, Chris J., John P. Frendreis, and Raymond Tatalovich. 2007. *The Presidency and Economic Policy.* Lanham, MD: Rowman and Littlefield.

Donaldson, Gary A. 1979. *Truman Defeats Dewey.* Lexington: University Press of Kentucky.

Downs, George W., Jr. and Lawrence B. Mohr. 1979. "Toward a Theory of Innovation." *Administration & Society* 10 (February): 379–408.

Druckman, James N. and Lawrence R. Jacobs. 2006. "Lumpers and Splitters: The Public Opinion Information that Politicians Collect and Use." *Public Opinion Quarterly* 70 (Winter): 453–476.

Druckman, James N., Lawrence R. Jacobs, and Eric Ostermeier. 2004. "Candidate Strategies to Prime Issues and Image." *Journal of Politics* 66 (November): 1180–1202.

Durant, Robert F. and Paul F. Diehl. 1989. "Agendas, Alternatives, and Public Policy: Lessons from the U.S. Foreign Policy Arena." *Journal of Public Policy* 9 (April/June): 179–205.

Durr, Robert H. 1993. "What Moves Policy Sentiment?" *American Political Science Review* 87 (March): 158–170.

Edelman, Murray J. 1967. *The Symbolic Uses of Politics.* Urbana: University of Illinois Press.

Edwards, George C. III. 1985. "Measuring Presidential Success in Congress: Alternative Approaches." *Journal of Politics* 47 (June): 667–685.

————. 1989. *At the Margins: Presidential Leadership of Congress.* New Haven, CT: Yale University Press.

————. 2003. *On Deaf Ears: The Limits of the Bully Pulpit.* New Haven, CT: Yale University Press.

———. 2009. "Presidential Approval as a Source of Influence in Congress." In George C. Edwards III and William G. Howell, eds. *The Oxford Handbook of the American Presidency.* New York: Oxford University Press, pp. 338–361.

——— and Andrew Barrett. 2000. "Presidential Agenda Setting in Congress." In Jon R. Bond and Richard Fleisher, eds. *Polarized Politics: Congress and the President in a Partisan Era.* Washington, DC: CQ Press, pp. 109–133.

Edwards, George C. III, Andrew Barrett, and Jeffrey Peake. 1997. "The Legislative Impact of Divided Government." *American Journal of Political Science* 41 (April): 545–563.

Edwards, George C. III and B. Dan Wood. 1999. "Who Influences Whom? The President, Congress, and the Media." *American Political Science Review* 93 (June): 327–344.

Eisinger, Robert M. 2003. *The Evolution of Presidential Polling.* New York: Cambridge University Press.

Epstein, David and Sharyn O'Halloran. 1999. *Delegating Powers: A Transaction Cost Politics Approach to Policy Making Under Separate Powers.* New York: Cambridge University Press.

Erikson, Robert S., Michael B. MacKuen, and James A. Stimson. 2002. *The Macro Polity.* New York: Cambridge University Press.

Eshbaugh-Soha, Matthew. 2003. "Presidential Press Conferences over Time." *American Journal of Political Science* 47 (April): 348–353.

Eshbaugh-Soha, Matthew. 2005. "The Politics of Presidential Agendas." *Political Research Quarterly* 58 (June): 257–268.

Eshbaugh-Soha, Matthew and Jeffrey S. Peake. 2004. "Presidents and the Economic Agenda." *Congress and the Presidency* 31 (Autumn): 161–181.

Eshbaugh-Soha, Matthew and Jeffrey S. Peake. 2005. "Presidential Influence over the Systemic Agenda." *Political Research Quarterly* 58 (March): 127–138.

Fett, Patrick J. 1992. "Truth in Advertising: The Revelation of Presidential Legislative Priorities." *Western Political Quarterly* 45 (December): 895–920.

Fiorina, Morris P., with Samuel J. Abrams and Jeremy C. Pope. 2005. *Culture War? The Myth of a Polarized America.* New York: Pearson Longman.

Fishel, Jeff. 1985. *Presidents & Promises: From Campaign Pledge to Presidential Performance.* Washington, DC: CQ Press.

Fisher, Louis. 1975. *Constitutional Conflicts between Congress and the President.* Princeton, NJ: Princeton University Press.

Fleisher, Richard and Jon R. Bond. 2000a. "Congress and the President in a Partisan Era." In Jon R. Bond and Richard Fleisher, eds. *Polarized Politics: Congress and the President in a Partisan Era.* Washington, DC: CQ Press, pp. 1–8.

Fleisher, Richard and Jon R. Bond. 2000b. "Partisanship and the President's Quest for Votes on the Floor of Congress." In Jon R. Bond and Richard Fleisher, eds. *Polarized Politics: Congress and the President in a Partisan Era.* Washington, DC: CQ Press, pp. 154–185.

Fleisher, Richard and Jon R. Bond. 2004. "The Shrinking Middle in the US Congress." *British Journal of Political Science* 34 (July): 429–451.

Flemming, Roy B., B. Dan Wood, and John Bohte. 1999. "Attention to Issues in a System of Separated Powers: The Macrodynamics of American Policy Agendas." *Journal of Politics* 61 (February): 76–108.

Formisano, Ronald P. 1993. "The New Political History and the Election of 1840." *Journal of Interdisciplinary History* 23 (Spring): 661–682.

Frendreis, John, Raymond Tatalovich, and Jon Schaff. 2001. "Predicting Legislative Output in the First One-hundred Days, 1897–1995." *Political Research Quarterly* 54 (December): 853–870.

Friedrich, Robert J. 1982. "In Defense of Multiplicative Terms in Multiple Regression Equations." *American Journal of Political Science* 26 (November): 797–833.

Galvin, Daniel J. 2010. *Presidential Party Building: Dwight D. Eisenhower to George W. Bush.* Princeton, NJ: Princeton University Press.

Galvin, Daniel and Colleen J. Shogan. 2004. "Presidential Politicization and Centralization across the Modern-Traditional Divide." *Polity* 36 (No. 3): 477–504.

Gates, John B. and Jeffrey E. Cohen. 1988. "Presidents, Supreme Court Justices, and Racial Equality Cases: 1954–1984." *Political Behavior* 10 (No. 1): 22–36.

Geer, John G. 1996. *From Tea Leaves to Opinion Polls: A Theory of Democratic Leadership.* New York: Columbia University Press.

Geer, John G. and Patrick Goorha. 2003. "Declining Uncertainty: Presidents, Public Opinion, and Polls." In *Uncertainty in American Politics,* ed. Barry C. Burden. New York: Cambridge University Press, pp. 139–160.

Gelpi, Christopher, Peter Feaver, and Jason Aaron Reifler. 2009. *Paying the Human Costs of War: American Public Opinion and Casualties in Military Conflicts.* Princeton, NJ: Princeton University Press.

Gerring, John G. 1998. *Party Ideologies in America, 1828–1996.* New York: Cambridge University Press.

Gilmour, John C. 1995. *Strategic Disagreement: Stalemate in American Politics.* Pittsburgh: University of Pittsburgh Press.

Gilmour, John C. 2002. "Institutional and Individual Influences on the President's Veto." *Journal of Politics* 64 (February): 198–218.

Gleiber, Dennis W., Steven A. Shull, and Colleen A. Waligora. 1998. "Measuring the President's Professional Reputation." *American Politics Research* 26 (October): 366–385.

Grant, J. Tobin and Nathan J. Kelly. 2008. "Legislative Productivity of the U.S. Congress, 1789–2004." *Political Analysis* 16 (No. 3): 303–323.

Greenstein, Fred I. 1969. *Personality and Politics: Problems of Evidence, Inference, and Conceptualization.* Chicago: Markham.

Greenstein, Fred I. 1978. "The Modern Presidency." In *The New American Political System,* ed. Anthony King. Washington, DC: American Enterprise Institute, pp. 45–85.

———. 1982. *The Hidden-Hand Presidency: Eisenhower as Leader.* New York: Basic Books.

Greenstein, Fred I., ed. 1988. *Leadership and the Modern Presidency.* Cambridge, MA: Harvard University Press.

———. 2004. *The Presidential Difference: Leadership Style from FDR to Clinton,* 2nd ed. Princeton, NJ: Princeton University Press.

———. 2006. "Presidential Difference in the Early Republic: The Highly Disparate Leadership Styles of Washington, Adams, and Jefferson." *Presidential Studies Quarterly* 36 (September): 373–390.

———. 2009. *Inventing the Presidency: Leadership Style from George Washington to Andrew Jackson.* Princeton, NJ: Princeton University Press.

Gronke, Paul, Jeffrey Koch, and Matthew Wilson. 2003. "Follow the Leader? Presidential Approval, Presidential Support, and Representatives' Electoral Fortunes." *Journal of Politics* 65 (September): 785–808.

Gronke, Paul and Brian Newman. 2003. "FDR to Clinton, Mueller to ?: A Field Essay on Presidential Approval." *Political Research Quarterly* 56 (December): 501–512.

Groseclose, Tim., Steven D. Levitt, and James M. Snyder. 1999. "Comparing Interest Group Scores across Time and Chambers: Adjusted ADA Scores for the U.S. Congress." *American Political Science Review* 93 (March): 33–50.

Groseclose, Timothy and Nolan McCarty. 2001. "The Politics of Blame: Bargaining before an Audience." *American Journal of Political Science* 45 (No. 1): 100–119.

Grossback, Lawrence J., David A. M. Peterson, and James A. Stimson. 2006. *Mandate Politics.* New York: Cambridge University Press.

Hacker, Jacob S. 1997. *The Road to Nowhere: The Genesis of President Clinton's Plan for Health Security.* Princeton, NJ: Princeton University Press.

Hager, Gregory L. and Terry Sullivan. 1994. "President-centered and Presidency-centered Explanations of Presidential Public Activity." *American Journal of Political Science* 38 (November): 1079–1103.

Hall, Wynton C. 2002. "'Reflections of Yesterday': George H. W. Bush's Instrumental Use of Public Opinion Research in Presidential Discourse." *Presidential Studies Quarterly* 32 (September): 531–558.

Hargreaves, Mary W. M. 1985. *The Presidency of John Quincy Adams.* Lawrence: University Press of Kansas.

Hargrove, Ervin C. 1988. *Jimmy Carter as President: Leadership and the Politics of the Public Good.* Baton Rouge: Louisiana State University Press.

Hartmann, Susan M. 1971. *Truman and the 80th Congress.* Columbia: University of Missouri Press.

Heith, Diane J. 1998. "Staffing the White House Public Opinion Apparatus 1969–1988." *Public Opinion Quarterly* 62 (Summer): 165–189.

Heith, Diane J. 2004. *Polling to Govern: Public Opinion and Presidential Leadership.* Stanford, CA: Stanford University Press.

Herbst, Susan. 1998. *Reading Public Opinion: How Political Actors View the Democratic Process.* Chicago: University of Chicago Press.

Herszenhorn, David M. 2010. "Congress Passes Tax Cut Package for $801 Billion." *New York Times,* December 17, 2010; accessed March 17, 2011 at http://www.nytimes.com/2010/12/17/us/politics/17cong.html?scp=1&sq=congress%20passes%20tax%20cut%20package%20for%20&st=cse.

Herszenhorn, David M. and Jackie Calmes. 2010. "Tax Deal Suggests New Path for Obama." *New York Times,* December 6, 2010; accessed March 17, 2011 at http://www.nytimes.com/2010/12/07/us/politics/07cong.html?_r=1&scp=7&sq=bush%20retreat&st=cse, accessed December 20, 2010.

Hetherington, Marc J. 1996. "The Media's Role in Forming Voters' National Economic Evaluations in 1992." *American Journal of Political Science* 40 (May): 372–395.

Hibbs, Douglas A., Jr. 1977. "Political Parties and Macroeconomic Policy." *American Political Science Review* 71 (December): 1467–1487.

Hill, Kim Quaile. 1998. "The Policy Agendas of the President and the Mass Public: A Research Validation and Extension." *American Journal of Political Science* 42 (October): 1328–1334.

Hoekstra, Douglas J. 1999. "The Politics of Politics: Skowronek and Presidential Research." *Presidential Studies Quarterly* 29 (September): 657–671.

Horvit, Beverly, Adam J. Schiffer, and Mark Wright. 2008. "The Limits of Presidential Agenda Setting: Predicting Newspaper Coverage of the Weekly Radio Address." *Harvard International Journal of Press/Politics* 13 (No. 1): 8–28.

Howell, William G. 2003. *Power without Persuasion: The Politics of Direct Presidential Action.* Princeton, NJ: Princeton University Press.

Howell, William G. 2005. "Introduction: Unilateral Powers: A Brief Overview." *Presidential Studies Quarterly* 35 (September): 417–439.

Howell, William, Scott Adler, Charles Cameron, and Charles Riemann. 2000. "Divided Government and the Legislative Productivity of Congress, 1945–94." *Legislative Studies Quarterly* 25 (May): 285–312.

Howell, William G. and Kenneth R. Mayer. 2005. "The Last One Hundred Days." *Presidential Studies Quarterly* 35 (September): 533–553.

Howell, William G. and Jon C. Pevehouse. 2007. *While Dangers Gather: Congressional Checks on Presidential War Powers.* Princeton, NJ: Princeton University Press.

Huntington, Samuel P. 1968. *Political Order in Changing Societies.* New Haven, CT: Yale University Press.

Huntington, Samuel P. 1973. "Congressional Responses to the Twentieth Century." In David Truman, ed. *Congress and America's Future,* 2nd ed. Englewood Cliffs, NJ: Prentice-Hall, pp. 6–38.

"In Crisis, Opportunity for Obama." *Wall Street Journal Online Edition,* November 21, 2008 (http://online.wsj.com/article/SB12272127805 6345271.html), accessed on January 28, 2010.

Jacobs, Lawrence R. and Melanie Burns. 2004. "The Second Face of the Public Presidency: Presidential Polling and the Shift from Policy to Personality Polling." *Presidential Studies Quarterly* 34 (September): 536–556.

Jacobs, Lawrence R. and Robert Y. Shapiro. 1995. "Issues, Candidate Image, and Priming: The Use of Private Polls in Kennedy's 1960 Presidential Campaign." *American Political Science Review* 88 (September): 527–540.

Jacobs, Lawrence R. and Robert Y. Shapiro. 1994 "The Rise of Presidential Polling: The Nixon White House in Historical Perspective." *Public Opinion Quarterly* 59 (Summer): 163–195.

Jacobs, Lawrence R. and Robert Y. Shapiro. 1995–1996. "Presidential Manipulation of Polls and Public Opinion: The Nixon Administration and the Pollsters." *Political Science Quarterly* 110 (Winter): 519–538.

Jacobs, Lawrence R. and Robert Y. Shapiro. 2000. *Politicians Don't Pander: Political Manipulation and the Loss of Democratic Responsiveness.* Chicago: University of Chicago Press.

Jacobson, Gary C. 2000. "Party Polarization in National Politics: The Electoral Connection." In Jon R. Bond and Richard Fleisher, eds. *Polarized Politics: Congress and the President in a Partisan Era.* Washington: CQ Press, pp. 9–30.

Jacobson, Gary C. 2007. *A Divider, Not a Uniter: George W. Bush and the American People.* New York: Longman.

James, Scott. 2009. "Historical Institutionalism, Political Development, and the Presidency." In George C. Edwards III and William G. Howell, eds. *The Oxford Handbook of the American Presidency.* New York: Oxford University Press, pp. 51–81.

Jenkins-Smith, Hank C., Carol L. Silva, and Richard W. Waterman. 2005. "Micro- and Macrolevel Models of the Presidential Expectations Gap." *Journal of Politics* 67 (August): 690–715.

Jones, Bryan D. and Frank R. Baumgartner. 2004. "Representation and Agenda Setting." *Policy Studies Journal* 32 (No. 1): 1–24.

Jones, Bryan D. and Frank R. Baumgartner. 2005. *The Politics of Attention: How Government Prioritizes Problems.* Chicago: University of Chicago Press.

Jones, Bryan D., Heather Larsen-Price, and John Wilkerson. 2009. "Representation and American Governing Institutions." *Journal of Politics* 71 (January): 277–290.

Jones, Bryan D., Frank R. Baumgartner, Christian Breunig, Christopher Wlezien, Stuart Soroka, Martial Foucault, Abel Francois, Christoffer Green-Pedersen, Chris Koski, Peter John, Peter B. Mortensen, Frederic Varone, and Stefaan Walgrave. 2009. "A General Theory of Public Budgets: A Comparative Analysis." *American Journal of Political Science* 53 (October): 855–873.

Jones, Charles O. 1977. *An Introduction to the Study of Public Policy.* North Scituate, MA: Duxbury Press.

Jones, Charles O. 1994. *The Presidency in a Separated System.* Washington, DC: Brookings Institution Press.

Katznelson, Ira and John S. Lapinski. 2006. "The Substance of Representation: Studying Political Content and Legislative Behavior." In E. Scott Adler and John S. Lapinski, eds. *The Macropolitics of Congress.* Princeton, NJ: Princeton University Press, pp. 96–126.

Kenny, Lawrence and Babak Lotfina. 2005. "Evidence on the Importance of Spatial Voting Models in Presidential Nominations and Elections." *Public Choice* 123: 439–462.

Kinder, Donald R., Mark D. Peters, Robert P. Abelson, and Susan T. Fiske. 1980. "Presidential Prototypes." *Political Behavior* 2 (No. 4): 315–337.

King, David C. 1997. "The Polarization of American Parties and Mistrust of Government." In Joseph S. Nye, Philip D. Zelikow, and David C. King, eds. *Why People Don't Trust Government.* Cambridge, MA: Harvard University Press, pp. 155–178.

King, David C. 2003. "Congress, Polarization, and Fidelity to the Median Voter." Working Paper, John F. Kennedy School of Government, Harvard University.

King, Gary. 1990. "When Not to Use R-Squared." *The Political Methodologist* 3(2): 11–12.

Kingdon, John W. 1995. *Agendas, Alternatives, and Public Policies,* 2nd ed. New York: HarperCollins.

Koger, Gregory. 2010. *Filibuster: A Political History of Obstruction in the House and Senate.* Chicago: University of Chicago Press.

Korzi, Michael J. 2003. "Our Chief Magistrate and His Powers: A Reconsideration of William Howard Taft's 'Whig' Theory of Presidential Leadership." *Presidential Studies Quarterly* 33 (June): 305–324.

Krause, George A. 2002. "Separated Powers and Institutional Growth in the Presidential and Congressional Branches: Distinguishing between Short-Run versus Long-Run Dynamics." *Political Research Quarterly* 55 (March): 27–57.

Krause, George A. and David B. Cohen. 1997. "Presidential Use of Executive Orders, 1953–1994." *American Politics Research* 25 (October): 458–481.

Krause, George A. and Jeffrey E. Cohen. 2000. "Opportunity, Constraints, and the Development of the Institutional Presidency: The Issuance of Executive Orders, 1939–96." *Journal of Politics* 62 (February): 88–114.

Krehbiel, Keith. 1998. *Pivotal Politics: A Theory of U.S. Lawmaking.* Chicago: University of Chicago Press.

Krukones, Michale G. 1984. *Promises and Performance: Presidential Campaigns as Policy Predictors.* Lanham, MD: University Press of America.

Krutz, Glen S. 2005. "Issues and Institutions: 'Winnowing' in the U.S. Congress." *American Journal of Political Science* 49 (April): 313–326.

Krutz, Glen S., Richard Fleisher, and Jon R. Bond. 1998. "From Abe Fortas to Zöe Baird: Why Some Presidential Nominations Fail in the Senate." *American Political Science Review* 92 (December): 871–881.

Landy, Marc and Sidney M. Milkis. 2000. *Presidential Greatness.* Lawrence: University Press of Kansas.

Lapinski, John S. 2008. "Policy Substance and Performance in American Lawmaking, 1877–1994." *American Journal of Political Science* 52 (April): 235–251.

Laracey, Mel. 2002. *Presidents and the People: The Partisan Story of Going Public.* College Station: Texas A & M University Press.

Larocca, Roger T. 2006. *The Presidential Agenda: Sources of Executive Influence in Congress.* Columbus: Ohio State University Press.

Layman, Geoffrey C., Thomas M. Carsey, and Juliana Menasce Horowitz. 2006. "Party Polarization in American Politics: Characteristics, Causes, and Consequences." *Annual Review of Political Science* 9 (No. 1): 83–110.

Layman, Geoffrey C., Thomas M. Carsey, John C. Green, Richard Herrera, and Rosalyn Cooperman. 2010. "Activists and Conflict Extension in American Party Politics." *American Political Science Review* 104 (May): 324–346.

Lebo, Matthew J. and Andrew O'Geen. 2011. "The President's Role in the Partisan Congressional Arena." *Journal of Politics* 73 (July): 1–17.

Lee, Jong R. 1975. "Presidential Vetoes from Washington to Nixon." *Journal of Politics* 37 (May): 522–546.

Leibiger, Stuart. 1999. *Founding Friendships: George Washington, James Madison and the Creation of the American Republic.* Princeton, NJ: Princeton University Press.

Leuchtenburg, William E. 1983. *In the Shadow of FDR: From Harry Truman to Ronald Reagan.* Ithaca, NY: Cornell University Press.

Lewis, David E. 2005. "Staffing Alone: Unilateral Action and the Politicization of the Executive Office of the President, 1988–2004." *Presidential Studies Quarterly* 35 (September): 496–514.

Lewis, David E. 2008. *The Politics of Presidential Appointments: Political Control and Bureaucratic Performance.* Princeton, NJ: Princeton University Press.

Lewis, David E. 2009. "Revisiting the Administrative Presidency: Policy, Patronage, and Agency Competence." *Presidential Studies Quarterly* 39 (March): 60–73.

Lewis-Beck, Michael S. and Andrew Skalaban. 1990a. "The R-Squared: Some Straight Talk." *Political Analysis* 2(1): 153–171.

Lewis-Beck, Michael S. and Andrew Skalaban. 1990b. "When to Use R-Squared." *The Political Methodologist* 3(2): 9–11.

Light, Paul C. 1991. *The President's Agenda: Domestic Policy Choice from Kennedy to Reagan,* Revised ed. Baltimore: Johns Hopkins University Press.

Light, Paul C. 1999a. *The President's Agenda: Domestic Policy Choice from Kennedy to Clinton,* 3rd edition. Baltimore: Johns Hopkins University Press.

———. 1999b. *The True Size of Government.* Washington, DC: Brookings.

———. 2000. "Domestic Policy Making." *Presidential Studies Quarterly* 30 (March): 109–132.

Lim, Elvin T. 2002. "Five Trends in Presidential Rhetoric: An Analysis of Rhetoric from George Washington to Bill Clinton." *Presidential Studies Quarterly* 32 (June): 328–366.

Loomis, Burdette A. 2009. "Connecting Interest Groups to the Presidency." In George C. Edwards III and William G. Howell, eds. *The Oxford Handbook of the American Presidency.* New York: Oxford University Press, pp. 403–414.

Lowi, Theodore J. 1964. "American Business, Public Policy, Case-studies, and Political Theory." *World Politics* 16 (July): 677–715.

Lynch, G. Patrick. 1999. "Presidential Elections and the Economy 1872 to 1996: The Times they are a 'Changin or the Song Remains the Same?" *Political Research Quarterly* 52 (December): 825–844.

Lynch, G. Patrick. 2002. "U.S. Presidential Elections in the Nineteenth Century: Why Culture and the Economy Both Mattered." *Polity* 35 (Autumn): 29–50.

Macmahon, Arthur W. 1956. "Woodrow Wilson as Legislative Leader and Administrator." *American Political Science Review* 50 (September): 641–675.

Malone, Dumas. 1974. *Jefferson and His Times.* Boston: Little Brown, vol. 4 and 5.

Manza, Jeff and Fay Lomax Cook. 2002. "A Democratic Polity?: Three Views of Policy Responsiveness to Public Opinion in the United States." *American Politics Research* 30 (No. 6): 630–667.

Marshall, Bryan W. and Richard L. Pacelle Jr. 2005. "Revisiting the Two Presidencies: The Strategic Use of Executive Orders." *American Politics Research* 33 (January): 81–105.

Marshall, Bryan W. and Brandon C. Prins. 2007. "Strategic Position Taking and Presidential Influence in Congress." *Legislative Studies Quarterly* 32 (May): 257–284.

Masket, Seth. 2007. "It Takes an Outsider: Extra-legislative Organization and Partisanship in the California Assembly, 1849–2006." *American Journal of Political Science* 51 (July): 482–497.

Mason, Jeff. 2010. "Obama's Healthcare Win Could Boost Foreign Policy." Reuters, March 26, 2010, http://www.reuters.com/article/idUSTRE62P0P320100326, accessed December 6, 2010.

Matthews, Steven A. 1989. "Veto Threats: Rhetoric in a Bargaining Game." *Quarterly Journal of Economics* 104: 347–369.

Mayer, Kenneth. 2001. *With the Stroke of a Pen: Executive Orders and Presidential Power.* Princeton, NJ: Princeton University Press.

Mayer, Kenneth R. 1999. "Executive Orders and Presidential Power." *Journal of Politics* 61 (May): 445–466.

Mayer, Kenneth R. 2009. "Going Alone: The Presidential Power of Unilateral Action." In George C. Edwards III and William G. Howell, eds. *The Oxford Handbook of the American Presidency.* New York: Oxford University Press, pp. 427–454.

Mayer, Kenneth R. and Kevin Price. 2002. "Unilateral Presidential Powers: Significant Executive Orders, 1949–99." *Presidential Studies Quarterly* 32 (June): 367–386.

Mayhew, David R. 1974. *Congress: The Electoral Connection.* New Haven, CT: Yale University Press.

Mayhew, David R. 1991. *Divided We Govern: Party Control, Lawmaking and Investigations.* New Haven, CT: Yale University Press.

Mayhew, David R. 2005. *Divided We Govern: Party Control, Lawmaking and Investigations, 1946–2002,* 2nd ed. New Haven, CT: Yale University Press.

Mayhew, David R. 2008. *Parties and Policies: How the American Government Works.* New Haven, CT: Yale University Press.

McCarty, Nolan M. 1997. "Presidential Reputation and the Veto." *Economics and Politics* 9 (No. 1): 1–27.

McCarty, Nolan M. 2009. "Presidential Vetoes in the Early Republic: Changing Constitutional Norms or Electoral Reform." *Journal of Politics* 71 (April): 369–384.

McCarty, Nolan and Keith Poole. 1995. "Veto Power and Legislation: An Empirical Analysis of Executive-Legislative Bargaining from 1961–1986." *Journal of Law, Economics, and Organization* 11 (2): 282–312.

McDonald, Forrest. 1974. *The Presidency of George Washington.* Lawrence: University Press of Kansas.

McDonald, Forrest. 1976. *The Presidency of Thomas Jefferson.* Lawrence: University Press of Kansas.

McDonald, Forrest. 1994. *The American Presidency: An Intellectual History.* Lawrence: University Press of Kansas.

Merry, Robert W. 2009. *A Country of Vast Designs: James K. Polk, The Mexican War, and the Conquest of the American Continent.* New York: Simon and Schuster.

Milkis, Sidney M. and Michael Nelson. 2008. *The American Presidency: Origins and Development, 1776–2007,* 5th ed. Washington, DC: CQ Press.

Miller, Gary and Norman Schofield. 2003. "Activists and Partisan Realignment in the United States." *American Political Science Review* 97 (May): 245–260.

Moe, Ronald C. 1987. "The Founders and Their Experience with the Executive Veto." *Presidential Studies Quarterly* 17: 416.

Moe, Ronald C. and Stephen C. Teel. 1970. "Congress as Policy-Maker: A Necessary Reappraisal." *Political Science Quarterly* 85 (xx): 443–470.

Moe, Terry. 1985. "The Politicized Presidency." In John E. Chubb and Paul E. Peterson, eds. *The New Direction in American Politics.* Washington, DC: The Brookings Institution, pp. 235–271.

Moe, Terry. 1993. "Presidents, Institutions, and Theory." In George C. Edwards III, John H. Kessel, and Bert A. Rockman, eds. *Researching the Presidency: Vital Questions, New Approaches.* Pittsburgh: University of Pittsburgh Press, pp. 337–385.

Moe, Terry. 2009. "The Revolution in Presidential Theory." *Presidential Studies Quarterly* 39 (December): 701–724.

Moe, Terry M. and William G. Howell. 1999. "Unilateral Action and Presidential Power: A Theory." *Presidential Studies Quarterly* 29 (December): 850–873.

Morgan, Ruth. 1970. *The President and Civil Rights: Policy Making by Executive Order.* New York: St. Martin's.

Mueller, John E. 1970. "Presidential Popularity from Truman to Johnson." *American Political Science Review* 64 (March): 18–34.

Mueller, John E. 1973. *War, Presidents, and Public Opinion.* New York: Wiley.

Murphy, Chad. 2008. "The Evolution of the Modern Rhetorical Presidency: A Critical Response." *Presidential Studies Quarterly* 38 (June): 300–307.

Murray, Shoon Kathleen. 2006. "Private Polls and Presidential Policymaking: Reagan as a Facilitator of Change." *Public Opinion Quarterly* 70 (Winter): 477–498.

Murray, Shoon Kathleen and Peter Howard. 2002. "Variation in White House Polling Operations: Carter to Clinton." *Public Opinion Quarterly* 66 (Winter): 527–558.

Neustadt, Richard E. 1954. "Presidency and Legislation: The Growth of Central Clearance." *American Political Science Review* 48 (September): 641–671.

Neustadt, Richard E. 1955. "Presidency and Legislation: Planning the President's Program." *American Political Science Review* 49 (December): 980–1021.

———. 1960. *Presidential Power: The Politics of Leadership.* New York: Wiley.

———. 1990. *Presidential Power and the Modern Presidents: The Politics of Leadership from Roosevelt to Reagan.* New York: Free Press.

Newman, Brian and Emerson Siegle. 2010. "Polls and Elections: The Polarized Presidency: Depth and Breadth of Public Partisanship." *Presidential Studies Quarterly* 40 (June): 342–363.

Nichols, David. 1994. *The Myth of the Modern Presidency.* University Park: Pennsylvania State University Press.

Ostrom, Charles W., Jr. and Dennis M. Simon. 1985. "Promise and Performance: A Dynamic Model of Presidential Popularity." *American Political Science Review* 79 (June): 334–358.

Page, Benjamin I. 1978. *Choices and Echoes in Presidential Elections: Rational Man and Electoral Democracy.* Chicago: University of Chicago Press.

Peake, Jeffrey S. 2001. "Presidential Agenda Setting in Foreign Policy." *Political Research Quarterly* 54 (March): 69–86.

Peake, Jeffrey S. and Matthew Eshbaugh-Soha. 2008. The Agenda-Setting Impact of Major Presidential TV Addresses." *Political Communication* 25 (No. 2): 113–137.

Peterson, David A. M., Lawrence J. Grossback, James A. Stimson, and Amy Gangl. 2003. "Congressional Response to Mandate Elections." *American Journal of Political Science* 47 (July): 411–426.

Peterson, Mark A. 1990. *Legislating Together: The White House and Capitol Hill from Eisenhower to Reagan.* Cambridge, MA: Harvard University Press.

Peterson, Mark A. 1992. "The Presidency and Organized Interests: White House Patterns of Interest Group Liaison." *American Political Science Review* 86 (September): 612–625.

Petrocik, John R. 1996. "Issue Ownership in Presidential Elections, with a 1980 Case Study." *American Journal of Political Science* 40 (August): 825–850.

Pfiffner, James P. 2008. *The Modern Presidency,* 5th ed. New York: Wadsworth.

Phelps, Glenn. 1989. "George Washington: Precedent Setter" in Thomas C. Cronin, ed. *Inventing the American Presidency*. Lawrence: University Press of Kansas, pp. 259–281.

Pious, Richard M. 2009. "Prerogative Power and Presidential Politics." In George C. Edwards III and William G. Howell, eds. *The Oxford Handbook of the American Presidency*. New York: Oxford University Press, pp. 455–476.

Polsby, Nelson W. 1968. "The Institutionalization of the U.S. House of Representatives." *American Political Science Review* 62 (March): 144–168.

Polsby, Nelson W. 1984. *Political Innovation in America: The Politics of Policy Initiation*. New Haven, CT: Yale University Press.

Pomper, Gerald M. 2003. "Parliamentary Government in the United States: A New Regime for a New Century?" In John C. Green and R. Farmer, eds. *The State of the Parties*, Lanham, MD: Rowman & Littlefield. 4th ed., pp. 267–286.

Pomper, Gerald M. and Susan S. Lederman. 1980. *Elections in America: Control and Influence in Democratic Politics*, 2nd ed. New York: Longman.

Poole, Keith T. and Howard Rosenthal. 1997. *Congress: A Political-Economic History of Roll Call Voting*. New York: Oxford University Press.

Ragsdale, Lyn. 1998. *Vital Statistics on the Presidency*, revised ed. Washington, DC: CQ Press.

Ragsdale, Lyn. 2009. *Vital Statistics on the Presidency*, 3rd ed. Washington, DC: CQ Press.

Ragsdale, Lyn and John J. Theis, III. 1997. "The Institutionalization of the American Presidency, 1924–92." *American Journal of Political Science* 41 (October): 1280–1318.

Randall, Ronald. 1979. "Presidential Power versus Bureaucratic Intransigence: The Influence of the Nixon Administration on Welfare Policy." *American Political Science Review* 73 (September): 795–810.

Rivers, Douglas and Nancy Rose. 1985. "Passing the President's Program: Public Opinion and Presidential Influence in Congress." *American Journal of Political Science* 92 (No. 2): 183–196.

Rogers, Everett M. 1995. *Diffusion of Innovations*, 4th ed. New York: Free Press.

Rohde, David W. and Meredith Barthelemy. 2009. "The President and Congressional Parties in an Era of Polarization." In George C. Edwards III and William G. Howell, eds. *The Oxford Handbook of the American Presidency*. New York: Oxford University Press, pp. 289–310.

Rohde, David W. and Dennis M. Simon. 1985. "Presidential Vetoes and Congressional Response: A Study of Institutional Conflict." *American Journal of Political Science* 29 (August): 397–427.

Romer, Thomas and Howard Rosenthal. 1978. "Political Resource Allocation, Controlled Agendas, and the Status Quo." *Public Choice* 33 (No. 4): 27–43.

Rottinghaus, Brandon. 2003. "Reassessing Public Opinion Polling in the Truman Administration." *Presidential Studies Quarterly* 33 (June): 325–332.

Rottinghaus, Brandon. 2006. "Rethinking Presidential Responsiveness: The Public Presidency and Rhetorical Congruency, 1953–2001." *Journal of Politics* 68 (August): 720–732.

Rudalevige, Andrew. 2002. *Managing the President's Program: Presidential Leadership and Legislative Policy Formulation*. Princeton, NJ: Princeton University Press.

Rudalevige, Andrew. 2005. *The New Imperial Presidency: Renewing Presidential Power after Watergate*. Ann Arbor: University of Michigan Press.

Saunders, Kyle L. and Alan I. Abramowitz. 2004. "Ideological Realignment and Active Partisans in the American Electorate." *American Politics Research* 32 (No. 3): 285–309.

Schlesinger, Arthur M., Jr. 2004. *War and the American Presidency*. New York: W. W. Norton.

Seligman, Lester G. 1956. "Presidential Leadership: The Inner Circle and Institutionalization." *Journal of Politics* 18 (August): 410–426.

Seligman, Lester G. 1980. "On Models of the Presidency." *Presidential Studies Quarterly* 10 (Summer): 353–363.

Seligman, Lester G. and Cary R. Covington. 1989. *The Coalitional Presidency*. Chicago: Dorsey.

Shafer, Byron E. 2003. *The Two Majorities and the Puzzle of Modern American Politics*. Lawrence: University Press of Kansas.

Shapiro, Robert Y. and Lawrence R. Jacobs. 2001. 'Source Material': Presidents and Polling: Politicians, Pandering, and the Study of Democratic Responsiveness." *Presidential Studies Quarterly* 31 (March): 150–167.

Shaw, Malcolm. 1987. "The Traditional and Modern Presidencies." In Shaw, Malcolm, ed. *The Modern Presidency: From Roosevelt to Reagan*. New York: Harper and Row, pp. 244–310.

Shields, Todd and Chi Huang. 1997. "Executive Vetoes: Testing Presidency versus President-Centered Perspectives of Presidential Behavior." *American Politics Quarterly* 25 (4): 431–457.

Shipan, Charles R. 2006. "Does Divided Government Increase the Size of the Legislative Agenda?" In E. Scott Adler and John S. Lapinski, eds. *The Macropolitics of Congress*. Princeton, NJ: Princeton University Press, pp. 151–170.

Shull, Stephen A., ed. 1991. *Two Presidencies: A Quarter Century Assessment*. Chicago: Nelson Hall.

Simon, Dennis M. 2009. "Public Expectations of the President." In *The Oxford Handbook of the American Presidency*, eds. George C. Edwards III and William G. Howell. New York: Oxford University Press, pp. 135–159.

Simon, James F. 2012. *FDR and Chief Justice Hughes: The President, the Supreme Court, and the Epic Battle over the New Deal.* New York: Simon & Schuster.

Sinclair, Barbara. 1997. *Unorthodox Lawmaking: New Legislative Processes in the U.S. Congress.* Washington, DC: CQ Press.

Sinclair, Barbara. 2000. "Hostile Partners: The President, Congress, and Lawmaking in the Partisan 1990s." In Jon R. Bond and Richard Fleisher, eds. *Polarized Politics: Congress and the President in a Partisan Era.* Washington, DC: CQ Press, pp.134–153.

Sinclair, Barbara. 2002. "The Dream Fulfilled? Party Development in Congress, 1950–2000," in John C. Green and Paul S. Herrnson, eds. *Responsible Partisanship?* Lawrence: University Press of Kansas, pp. 181–200.

Sinclair, Barbara Deckard. 1977. "Party Realignment and the Transformation of the Political Agenda: The House of Representatives, 1925–1938." *American Political Science Review* 71 (September): 940–953.

Skinner, Richard M. 2008–2009. "George W. Bush and the Partisan Presidency." *Political Science Quarterly* 123 (No. 4): 605–622.

Skowronek, Stephen. 1993. *The Politics that Presidents Make.* Cambridge, MA: Belknap.

Skowronek, Stephen. 2002. "Presidency and American Political Development: A Third Look." *Presidential Studies Quarterly* 32 (December): 743–752.

Skowronek, Stephen. 2008. *Presidential Leadership in Political Time.* Lawrence: University Press of Kansas.

Skowronek, Stephen. 2009. "The Paradigm of Development in Presidential History." In *The Oxford Handbook of the American Presidency,* eds. George C. Edwards III and William G. Howell. New York: Oxford University Press, pp. 749–770.

Smith, Kevin B. 2002. "Typologies, Taxonomies, and the Benefits of Policy Classification." *Policy Studies Journal* 30 (August): 379–395.

Smith, Steven S. 2007. *Party Influence in Congress.* New York: Cambridge University Press.

Spitzer, Robert J. 1983. *The Presidency and Public Policy: The Four Arenas of Presidential Power.* Tuscaloosa: University of Alabama Press.

Spitzer, Robert J. 1988. *The Presidential Veto: Touchstone of the American Presidency.* Albany: SUNY Press.

Stanley, Harold and Richard Niemi. 2009. *Vital Statistics on American Politics Online Edition, 2009–10.* Washington, DC: CQ Press (http://www.cqpress.com.avoserv.library.fordham.edu/product/Vital-Statistics-on-American-Politics-7.html, accessed on December 19, 2010).

Steger, Wayne P. 2005. "The President's Legislative Program: An Issue of Sincere versus Strategic Behavior." *Politics and Policy* 33 (June): 312–329.

Stolberg, Sheryl Gay and David M. Herszenhorn. 2010. "Obama's Health Bill Plan Largely Follows Senate Version." *New York Times*, February 22, 2010 (http://www.nytimes.com/2010/02/23/health/policy/23health.html?scp=4&sq=obama%20public%20option%20health%20care&st=cse, accessed December 20, 2010).

Talev, Margaret and Steven Thomma. 2010. "Obama's Health Care Win Ensures his Legacy – and May Help in November." *McClatchy Newspapers*, March 21, 2010. http://www.mcclatchydc.com/2010/03/21/90800/battered-and-bruised-obama-wins.html#ixzz17L1rAWMK, accessed December 6, 2010.

Teten, Ryan L. 2003. "Evolution of the Modern Rhetorical Presidency: Presidential Presentation and Development of the State of the Union Address." *Presidential Studies Quarterly* 33 (June): 333–346.

Teten, Ryan L. 2007. 'We the People': The 'Modern' Rhetorical Popular Address of the Presidents during the Founding Period." *Political Research Quarterly* 60 (December): 669–682.

Teten, Ryan L. 2008. "The Evolution of the Rhetorical Presidency and Getting Past the Traditional/Modern Divide." *Presidential Studies Quarterly* 38 (June): 308–314.

Theriault, Sean M. 2008. *Party Polarization in Congress*. New York: Cambridge University Press.

Tilly, Charles. 1985. "War Making and State Making as Organized Crime." In *Bringing the State Back In*, eds. Peter B. Evans, Dietrich Rueschemeyer, and Theda Skocpol. New York: Cambridge University Press, pp. 169–191.

Travis, Rick and Nikolaos Zahariadis. 2002. "A Multiple Streams Model of U.S. Foreign Aid Policy." *Policy Studies Journal* 30 (No. 4): 495–514.

Tulis, Jeffrey. 1987. *The Rhetorical Presidency*. Princeton, NJ: Princeton University Press.

Walker, Jack L. 1977. "Setting the Agenda in the U.S. Senate: A Theory of Problem Selection." *British Journal of Political Science* 7 (October): 423–445.

Walker, Jack L. 1991. *Mobilizing Interest Groups in America: Patrons, Professions, and Social Movements*. Ann Arbor: University of Michigan Press.

Walker, Stephen G. 2009. "The Psychology of Presidential Decision Making." In the *Oxford Handbook of the American Presidency*, edited by George C. Edwards III and William G. Howell. New York: Oxford University Press, pp. 550–574.

Waterman, Richard W. 2009. "Assessing the Unilateral Presidency," in George C. Edwards III and William G. Howell, eds. *The Oxford Handbook of the American Presidency*. New York: Oxford University Press, pp. 477–498.

Waterman, Richard W., Robert Wright, and Gilbert St. Clair. 1999. *The Image-Is-Everything Presidency: Dilemmas in American Leadership*. Boulder, CO: Westview Press.

Waterman, Richard W., Hank C. Jenkins-Smith, and Carol L. Silva. 1999. "The Expectations Gap Thesis: Public Attitudes toward an Incumbent President." *Journal of Politics* 61 (November): 944–966.

Watson, Richard. 1993. *Presidential Vetoes and Public Policy*. Lawrence: University Press of Kansas.

Wawro, Gregory J. and Eric Schickler. 2006. *Filibuster: Obstruction and Lawmaking in the U.S. Senate*. Princeton, NJ: Princeton University Press.

Wayne, Stephen J. 1978. *The Legislative Presidency*. New York: Harper Collins.

Wayne, Stephen J. 1982. "Great Expectations: What People Want from Presidents." In Thomas Cronin, ed. *Rethinking the Presidency*. Boston: Little Brown, pp. 185–199.

Wayne, Stephen J., Richard L. Cole, and James F. C. Hyde, Jr. 1979. "Advising the President on Enrolled Legislation: Patterns of Executive Influence." *Political Science Quarterly* 94 (Summer): 303–317.

Welch, Richard E., Jr. 1988. *The Presidencies of Grover Cleveland*. Lawrence: University Press of Kansas.

Wildavsky, Aaron. 1966. "The Two Presidencies." *Trans-Action* 4 (December): 7–14.

Williams, Robert J. 1979. "Harry S. Truman and the American Presidency." *Journal of American Studies* 13 (December): 393–408.

Winter, David. 2003. "Measuring the Motives of Political Actors at a Distance." In *The Psychological Assessment of Political Leaders*, Jerrold Post, ed. Ann Arbor: University of Michigan Press, pp. 153–177.

Wood, B. Dan. 2007. *The Politics of Economic Leadership: The Causes and Consequences of Presidential Rhetoric*. Princeton, NJ: Princeton University Press.

Wood, B. Dan. 2009a. *The Myth of Presidential Representation*. New York: Cambridge University Press.

Wood, B. Dan. 2009b. "Presidents and the Political Agenda." In George C. Edwards III and William G. Howell, eds. *The Oxford Handbook of the American Presidency*. New York: Oxford University Press, pp. 108–132.

Wood, B. Dan and Jeffrey S. Peake. 1998. "The Dynamics of Foreign Policy Agenda Setting." *American Political Science Review* 92 (March): 173–184.

Woolley, John. 2005. "Drawing Lines or Defining Variables: Studying Big Changes in the Presidency." Paper presented at the annual meeting of the American Political Science Association, Washington, DC, September, 2005.

Woolley, John T. 1991. "Institutions, the Election Cycle and the Presidential Veto." *American Journal of Political Science* 35 (2): 279–304.

Wright, Gerald C., Jr. 1976. "Linear Models for Evaluating Conditional Relationships." *American Journal of Political Science* 20 (May): 349–373.

Wyszomirski, Margaret, J. 1982. "The De-Institutionalization of Presidential Staff Agencies." *Public Administration Review* 42 (September-October): 448–458.

Yates, Jeff and Andrew Whitford. 2005. "Institutional Foundations of the President's Issue Agenda." *Political Research Quarterly* 58 (December): 577–585.

Yoo, Christopher S., Steven G. Calabresi, and Anthony J. Colangelo. 2005. The Unitary Executive in the Modern Era, 1945–2004. *Iowa Law Review* 90 (No. 2): 601–732.

Yoo, Christopher S., Steven G. Calabresi, and Laurence Nee. 2004. "The Unitary Executive During the Third Half-Century, 1889–1945." *Notre Dame Law Review* 80 (No. 1): 1–110.

Young, Garry and William B. Perkins. 2005. "Presidential Rhetoric, the Public Agenda, and the End of Presidential Television's 'Golden Age'." *Journal of Politics* 67 (November):1190–1205.

Zellner, Arnold. 1962. "An Efficient Method of Estimating Seemingly Unrelated Regressions and Tests for Aggregation Bias." *Journal of the American Statistical Association* 57 (June): 348–368.

Zengerle, Patricia. 2010. "What Does Health Care Passage Mean for Obama?" *Reuters,* March 22, 2010 (http://www.reuters.com/article/idUSTRE62L0KY20100322, accessed December 20, 2010).

Index